**People
in Poverty**
A Melbourne
Survey

Institute of Applied Economic
and Social Research
University of Melbourne

Monographs
This series of Institute Monographs
presents the results of research
by members of the Institute staff
and others working in close association
with the Institute.
The views expressed are those
of the authors.

People
in Poverty
A Melbourne
Survey

Ronald F. Henderson
Alison Harcourt
R. J. A. Harper

Published by Cheshire for the
Institute of Applied Economic
and Social Research,
University of Melbourne.

This book is copyright
and reproduction of the
whole or part without the
publisher's written permission
is prohibited.
© 1970 University of Melbourne
First Published 1970
SBN 7015 1237 7 (cased)
SBN 7015 1265 2 (limp)
Printed in Australia for
F. W. Cheshire Publishing Pty Ltd
346 St Kilda Road, Melbourne
142 Victoria Road, Marrickville, NSW
at The Griffin Press
Marion Road, Netley, South Australia
Registered in Australia
for transmission by post as a book

Contents

List of Tables

Preface

This survey is of poverty due to inadequate income—inadequate for the needs of the family whom the income has to support. We believe it is the first attempt to measure the extent and causes of such poverty in Australia. Our survey was restricted to the metropolitan area of Melbourne, but since a large proportion of the Australian population live in big cities like Melbourne we believe that our results are a good indication of the extent of poverty in urban Australia.

There are, however, three groups in poverty which are not described in this book and which, no doubt, are important when considering the total numbers in poverty in Australia. The sample used in our survey was drawn from those living in private dwellings; those living in institutional accommodation like hospitals, hostels and boarding houses were not sampled. This means that homeless men and a number of the poor, particularly the aged poor, were omitted. Our estimates of poverty are understated to this extent.

As the survey was based on Melbourne only, and as, by chance, it contained no Aborigines we have not been able to comment on poverty among the people of rural Australia or among the Aborigines. We believe, however, that in both groups the incidence of poverty is high and in urgent need of attention.

There are other kinds of poverty—cultural poverty, poverty due to mis-spending of income. But examination of poverty in terms of inadequate income is the most fundamental, basic approach to the problem and the provision of adequate income is a primary need which in a rich, civilised community can and should be met.

The statistical material that is contained in this book has been limited to that which was relevant to the practical problems of the relief of poverty. Further statistical material will be presented in a Technical Paper which is now in preparation.

This book, we hope, will serve to stimulate concern and provide a basis for more informed discussion on the community's attitudes and responsibilities to the poor.

Postscript—21st August, 1970

In the 1970 budget the basic pension rate was raised by only 50 cents a week to $15.50 for a single pensioner. This is an increase of $3 \cdot 3$ per cent. A married couple will receive $27.50—an increase of $1. Since there has been no increase in allowances for children, for a widow with three children the increase in income is only 1·8 per cent. By comparison, the average wage earner is enjoying increases of income of 8 per cent and receiving a substantial reduction in income tax. So the gap between the incomes of the pensioner and the average wage earner will continue to widen rapidly throughout 1970-71. As rents and prices rise, more pensioners fall into dire poverty. Long term sickness benefits have been raised from $10 a week to $15.50, and in addition Supplementary Assistance of $2 a week has been extended to this group. This extension is welcome, but it will still leave many of those dependent on these benefits below the poverty line.

Since no increase is made in the money value of child endowment payments, their real value will decline further and more large families will sink into poverty.

Since poor large families and pensioners pay very little or no income tax the reduction in income tax rates in the 1970 budget will be more than offset for them by the rises in indirect taxes.

Our conservative estimate of the amount by which the poverty line should be updated to July 1970 for a standard family was based on the assumption that average earnings would rise by 5·4 per cent for the year. In fact, they have risen by 8 per cent, so the poverty line should be $43.40 instead of $42.40. Hence many recommendations for increased rates of pension and benefits included in this book are understatements of what is needed and the amounts required should be increased accordingly.

Acknowledgments

The study described in this book was essentially a counting—a counting of people with low incomes and their characteristics. So a major part of the responsibility and work involved was borne by Mrs Alison Harcourt (née Doig) who carried out the design of the sample and the programming for analysis by computer of the large volume of material collected in the survey. Her devotion to accuracy in pursuit of even one straying income unit among thousands, and her persistence in re-arrangement of data to achieve clear and relevant presentation have been the core of the enterprise.

Mr John Harper has been in a key position from the very start and it is right that the first account of the project should have been given by him (at the ANZAAS Congress in Melbourne in January 1967). There is no aspect of the project—design of questionnaires, organisation of survey, methods of analysis or writing up—in which he has not made a major contribution.

Miss Sheila Shaver has been in the midst of the project for several years as coder, editor of questionnaires, analyser of data and author of text—so much so that the news that she was willing to return from America for a further spell of work on it still remains one of the brightest memories of the whole period.

Many people have been involved in this project. Professor Jean Martin brought her knowledge of sociology to achieve the design of the first questionnaire. That such a high response rate was achieved and so much information collected on the delicate subject of income was largely due to her skill. Professor Roger Layton gave a great deal of time and thought on repeated visits from Sydney to the choice of the technique— a stratified two-stage sample survey—which enabled us at minimum cost to discover 'how many are poor?' and 'what are their disabilities and needs?'. Miss Margaret Harris was mainly responsible for the design of the long second questionnaire to obtain this information on disabilities and needs, and for the recruitment, briefing and supervision of the team of social workers and others with similar skill and experience who carried out the long and detailed interviews. She then went on to check and edit this material for us.

Mrs Jean Strecker (née Lydall), Mrs Diana Gower, Mrs Penny Pollitt, Mrs Helen Wisdom and Mrs Elizabeth Rouch all carried out much detailed work with enthusiasm and care to enable the analysis of food diaries, preparation of case studies and consideration of needs for welfare services to be carried out with accuracy and discrimination.

For the large first part of the survey we are grateful for the co-operation of the firm of Anderson Analysis and especially for the care with which Dr Peter Kenny, then with that firm, adapted the organisation to meet the exacting requirements of an academic survey.

Teams of interviewers and of coders carried out their work with a conviction that the whole enterprise was really worthwhile, in spite of the inevitable dullness and discouragement of these jobs from time to time.

The secretary of the Institute, Miss Mary Davis, and her assistants, and Mrs Nancy Hempel, secretary to Professor Downing, have undertaken the mass of typing and retyping that reflects the pioneering nature of this enterprise—at least to its authors. They have done it with a speed and efficiency for which we are most grateful.

Mrs Jean McCaughey has brought together a concern for welfare services and knowledge of computer programming to describe both the situation of the large migrant groups included in this survey and the need for improvements in personal welfare services.

Mrs Helen Ferber has organised a hundred and one details of the whole enterprise, and undertaken much of the demanding editorial work necessary in a book with several authors and some indigestible technical material. She has also prepared the index.

Professor R.I. Downing has been expert in social problems and public finance in Australia for many years. Without the knowledge that we could always rely on his unstinted help and guidance the project would probably never have been launched—it is even less likely that it would have been completed.

For the financial support required to enable this expensive project to be carried out we are grateful to the Myer and Potter Foundations for most generous donations, as well as to the Howard Norman Trust and a number of private individuals. A substantial grant was also received from the Australian Research Grants Commission, while one from the Social Science Research Council made possible the study of poverty among migrants.

Finally, we would wish to thank most sincerely all those who consented to be interviewed and gave us the information on which this whole project rests. We have tried to use it as fairly and constructively as possible.

Ronald F. Henderson

1 Economic and Social Background to Poverty in Melbourne*

Melbourne has been described by its city fathers as 'big, rich and beautiful'. It is certainly big. Its two million people are spread over 440 square miles; London's eight millions live on 620 square miles. It is also rich. Its workers are fully employed and their average living standards among the highest in the world.

Its population is growing rapidly, by over 2·5 per cent a year. With 73 per cent of families owning their own homes, usually detached houses with gardens, the suburban sprawl spreads apace, beautiful always in the eyes of the individual property-owners, less often so to the beholder.

In this serene and complacent scene, he who would find poverty must work hard, as we did. Poverty in Melbourne is, to invert a phrase, the submerged tip of an iceberg. It exists, nevertheless, and it is a disgrace to such a community.

The Poverty Line

For our survey of income and needs in Melbourne in 1966, we have accepted as a state of poverty the situation of a man with a wife (not working) and two children whose total weekly income at that time was less than the basic wage plus child endowment. We set our poverty line at $33 for such a standard family. The incomes of different-sized family units have been standardised to make them comparable with a unit of the basic size. This is a definition of poverty so austere as, we believe, to make it unchallengeable. No one can seriously argue that those we define as being poor are not so.

We chose this basic-wage content of the poverty line because of its relevance to Australian concepts of living standards—the basic wage being the lowest wage which can be paid to an unskilled labourer on the basis of, in the famous phrase of Mr Justice Higgins, 'the normal needs of an average employee regarded as a human being living in a civilised community.' This poverty line also has international relevance since, in its relationship to average earnings, to average incomes and to basic social service rates, it is comparable to the poverty lines that have been adopted in some surveys carried out overseas, particularly in the United Kingdom, the United States of America and Denmark.

We have deliberately confined ourselves to a study of poverty as determined by the relationship between the income of a family and its normal needs. We have not attempted to study, apart from housing expenditures, the use which families actually make of their incomes,

* This chapter was written by R.I. Downing.

which would have taken us into the much wider problem of secondary poverty. We have not attempted to study the personal causes of poverty, its life cycle or its perpetuation, which would have taken us into the deep waters of the sociology of poverty.

Finally we consider poverty to be a relative concept, to be defined in relationship to the living standards typical of the community in which we exist. That the Australian family which we define as poor would be well off in India is irrelevant. Further, since we assess poverty in relation to average living standards in Australia, we believe that the poverty line should be adjusted each year in step with the index of average earnings. This does not mean that we believe the proportion of the population in poverty can never change: the relationship of neither the minimum wage nor cash social benefit rates to average earnings is sacrosanct.

The Cost of Eliminating Poverty

Some large families were in poverty, but apart from these we found hardly any other family headed by a male breadwinner in regular employment to be poor.

Most poverty is among the existing social service beneficiaries—above all the aged, the widowed, the invalid and the sick. The machinery exists, therefore, for coping with most of the problem of poverty. It can largely be eliminated by quite moderate increases in rates of cash social benefit.

If our proposals for improved cash social benefits had been introduced for Australia as a whole in the financial year 1968-69, their total cost should not have exceeded $189 million or $0 \cdot 7$ per cent of gross national product in that year. Most of this cost could have been met simply by raising expenditure on cash social benefits from the actual $5 \cdot 3$ per cent of gross national product of 1968-69 to the $5 \cdot 9$ per cent that was spent in the four years 1960-61 to 1963-64.

The net cost of these proposals could be brought to about $100 million by the elimination of tax deductions for dependent children, which would be made redundant by our proposals for higher rates of child endowment.

This small amount of extra expenditure would, of course, eliminate poverty only in the very narrow sense with which we have concerned ourselves. The cheapness of our proposals is made possible by the fact that they concentrate on minimum essential increases for those groups eT

TABLE 1·1

ANNUAL EXPENDITURE ON CASH SOCIAL BENEFITS*

	Amount	Percentage of gross national product
	$ million	%
1952–53 to 1955–56	480	5·1
1956–57 to 1959–60	664	5·4
1960–61 to 1963–64	935	5·9
1964–65 to 1967–68	1,218	5·6
1968–69	1,442	5·3

*Expenditure on cash social benefits in 1968-69 totalled $1,442m, comprising:

	$m		$m
Age and invalid pensions	559	Medical benefits	66
Child endowment	193	Other health benefits	22
Widows' pensions	69	Scholarships	33
Other welfare benefits	46	Other education benefits	21
Pharmaceutical benefits	119	Repatriation benefits	220
Hospital benefits	86	Other benefits	8

which the survey reveals to be in the worst difficulties—single age pensioners, invalid pensioners, widow pensioners, rent-paying pensioners, non-pensioner wives of pensioners, non-pensioner parents of migrants, the unemployed and the sick, and children in large families.

The Size of the Problem

The figures derived from the first stage of our survey—of incomes during a particular week—suggested that some 7 per cent of income units in Melbourne might be in poverty. Further information collected in the subsequent second stage of the survey—which, for a smaller number of people, went into much more detail about their circumstances—supplemented by a detailed consideration of what inferences could be drawn from all the information collected at the first stage, has led us to conclude that, as a minimum estimate, 4 per cent of income units in Melbourne in 1966 were in need.

The deterioration since 1966 in the relationship between rates of cash social benefits and average earnings leads us to presume that the proportion in poverty and in need would now be larger.

The survey confirmed our expectation that the incidence of poverty and need in Melbourne would be low. There is no reason to suppose that the incidence would be significantly higher in any of the other cities of Australia. There might possibly be a little more poverty in rural areas where, however, only a small part of the population lives.

International statistical comparisons are always dangerous, especially in this field of poverty which bristles with problems of definition and measurement. It is nevertheless worth noting that, on the basis of not obviously very different criteria, it has been estimated that 14 per cent of the people are in poverty in the United Kingdom, which has made great efforts particularly over the last thirty years to improve social welfare; and that in the United States, by far the richest country in the world, 20 per cent of families have been found to be in poverty. The incidence of poverty in Melbourne, and by inference in Australia, can be confidently asserted to be much less than in those two countries. Only New Zealand and Scandinavia, with which countries Australia enjoys roughly comparable living standards, are likely to have as little poverty.

The reasons for this lower incidence of poverty are easy to identify. Without venturing into a discussion of the higher qualities of life in Australia, there is enough literacy and absence of discrimination, and enough pressure of demand to make employment available to virtually everyone capable of earning a living. The average level of wages is high and the minimum level is not uncomfortably far below the average. Despite some gaps and not very generous levels of expenditure, universal welfare provisions bring some assistance to all members of the community in respect of maternity, children, education, health expenditures, housing and provision for retirement.

An expenditure on cash social benefits which is not high by international standards but which, on the other hand, is concentrated by the means test on those demonstrably in need, ensures at least a minimum subsistence for those not in the work force—though it is among this group, naturally, that most of our poverty and need is found.

Full Employment and High Wages

Early in this century Australia determined that no industry should be allowed to employ labour unless it could pay a decent minimum wage. The arbitration system, building on the so-called 'Harvester' judgment of Mr Justice Higgins, established the minimum wage at the relatively high level being paid by better employers and varied it each quarter in step with retail prices. The legal minimum wage was, up to the end of the Second World War, much nearer to the average wage than was usual in other countries.

The maintenance of very high levels of employment ever since 1940 has made good wages available to virtually every man or woman seeking to work, with at worst but short periods of unemployment. (In rural areas and in some provincial cities there are insufficient employment opportunities for women.) It has also created a situation in which actual earnings have tended to drift increasingly above the legal minimum award rates. In 1968-69 average male weekly earnings were $69 a week and the minimum wage was fixed for Melbourne at $42.30 in November 1969. The shortage of labour has been such that the great majority of workers have shared in the earnings drift. Even the traditionally lower paid workers—women, juveniles, farm labourers, school dropouts and unskilled workers generally—have been able to secure rates of pay in better relation to other wage earners than formerly. Full employment has also made it possible for breadwinners to work overtime and to get second jobs, and for wives to get full-time or part-time jobs, so that family incomes have been high for those who wished and were able to take advantage of the tight labour market.

Full employment and high minimum wages have had the important additional advantage of reducing social and economic conflict. Since 1947 a huge flood of migrants from all parts of Europe, and a small but significant flow from non-European countries, have contributed nearly half of the total population increase of over 2 per cent a year. These migrants have been assimilated without strain into the economy and society. Automation, a rapidly growing work force, high migration, redundancy and high productivity are not feared in a full-employment economy. It is significant that in the post-war period it has been only during occasional and short periods of slight recession that migration and automation have been mentioned as possible sources of economic or social difficulty.

Universal Welfare Provisions

Various welfare provisions are available to the Australian community at large.

Children

Maternity allowances of $30 are paid for first confinements, with slightly higher amounts for subsequent children and multiple births. Child endowment is paid to the mothers or guardians of all children up to the age of sixteen, at the rate of 50 cents a week for the first child, $1 for the second, $1.50 for the third, and rising thereafter, as a result of changes introduced in the 1967-68 Budget Speech, by 25 cents a week for each child after the third: for the fourth child, $1.75, the fifth, $2.00 and so on. Child endowment is continued up to the age of twenty-one in the case of full-time students at the rate of $1.50 per child.

These and all other social benefit payments are not assessed as income for tax purposes; and taxpayers are, in addition, allowed to deduct from their taxable incomes $312 for a dependent spouse, $208 for the first dependent child or for students aged sixteen to twenty-one and $156 for other dependent children. As with all other deductions mentioned below, this concession is inevitably of greatest assistance to taxpayers in the higher income brackets where marginal tax rates are high.

Education

Education is available up to matriculation level at State schools which charge no tuition fees. Here, as in most countries, nominally free education involves quite high costs for books and school amenities as well as the cost of keeping the children. These factors often force many children of poor families to leave school as soon as they reach the legal minimum age. Moreover, the quality of State schools varies greatly, usually in direct ratio to the economic and social status of the areas in which the schools are located; just as the motivation of children to acquire education usually varies directly with the economic and social status of their families.

About 77 per cent of Australian children attend government schools, another 18 per cent are at Roman Catholic schools and the remaining 5 per cent are at other independent schools. A substantial and increasing amount of government aid is being provided for these Catholic and other independent schools.

Scholarships are offered, on a competitive basis, by both Commonwealth and State governments to encourage students to continue past the minimum school-leaving age (which in Victoria is fifteen) with secondary, tertiary and post-graduate education. These scholarships tend, inevitably, to be won by students at better schools and from backgrounds sympathetic to education. They are therefore not often enjoyed by the children of poor families even though living allowances are paid, subject to a means test, to holders of Commonwealth tertiary scholarships.

Taxpayers are allowed to deduct education expenses, up to a maximum of $300 per student aged less than twenty-one, from their taxable income.

Health

Age, invalid and widow pensioners get most health services free. For the community as a whole, the Commonwealth pays all pharmaceutical costs in excess of fifty cents on most prescriptions, except in the case of pensioners who usually pay nothing. For hospital services the Commonwealth pays a small basic rate in respect of any patient. For all who contribute on behalf of themselves and their families to one of the voluntary medical and hospital benefits associations, the Commonwealth in addition contributes to the refunds paid by these schemes, substantially in the case of medical care and rather less in the case of hospitalisation.

The drawback is that these schemes are voluntary and the rates of contribution high, with the result that even allowing for those who are eligible for treatment under the pensioner medical service some 15 per cent of the population are not covered, and, of those who are insured, many contribute at less than the maximum rate of contribution and receive a correspondingly lower level of refund. Many of the poorer families have inadequate or no cover. For these reasons illness involves financial hardship and anxiety for a number of families.

Some specialised services are excluded from the cover offered and others are included only at low rates of refund. There is no cover for dental treatment. All health expenditures not covered by refunds are allowed as deductions from taxable income.

The public hospital systems run by the States provide an important source of subsidised health services for the poor, and in practice further fee concessions are made to the very poor. Although some incur substantial debt, there is no evidence that anyone does not receive needed care, provided he is not deterred by costs, inconvenience or the means test.

There is also a patchwork of domiciliary services to assist the aged and the sick in their homes. The coverage of these services is uneven and many who need such help fail to receive it.

Housing

The great majority of Australians are well-housed at costs not unduly burdensome to the occupiers, even if standards of design and town-planning leave something to be desired. About 73 per cent of occupiers own or are buying their homes. There is limited assistance for young couples towards the cost of acquiring a house. For some lower-income families State Housing Commissions have been of great assistance. They offer low deposit requirements and long repayment terms to purchasers, flats for rental at less than current economic rents and rent rebates to tenants qualifying under a means test. However, waiting-lists for Commission housing are still lengthening; and it is families with low and irregular earnings who often find it most difficult to obtain and to keep Commission houses or flats. There is a shortage of cheap accommodation for rental and a number of families suffer from the high cost of housing.

Self-provision for Retirement

Some assistance is given to those who wish to provide for their own retirement by the allowance of contributions to assurance and super-annuation schemes, up to $1,200 a year, as deductions in determining taxable income. Men aged sixty-five or more, and women aged sixty or more, whose taxable incomes are comparable to those permitted to age pensioners, receive substantial tax exemptions and concessions.

Means-tested Cash Social Benefits

With full employment, high minimum wages and the universal welfare provisions described above, those regularly in the work-force and with small families are not likely to fall into serious poverty. For people out-side the work force—the aged and invalid, widows (especially the older ones and those with dependent children), the unemployed and the sick, there is an extensive network of cash social benefits. The rates of benefit provide, at best, no more than a minimum subsistence, and some people fail to receive them through ignorance (see Chapter 11).

Table 1·2 shows the current rates of benefit for Australia as a whole, as announced in the Budget Speech for 1969-70, compared with those announced for 1965-66 when most of the fieldwork for our survey was undertaken. During the intervening four years, average earnings in Australia rose by 28·1 per cent, while the basic pension rate rose by only 25 per cent for single pensioners and by 20·5 per cent for married-couple pensioners.

All cash social benefits are paid out of consolidated revenue, raised according to the government assessment of how best to levy taxes. There are no specific contributions from potential beneficiaries. Benefits continue as long as the need lasts. For some benefits there is a residence qualification, but special benefits and compassionate allowances can be granted in cases of hardship.

The unusual feature of the Australian system of cash benefits of the income-maintenance type is that they are all paid subject to a means test, except for blind persons.[1]

TABLE 1·2

COMMONWEALTH CASH SOCIAL BENEFITS   Weekly Rates

	Budget 1965-66 $	Budget 1969-70 $
Standard (Single) Rates		
Aged, invalids, widows with children (Class A Widows)	12.00	15.00
Widows, no children but 50 or over (Class B Widows)	10.75	13.25
Unemployment, sickness, special beneficiaries (adults or married minors)	8.25	10.00
Married Rate		
Age and invalid pensioners, both eligible for pension	22.00	26.50
Additions for Wife		
Non-pensioner dependent wife of invalid pensioner, or wife of unemployment, sickness or special beneficiary, or wife of age pensioner with dependent children or permanently incapacitated husband	6.00	7.00
Additions for Children		
Guardians' or mothers' allowance for single pensioners with children		
—at least one child under 6 years	4.00	6.00
—all children 6 years or older	4.00	4.00
Dependent children of pensioners and beneficiaries (additional to child endowment*)		
—first child	1.50	2.50
—subsequent children, each	1.50	3.50
Supplementary Assistance		
For standard (single-rate) age and invalid pensioners, and widow pensioners, if paying rent and entirely or substantially dependent on pension	2.00	2.00

*At the time of the survey, child endowment was paid in respect of all children under sixteen years, regardless of the parents' means, at the weekly rate of 50 cents for the first child, $1 for the second and $1.50 for the third and subsequent children. $1.50 was also paid for student children between the ages of sixteen and twenty-one. In the 1967-68 Budget payments for the fourth and subsequent children were increased in steps of 25 cents, so that the rate for the fourth child became $1.75, for the fifth, $2.00 and so on.

[1] Repatriation Department payments to ex-servicemen and their dependants in respect of incapacity or death attributed to war service are not subject to any test of means. It can be argued that these more closely resemble compensation than cash social benefits.

There is, then, in respect of the 2·4 per cent of gross national product which passes through these means-tested social benefits, a substantial redistribution of income to the poor from the not-so-poor. Revenue is collected according to capacity to pay; benefits go only to those who can prove need under the means test.

The means test is, however, fairly liberal. For age, invalid and widow pensioners without dependent children a house owned and occupied by a pensioner, its land and contents, a car or any personal effects are excluded from the valuation of assets. Income from property, gifts from relatives and benefit payments (other than annuities) from friendly societies and trade unions are ignored. 'Means as assessed' include only earnings, annuities and superannuation plus 10 per cent of the value of any other assets in excess of $400 for a single pensioner and $800 for a married couple. A single age pensioner can have means equivalent to $10 a week, and a married couple without dependent children, $17 a week, and still receive full pension. Until the introduction of the 'tapered' means test in the 1969-70 Budget Speech, the pension was reduced by $1 for each $1 of means in excess of these limits; now, the pension is reduced by only 50 cents for each $1 excess.

Attitudes to the Means Test

The adequacy of the various rates of benefit and the impact of the means test are discussed in the relevant chapters. It is appropriate here to discuss the general attitude of Australians to the concept of the means test.

It may seem surprising that a country which prides itself on its riches, its social justice and its egalitarianism (each to some extent, in any case, mythical) should be the only advanced country to retain a means test as a central feature of most of its cash social benefits. Other countries are said to regard the means test as an abhorrent affront to social justice. It does not seem to be so regarded in Australia.

There is certainly some opposition to the means test—but this opposition is probably strongest among those who are excluded by it from the benefits, rather than among those who submit themselves to it and thereby qualify for the benefits.

All major political parties have expressed their intention of getting rid of the means test. None of them, when in office, has done so; they have all been content merely to liberalise its provisions. In recent years the Liberal Party, which has been in office since 1949, has more or less explicitly abandoned the intention it expressed, when in opposition, of abolishing the means test. A Labor Party view on the matter was stated by the one-time Prime Minister Chifley: 'I am not greatly concerned about abolishing the means test so that everybody in the community above the prescribed age-limit may receive an age pension, even though that is part of Labor's policy. . . . I am concerned about people on the lowest rung of the economic ladder, who suffer great hardship under present living conditions . . .'[2]

Some reasons for the acceptance of the means test can be suggested. Firstly, the means test as it is operated in Australia is not only fairly liberal, but also the 'poor-house' and 'work-house' connotations, which attach to the concept of the means test in some other countries, do not exist in Australia which had no experience of such institutions, at least under those names.

Secondly, the price paid in most countries for having universal benefits not subject to a means test is the levy of social security contributions, sometimes in the form of a poll-tax, sometimes in the form of a proportionate income tax, but always falling more heavily on the lower-income groups than, it is popularly believed, do the sources of consolidated revenue in Australia.[3] From the beginning of discussion on the the provision of social services here, there has been fierce opposition to any form of social security contribution which could be regarded as falling with particular weight on lower incomes.

Thirdly, it was widely accepted during such discussions that all benefits should be provided on a universal basis to all those who might be eligible —for example, by age, invalidity or widowhood. But, in practical politics subject to Treasury advice, no government has ever been willing to face the cost of providing such universal services. In this situation, the means test was brought in not so much as a test of poverty—and certainly not

[2] Quoted by T. H. Kewley, *Social Security in Australia,* Sydney University Press, 1965 p. 292.

[3] Australia's income tax used to be described as the Income Tax and Social Service Contribution. The Social Service Contribution was first introduced as a separate tax, earmarked for payment into the National Welfare Fund; but it was always levied on a progressive basis, with higher incomes paying a higher proportion than lower incomes. Later, it was merged into the income tax schedule and now even the name has gone. The National Welfare Fund is financed by transfers, as required, from consolidated revenue. However, the introduction of this concept probably contributed significantly to the change of attitude towards the receipt of pensions.

There is also a 2·5 per cent payroll tax, which was introduced at the same time as child endowment. The proceeds of this tax were originally paid direct to the National Welfare Fund, but are now treated as part of consolidated revenue.

of pauperism—but rather as a test of need, by which total expenditure might be kept within reasonable bounds.

The perhaps surprising outcome of this route to the adoption of the means test is that the typical Australian regards cash social benefits as a right, provided he is eligible to receive them under the means test, and not as a charity; he accepts that it is reasonable to abrogate this right in the case of people who are well enough off not to qualify under a fairly liberal means test.

Up to about the beginning of the Second World War, there was some stigma attached to the acceptance of age and invalid pensions. This was, however, always what might be regarded as a 'class' rather than a 'social' stigma—the recipients were stigmatised as 'working class' rather than as 'paupers'. No 'gentleman' would have liked being seen in a queue in a post office collecting his pension (then the standard method of distribution), but this hardly worried 'others' who, after all, were in the company of their eligible social equals. Moreover, the introduction in 1912 of maternity allowances, payable to all mothers without means test (except for a decade or so during and after the depression of the early 1930s) and in fact taken by mothers of all classes, did something to break down what stigma attached to the means-tested age and invalid pensions.

Of the greatest significance in this regard, however, was firstly the introduction in 1941, without means test, of child endowment for all mothers. Secondly, the Commonwealth Government established an optional system of receiving cash social benefits through cheques sent by post or, in the case of child endowment, through deposits in recipients' bank accounts. With so many in the community accepting some cash social benefits, and with their receipt made anonymous and convenient, the eligibility for means-tested benefits became to some extent an object of envy and competition rather than a stigma.

It has frequently been argued that the means test discourages thrift. There was never very much to this argument. Given that the means test permitted, without loss of pension, an accumulation of assets well beyond the capacity of most workers, and that it had no effect whatever on people with means in excess of the prescribed limits, it could affect only a narrow band of savers. The introduction in 1969 of the tapered means test greatly weakens even that limited objection.

The most effective opposition has come recently from middle-income groups whose savings for retirement have been badly eroded by inflation but who have still had enough left to be excluded, by the means test, from eligibility for the pension. Their problem, too, has been significantly eased by the introduction of the tapered means test.

Benefit Expenditures and Impact on Poverty

Australia can be judged to have established a reasonably good economic and social structure from the point of view of its capacity to reduce the impact of poverty. This has not, however, been achieved by any lavish expenditure on social welfare. In 1966 Australia spent only 5·6 per cent of her gross national product on cash social benefits. This is a low figure compared with about 14·7 per cent in the Common Market countries; 12·6 per cent in Austria; between 9 and 11 per cent in Sweden, Norway, Denmark, Chile and Uruguay; between 7·5 and 8·5 per cent in Canada, Finland, Switzerland, Ireland, Greece and the United Kingdom; and 6·3 per cent in New Zealand. In fact, among advanced countries only the United States (5·3 per cent), Israel (5·4 per cent) and Japan (4·5 per cent) record expenditures lower than Australia's in relation to their gross national products.

Australia, while maintaining full employment and high wages, has made only very moderate social security expenditures and yet has had considerable success in reducing poverty. This must be attributed largely to her extensive reliance, unique among advanced countries, on the means test as a device for concentrating social expenditures where they are needed. This effect is reinforced by her avoidance, in revenue-raising, of contributions falling relatively heavily on lower incomes, which are an important source of social security finance in most other countries.

The arguments in favour of the means test are formidable. It concentrates benefits where they are most needed and so permits rates of benefit to rise more rapidly than they would if benefits were paid more indiscriminately. It offers a major instrument for redistribution of income in favour of those in need, in a situation where for many reasons— economic, social, political and administrative—the tax system alone is unable to achieve enough. And it retains an incentive to self-reliance among a large part of the population to provide at least some income for their retirement.

The main objection to this non-contributory, means-tested system is that it is unlikely ever to offer more than a minimum subsistence rate of benefit. Moreover, average earnings in Australia over the last thirty years have been rising by some 6 per cent a year and retail prices by 3 per cent. The financial institutions which look after most people's savings have not been enterprising enough to earn and distribute rates of return on funds adequate to offset the consequent erosion of the real value of people's savings. It has therefore been difficult for the average person, either because of ignorance or lack of foresight, to accumulate enough to provide a decent supplement to the pension let alone to provide an adequate independent income for retirement.

It is this sort of consideration which has presumably led the Labor Party, while still in opposition, to promise to examine the possibility of introducing a national superannuation scheme with retirement income related to past earnings, updated in step with the index of average earnings. The proposed retirement income would also be updated, after retirement, in step with that index. The essential advantages of the means test would be retained by a schedule of contributions graduated so as to rise progressively in relation to earnings. The payments to lower-paid earners would be heavily subsidised from consolidated revenue. The existing test on current means of pensioners would be replaced by a test based on past earnings.

A scheme along these lines, especially if extended to cover other aspects of social security, could provide adequate cash benefits on a basis compatible with what appear to be Australian social attitudes. It will be interesting to see whether the Labor Party takes up the proposal seriously if it does gain office.

2 Stage I of the Survey*

The ultimate purpose of our investigation into poverty in Melbourne was to discover sufficient quantitative information to meet the needs of both governments and voluntary agencies in the planning of their welfare activities. We needed, therefore, to estimate the numbers of people who were in poverty according to some clearly defined criteria. We needed also to know the characteristics of those in poverty. Were the poor mainly the aged, were they children, migrants, or the unemployed or did they have some other distinguishing characteristic? Such questions on the characteristics of the poor had to be answered if any remedial action were not to be misdirected.

These questions could not be answered from information already existing in the files of government departments or welfare agencies. These sources, and the work of individual researchers, contained plenty of relevant information and provided ample evidence that there was a section of the community in need. From none, however, could an estimate of the extent of poverty be made, nor a comprehensive picture of its nature and causes be obtained. In some cases the information was descriptive or impressionistic; in others it dealt only with certain groups or areas. No consistent criteria were used. It was also evident that the poor who sought help from several organisations might be counted many times, while many other needy cases who had not sought help would go unrecorded. It was apparent that if we wanted reliable quantitative information, it would be necessary to conduct a survey ourselves and gather the raw data by personal interview.

Collection of Information

The area in which the survey was conducted was not restricted to the old inner suburbs of Melbourne, as there was evidence that some of the newer suburbs and the more sparsely settled outer suburbs were by no means free of poverty. The area examined was that described as metropolitan Melbourne by the Commonwealth Bureau of Census and Statistics in the 1961 census. Using the census boundaries had the advantage of allowing us to draw on the detailed information that had been collected about the population of Melbourne in 1961. At the time of the survey the 812[1] square miles of the metropolis, most of which could correctly

---

* This chapter was written by R. J. A. Harper.

[1] The survey area is greater than the 440 square miles mentioned in Chapter 1. The smaller area is the new definition of the metropolitan area formulated after the 1966 census and includes only areas in which the population density was greater than 500 per square mile.

be described as suburbia, contained about 2·1 million people. It consisted of forty-six cities and shires and it ranged from Whittlesea in the north to Frankston in the south, and from Keilor, Sunshine and Altona in the west to Lilydale, Ferntree Gully and Berwick in the east.

Poor people may live in private accommodation or in institutions like boarding houses, hostels, hospitals, charitable institutions and gaols. In seeking to identify those who were in poverty we recognised that these two groups presented very different problems. Their patterns of living were different, the problems of collecting data from them were different and, in fact, to establish any comparable criteria for the measurement of poverty in the two groups was almost impossible. We therefore decided to limit our enquiry to an investigation of poverty in private dwellings only. We did not underestimate the importance of poverty among the 5 per cent of the population living in institutions but rather we thought it should be the subject of a separate and differently planned enquiry. The exclusion of the institutional poor from all of the estimates that are made throughout this book should constantly be remembered.

The range of information that we collected in our survey was narrowed by the meaning we attached to the term 'poverty' and the way in which we decided to measure it. Probably, to most people poverty means an inadequacy of income and this was the way we defined it. Limiting our investigation to an objective study of the needs of families of various sizes and whether they had sufficient income to meet these needs meant that we avoided the subjectivity and the moral overtones that would be involved had we adopted some of the possible alternative criteria. It is true that poverty in the eyes of some is the result of misuse of income: the poor are categorised as improvident, ignorant and intemperate. For us to have taken a view in any way like this would have meant imposing value judgments, many of which would have been quite inappropriate, on our analysis.

Another alternative view is that a study of poverty should embrace the whole life-style of the poor. Poverty is seen as a cultural and social as well as an economic condition. The life-style of the poor amounts to a self perpetuating cycle of impoverishment, indifference and ignorance. This suggests an examination of the whole sub-culture of poverty and all the social and economic forces that interact on it. Such an approach has much to recommend it but we have not pursued it. It would have required an amount of time and money far greater than was available to us.

Our analysis of poverty is, in the main, an economic analysis and our efforts have been directed largely towards making policy recommendations for the alleviation of inadequacy of income. Our work is, we feel, complementary to and a necessary preliminary to any broader sociological study. We have sought to provide an analytical framework and, for the first time, quantitative information on which others, perhaps with different interests and talents, can usefully build.

The Two Stages of the Survey

Since our objectives were to measure both the extent and the nature and causes of poverty we faced something of a dilemma. The measurement of the extent of poverty in the population and, more particularly, within certain groups in the population, could only be accurate if based on the results of a large representative sample covering rich and poor alike. On the other hand, useful information on the nature and causes of poverty could only be derived from long, detailed, and therefore costly interviews with those in poverty. These twin objectives seemed to indicate that a large number of lengthy interviews were needed. Such a survey would have been prohibitively expensive and, moreover, would have been wasteful, since many of the interviews would have been with respondents who were clearly not in poverty.

To resolve this problem we adopted a compromise and carried out the survey in two stages. Stage I was a survey of approximately 4,000 randomly selected households. These people were interviewed using a questionnaire which, though relatively short, enabled us to identify those in or near poverty. This stage of the survey was essentially a 'snapshot' picture recording the circumstances in households during the week in which the interviews took place. It was from this that our preliminary estimates of the extent of poverty were made. A description of this stage and the results it produced are set out in detail in this chapter.

Stage II of the survey consisted of a random selection of those found to be in or near poverty at the Stage I interview. These families were re-interviewed, with a much longer and more detailed questionnaire; information was collected on their economic circumstances over the previous year and any other factors in their background that had a bearing on their present impoverished state. This second stage material had a time dimension quite different from the first. It enabled us to qualify some of the results from the first stage and provided us with case studies

of the poor which added to our understanding of their problems. A discussion of this stage of the survey and of the food expenditure enquiry
that was carried out with it are to be found in Chapter 3.

Stage I Sample

A detailed discussion of the technicalities involved in the design of the
sample is not warranted here.[2] However, a brief description of how we
chose the people to be interviewed is necessary as it provides some
insight into the way in which the statistical estimates that appear
throughout this book have been made.

We anticipated that a cross-section of the population of Melbourne
would show that something less than 10 per cent of families were in
poverty. If this were so it raised two problems for us. Firstly, it meant
that if we sampled in this way only a small proportion of all the material
we collected would be relevant to the circumstances of the poor. Secondly, there was a risk that such a sample would produce insufficient
cases of poverty to provide a large enough sample for re-interview at
the second stage. We had decided that at the very least 400 second stage
interviews were necessary.

We tried to overcome these disadvantages by designing the Stage I
sample so that it was purposely slanted towards the poor. To do this we
needed to sample more intensively in areas in which we expected the
incidence of poverty to be high and to sample only lightly in areas
where we anticipated that poverty was rare. This deliberate attempt to
select a larger number of the poor in our sample does not invalidate the
results. Valid estimates can be made from such a sample so long as the
selection is made randomly and the chances of selection are known in
every case.

As we needed to know in which areas of Melbourne we should sample
more intensively we required some objective method of assessing the
likelihood of poverty in particular areas. No obvious criterion existed
for this purpose so we had to devise our own method of assessment. In
doing this we made considerable use of the data from the 1961 population census. Firstly, for census purposes Melbourne was divided into
2,111 collectors' districts. These were convenient area-units for us to
assess as they were small enough to be thought of as reasonably homogeneous, each containing on the average about 1,000 people and about
285 dwellings. Secondly, the census provided us with data for each

[2] For details of the sample design see R. J. A. Harper, 'Survey of Living Conditions
in Melbourne—1966', *The Economic Record*, vol. 43, no. 102, June 1967.

district on several variables that we believed to be associated with poverty. These included the percentage of the population in each district who were aged, the percentage who were under fifteen years, the percentage who were unemployed and the percentage who lived in rented accommodation. From other sources we added information on the incidence of pensioners and on the general levels of family income. By combining all these factors we were able to assess all districts and divide them into five groups or strata, ranging from the relatively affluent stratum I through to stratum V in which we expected the incidence of poverty to be the highest. The results of this stratification appeared convincing. Most of the inner suburbs were in stratum IV or V and all the districts that were known by welfare agencies to be poverty areas were in one or other of these two strata.

In each stratum a number of districts were randomly selected, each district being allowed a chance of selection proportional to its size. Within each of the selected districts the dwellings which were to comprise the sample were then chosen. In order to reduce the cost of travelling at the interviewing stage these were chosen in clusters averaging six dwellings. Fifty clusters were chosen in strata I and II, 70 in stratum III, 360 in stratum IV, and in stratum V (which was much smaller) 160.

TABLE 2·1

SAMPLE DESIGN

Stratum	Number of districts	Number of clusters	Approximate chance of selection
I	518	50	1 in 500
II	459	50	1 in 450
III	526	70	1 in 350
IV	468	360	1 in 54
V	79	160	1 in 16
Total	2,050*	690	1 in 137

*Sixty-one collectors' districts were omitted as being unsatisfactory for future sampling purposes. They contained too few dwellings or too many institutions for a satisfactory sampling of private dwellings to be made.

The actual selection of the dwellings in each cluster was done with great care by specially trained field staff in a manner that ensured complete randomness. It should be emphasised that throughout the process of selection we had no information about individual dwellings or the people within them, so prior knowledge did not influence the selection in any way. This complete absence of any form of bias in the selection procedure was essential if we were to calculate the probability of selection attaching to each dwelling. It was necessary to know these probabilities if, from a sample of less than one per cent, we were to make accurate estimates of the characteristics of the whole population.

The figures that appear throughout this book are estimates for the Melbourne metropolitan area derived from this relatively small sample. They are the result of a 'grossing up' procedure. To make these estimates each completed interview in the survey had a weighting attached to it which depended primarily on its chances of selection. Differences in weighting were necessary to 'correct' for the way in which we had slanted our sample towards the poverty strata. From Table 2·1 it can be seen, for example, that interviews in stratum I carried much higher weights (approximately 500) than interviews in stratum V where the weights were about 16.

The Questionnaire

The design of the questionnaire and the formulation of the exact questions stemmed from the objectives of the survey. Before discussing the questionnaire in any detail, however, it is worthwhile setting out certain of the basic definitions which had a bearing on its design.

Although the selected sample was in terms of dwellings, the questionnaire was designed to record information relating to a household only. It was realised that many dwellings would contain multiple households and in these situations the interview would be hopelessly complex unless each household was treated separately. A 'household' was defined as 'a group of persons who eat their meals together or whose meals are prepared by a common cook out of a common pot.'

It was decided that while some of the data could suitably be analysed on a household basis, it would be desirable for the bulk of the data, and in particular the income data, to be analysed on the basis of a more appropriate economic unit. For many purposes the household was too heterogeneous a unit, particularly if it contained boarders or consisted of an 'extended' family. As an alternative, the 'family' as a unit of analysis raised difficulties of definition which would lead to ambiguity. To frame a family definition that would be analytically useful and deal satisfactorily with in-laws, distant relatives and several generations seemed impossible. It was decided therefore to use as our basic unit of analysis

an 'income unit' which was defined as either: (i) a married couple and
their dependent children, i.e. their children less than fifteen years and
also any children aged fifteen years or older still engaged in full-time
secondary education; or (ii) a single person aged fifteen years or older,
no longer engaged in full-time secondary education. Thus an income
unit was defined as a maximum of a man, wife and dependent children:
an independent child or an aged parent, for example, was treated as a
separate income unit. In many households, of course, all persons fell
within the same income unit; in other households there were as many
income units as there were people.

The purpose of the questionnaire was to identify income units that
were in poverty and to record some of their basic characteristics. Bearing in mind the meaning we were attaching to poverty—the adequacy
of income in relation to the size and composition of the family for which
it had to provide—the main questions asked concerned the nature and
composition of the household and the income of all its members.

We wanted not only to collect information about the more obvious
elements of income, but to assess the importance of various sources of
additional income in the alleviation of poverty. These sources of additional income included child endowment, the profits made from non-
related boarders and intra-family board payments.

To pinpoint more exactly the information we needed, we built up a
large number of hypotheses which we hoped to test. We were, for
example, anxious to discover the incidence of certain economic 'disabilities' in the community and the extent to which poverty was associated with each disability and various combinations of them. The
disabilities that we chose as being important included old age, the lack
of a male head in the income unit, a large number of dependent children,
recent migration, low skill, sickness or accident preventing employment,
and unemployment. We were also interested in the standard and cost of
housing, particularly in relation to the level of income of the occupants.

The following is a brief description of the resultant eight-page questionnaire. The first section concerned the housing of the household.
Questions were asked on the type of accommodation, how many rooms
it contained and the extent to which rooms and bathing, toilet and
laundry facilities were shared with other households. The amounts of
weekly rent or instalment payments were recorded. Provision was also
made for interviewers to assess the standard of the housing on a five-
point scale ranging from very good to very poor.

The second section of the questionnaire dealt with the collection of personal information about each member of the household. Each person's relationship to the head of the household was recorded along with his sex, age, date and country of birth, year of arrival in Australia (in the case of a migrant) and his employment. In the case of anyone who worked either full-time or part-time questions were asked about work status, occupation and time off work during the past year.

The third section introduced questions on income. This was thought to be a difficult subject to broach. For this reason the first reference to income was left until this advanced stage of the interview, when it was hoped that rapport would have been established between the interviewer and the respondent. The first question concerning the level of income was: 'Could you tell me, of each person or married couple, whether their income last week was more or less than $80 after tax?' Only if income was said to be less than this amount were further questions asked about its composition. The figure of $80 was chosen as it was felt that if a man and wife had this income, no matter what size their family, they would not be in poverty.

All persons working full-time or part-time were then questioned as to whether that week's earnings were more or less than the earnings of a standard working week. Details of overtime, second jobs and time off from work were recorded.

Further questions about income were then asked of all whose income was less than $80 in the previous week. In all these cases we sought a detailed breakdown of income into earnings, social service pensions, gross amount received from non-related boarders, amounts from studentships and scholarships and any other income. Provision was made for the recording of annual income in the form of rent, interest and dividends and non-weekly earnings. Finally, women with eligible children were asked how much child endowment they received each week.

Because of our interest in intra-family board payments, details were sought of transactions involving money for board paid to, or received from relatives in the same household. The appropriate questions were asked whenever there were two or more related income units in the same household.

The questionnaire concluded with questions on the coverage of hospital and medical benefits, financial provision being made for retirement, and a couple of opinion questions designed to allow the respondents to 'have their say'.

Interviewing

During April, May and June of 1966 all interviews in Stage I were completed. The training of interviewers consisted of a detailed examination and discussion of the questionnaire and the *Guide to Interviewers* that had been specially prepared, practice in filling in questionnaire forms, simulated interviews and finally trial interviews in the field. In order to achieve greater accuracy in the interviewing of migrants, the interviewers were assisted in their work by a team of sixteen interpreters. Languages in which interviews were done included Greek, Italian, German, Maltese, Lebanese and Chinese.

Every reasonable attempt was made to secure an interview at the chosen addresses. Up to eight calls were made in order to establish contact and whenever an interview was refused a further attempt was made by another more experienced interviewer. These efforts were very successful in reducing the percentage of non-response.

The 4,306 interviews that were attempted produced 3,869 completed questionnaires (a response rate of 89·85 per cent). The 437 cases of non-response were made up of 155 cases of non-contact (3·60 per cent) and 282 refusals (6·55 per cent).

The completed questionnaires were checked carefully for any errors or inconsistencies. This very considerable mass of information was then coded and punched on to cards. Both the coding and punching were subjected to a series of tests to ensure that these processes were free of error before any analysis was done. Some of the basic statistics of the Stage I interviews are set out in Table 2·2.

TABLE 2·2

SUMMARY OF FIELD WORK

Number of income units included in the completed interviews	5,842
Number of people included in the completed interviews	12,056
Average number of income units per completed interview	1·51
Average number of people per income unit	2·06
Average number of people per completed interview	3·12
Typical length of interview	10–20 minutes

Method of Analysis of Income Data

There were two main problems in the analysis of the income data. Firstly, we had to decide what definition of income would be most appropriate for measuring the economic circumstances of people in or near poverty. Secondly, as we wished to compare the circumstances of different income units, some method of adjusting incomes to allow for the differing sizes and compositions of income units had to be devised.

Definition of Income: To frame a satisfactory definition of income for any purpose is notoriously difficult. The definition that should be used is the one most appropriate for the purpose in hand. Our main purpose was to measure as accurately as possible the income that was available to an income unit to meet its needs. However, as well as this we had a number of subsidiary purposes in mind. For example, we wanted to find out what bearing such additions to income as a wife's earnings, child endowment, profit from boarders or intra-family transfers had on whether a family was in poverty. Also we wondered about the extent to which high housing costs were contributing to poverty. These questions led us to frame a number of different definitions of income, but in this book only two of them are used.

The first is a fairly straightforward attempt to measure the disposable income of an income unit, and will be referred to simply as 'income'. It consisted of the weekly receipts (net of tax) of the head of the income unit and—in the case of a married couple, of his wife—in the form of earnings, pensions and benefits (both government and private), superannuation, rent, scholarships, etc. Any non-weekly receipts like rent, interest, dividends, profits, commissions, etc. were put on a weekly basis and included. In addition, child endowment and any income received by dependent children were taken into account.

As this measure is concerned with disposable income it takes no account of subsidies to various forms of expenditure. These subsidies may be important for some income units, particularly those containing pensioners who receive subsidies by way of the pensioner medical service and the concessional charges for telephone, television and radio licences, some forms of transport, rent and rates. However, these subsidies are contingent on the use of certain services and as some do not make much use of them they do not receive the benefits.

The second definition used may be referred to briefly as 'income after housing costs'. As the phrase implies, this was an attempt to measure what the income unit had left over after the cost of housing had been met. In some cases, because of high rents or instalment payments, families appeared to be in poverty by this measure although their income had apparently been adequate for their needs. In other cases, of course, where families were paying low rents or they owned their accommodation they appeared better off by this measure.

In the case of a household consisting of one income unit only (i.e. where there were no boarders) the calculation of 'income after housing costs' was quite simple. It was 'income' less whatever was paid in rent or instalments. For owner-occupiers or buyers no allowance was made for rates, land tax or maintenance and repair costs and to the extent that these costs are important the 'income after housing costs' may overestimate their true position.[3] The decision to omit these costs can be explained partly by the difficulty in collecting such information accurately and partly by the fact that at least some of the poor can defer such expenses as rates, repairs and maintenance.

In households in which there were boarders the calculation of 'income after housing costs' was more complex. It did not seem entirely satisfactory to attribute all the housing costs to the householder income unit: it seemed more reasonable that some part of the cost should be borne by the boarder who was also using the accommodation. For this reason the housing costs of the householder income unit were regarded as being equal to the rent or instalment payments made by him less any profit from boarders. That is, any profit from a boarder was regarded as an offset against the actual rent or instalments paid for the dwelling. In calculating this profit we assumed in all cases that $5.00 per week was the extra cost for food, etc. incurred by the householder because of the boarder; any board payment in excess of $5.00 per person represented profit to the householder. The choice of $5.00 as the 'cost' of the boarder is to some extent arbitrary—in actual cases the cost would vary enormously—but as our food expenditure enquiry showed, it does not seem unreasonable as a typical amount. In some cases, particularly when the boarder was related to the householder, the weekly board payments were less than $5.00. In these cases the householder was assumed to have made a loss equal to the deficiency and his 'income after housing costs' was reduced accordingly.

For the boarding income unit the cost of housing was regarded as the total board payment less the $5.00 which we assumed to be the cost of their food, etc. Their 'income after housing costs' was therefore equal to their 'income' less whatever this amount happened to be.

[3] An attempt to overcome the effect of this is made for the aged. See Chapter 5.

It will be apparent that except for the simplest household 'income after housing costs' contains a notional element. Whenever use is made of this measure it should be interpreted with this notional element in mind.

Income Adjustment: We wanted to make estimates of the number in poverty. Poverty, however, does not depend on income alone but on the size and type of family that it has to provide for. For example, a bachelor may live very comfortably on an income that would be quite insufficient for a married couple with several dependent children. Our problem was to know how we could bring all income units of varying sizes and compositions into a state of comparability. In some studies in the past this has been done by working in terms of equivalent adult males, regarding females as the equivalent of four-fifths of an adult male and children as one-half. This seems an unduly crude approach and we sought something more precise.

There is almost a complete lack of material in Australia on which to base adjustments of this kind. We examined many overseas approaches to the problem and eventually we decided to make use of data prepared in 1954 by the Budget Standard Service of New York, a co-operative organisation sponsored by the Welfare and Health Council in New York City for the use of social and health agencies in New York.[4] Their tabulations represented by far the most detailed approach that we could find to the problem of estimating costs and equivalent incomes for varying family groups. As well as allowing for the number of adults and children in the family unit, as is quite commonly done, allowance is also made for the age, sex and work status of the individuals. The costs of those who live alone are recognised as being higher than the costs of those who live with others. Their tabulations set out a method for calculating the total weekly costs of goods and services for various types of family units. Their data were based on 'the costs of prescribed quantities of goods and services in New York in October 1954. The quantities conform to standards based on scientific requirements for good nutrition and health, in so far as purely physical needs have been determined, and to social standards that have been revealed by studies of actual family purchases. The kinds of goods and services priced and used in the calculation of costs are typical of purchases made by families in the low to moderate income groups.'

[4] A detailed description of their data is published in *Low Income Families: Hearings before the Subcommittee on Low Income Families,* Joint Committee on the Economic Report, US Government Printing Office, Washington, DC, 1955, pp. 185-213.

The fact that the costs are in units of 1954 US dollars can be ignored as in using them we are not concerned with actual costs but rather with relative costs of goods and services. Thus the costs can be thought of as indices rather than money values. Their use assumes that the relationship between the costs of living of, say, a pre-school child and a working adult male is similar in New York in 1954 and in Melbourne in 1966. Of course, there is in fact an almost infinite variety in the patterns of costs among families but if one has to settle on a standard pattern, the New York data (as set out in Appendix B) do present a set of cost relationships that appears quite plausible for Melbourne.

Standard costs, which were made up of two parts, were calculated for every income unit in our survey. Firstly, there were the costs for each person, covering such items as food, clothing, education, recreation and transport that vary according to the age, sex and work status of the individual. Secondly, there were the housing and other costs like power, light, furniture, furnishings and equipment that vary with the size of the income unit.

Table 2·3 may clarify the way in which standard costs were built up for each income unit. The amounts shown are derived from Table B·1 in Appendix B.

The examples in Table 2·3 illustrate some of the assumptions underlying the construction of the standard costs. The costs for each person for personal requirements are assumed to be higher for males than for females and to vary with the age of the person. For children they rise as the child becomes older and for adults they are assumed to fall slightly at forty years and still further at sixty-five years. Costs are also assumed to be higher for those who work than for those who stay at home and they are higher for those living alone than for those who live with others. The examples also illustrate the spreading of such overhead costs of housing, power, furniture and equipment as the size of the family increases.

The necessary standard cost calculations have been made for all the income units in our survey. In order to have a point of reference for the adjustment of income we took the family group listed above—a man, wife and two children—to be a standard family. The incomes of all income units were then adjusted so that they became in each case the income that would have been equivalent had the income unit consisted of a man, wife and two children. The adjustment, which was made by multiplying the actual income by the ratio of the standard costs of the standard family to the standard costs of each particular unit, enabled us

TABLE 2·3

STANDARD COSTS FOR SELECTED INCOME UNITS

1 *Standard costs of a family*	
Male head (under 40 years—working)	19.70
Wife (under 40 years—at home)	10.00
Son (between 6 and 15 years)	8.48
Daughter (under 6 years)	5.80
Power, furniture, equipment (4 persons)	11.10
Housing (4 persons)	12.95
	67.31
2 *Standard costs for a single elderly person living alone*	
Male head (over 65 years—at home)	12.95
Power, furniture, equipment (1 person)	6.05
Housing (1 person)	11.20
	30.20
Female head (over 65 years—at home)	10.85
Power, furniture, equipment (1 person)	6.05
Housing (1 person)	11.20
	28.10
3 *Standard costs of an elderly married couple*	
Male head (over 65 years—at home)	11.85
Wife (over 65 years—at home)	8.10
Power, furniture, equipment (2 persons)	9.30
Housing (2 persons)	10.85
	40.10

to compare the economic circumstances of all income units as if they were of the same size and composition.

One example of this adjustment of income will suffice. The actual income of a single male age pensioner (without Supplementary Assistance or additional income) at the time of our survey was $12.00. His standard costs were 30.20. His 'adjusted income' then is

$$\$12.00 \times \frac{67.31}{30.20} = \$26.75.$$

The Poverty Line: Traditionally a 'poverty line' is drawn to separate the poor from the non-poor. It is drawn at a specific income level.

reflecting a current judgment as to the minimum standard below which a family should not fall. It depends on an assessment of what seems appropriate in a particular situation, taking account of community attitudes, economic conditions, customs and traditions. As a consequence the poverty line is drawn differently in different places. It is not easy to explain why, but there is no doubt that an income that would spell comfort in many countries means poverty in Australia. Similarly through time, the line must move upwards: we recognise that an income that would have kept a family quite comfortably at the turn of the century would be regarded as quite inadequate today.

We have assumed that if the standard family of a man, wife and two children had in 1966 an income that was equal only to the basic wage plus child endowment they would be likely to be in poverty. This amounted to $32.00, so it was assumed that $33.00 was a reasonable figure to use as a poverty line. The extra 80 cents was added so that the poverty line could be expressed in whole dollars, but the addition may also be regarded as a recognition that even among unskilled workers it was rare for them to receive only the basic wage.

Any income unit whose 'adjusted income' was below $33.00 was regarded as being in poverty. A comparison of the standard family and some categories of age pensioners, a group whose incomes before adjustment were quite different, illustrates the effect of this process of adjustment. Table 2.4 shows that after adjustment their incomes were much more alike, although only the aged married couple were above the poverty line.

TABLE 2·4

COMPARISON OF ADJUSTED INCOMES

	Income	Standard cost	Adjusted income
	$		$
(i) Standard family on basic wage plus child endowment	32.20	67.31	32.20
(ii) Male age pensioner living alone	12.00	30.20	26.75
(iii) Male age pensioner living alone and receiving Supplementary Assistance	14.00	30.20	31.20
(iv) Married age pensioner couple	22.00	40.10	36.93

There is, of course, a similar need to adjust 'income after housing costs'. This was done in a comparable manner, using the standard cost tabulations but excluding the housing element. In this way we were able to calculate standard costs excluding housing for all income units. Thus for the standard family these were 54·36, i.e. 67·31 less 12·95. The ratio of this measure for the standard family to that of a particular income unit was then used as the factor to adjust 'income after housing costs' for that income unit.

To illustrate, take the case in Table 2·4 of the male age pensioner receiving Supplementary Assistance and assume that he pays a rent of $5.00. His income was $14.00, his income after housing costs was $9.00 and his standard costs excluding housing costs were 19.00 (i.e. 30.20 less 11.20). His 'adjusted income after housing costs' was therefore

$$\$9.00 \times \frac{54.36}{19.00} = \$25.75.$$

As we wanted to measure poverty in terms of 'adjusted income after housing costs' we also had to set a poverty line in terms of this criterion. It is a fairly common assumption that housing costs for low income families should represent not more than 20 per cent of income: our survey data showed that there were very great variations in the relationship of housing costs to income but that if a single percentage had to be chosen a figure around 20 per cent was not unrealistic. In addition, in the standard costs of the standard family, housing was 19 per cent of the total costs. We therefore adopted a poverty line for 'adjusted income after housing costs' of $27.00: this seemed the most appropriate whole dollar amount, being 18 per cent below the $33.00 poverty line.

Updating the Poverty Line: The two poverty lines that have been set above relate to the period of the Stage I survey, the June quarter of 1966. Although in interpreting the results of the survey these are the relevant poverty lines, their appropriateness diminishes as we move from that date. As recommendations which relate to 1970 are made in this book it is necessary to update the poverty line.

We have assumed that the movement of the poverty line should allow not only for price changes but also for rising productivity and the increasing standards of the general community. More precisely, we maintain that the standard of living of pensioners should not be allowed to decline in relation to that of the average worker. For this reason we have linked it to the movements in the average weekly earnings per employed male unit in Victoria. In the June quarter of 1966, the poverty line of $33.00 was 54·55 per cent of the average weekly earnings. If this relationship were maintained, the poverty line would have risen to $40.20 by the June quarter of 1969, when average earnings had risen to $73.70. At the time of writing the best estimate that can be made of the change in average earnings in the period from June 1969 to June 1970 is that they will increase by at least a further 5·4 per cent. Raising the $40.20 poverty line by this percentage gives us an estimate of approximately $42.40 for the June quarter in 1970. In terms of income after housing costs the appropriate poverty line would be about $34.50.

Results of Stage I

As has been mentioned before, there were 5,842 income units in the completed interviews. When appropriate 'weights' are attached to each of these we get an estimate of 959,000 income units for the Melbourne metropolitan area. From this total there are two groups, however, that have been omitted when making the estimates that appear in most of the following tables.

The first group consists of those income units for whom insufficient income data were available. These constituted less than 5 per cent of the total and have been omitted from the income tabulations in order to simplify presentation. We believe that little or no distortion results from this as the evidence suggests that the characteristics of those with unknown incomes were not significantly different from those of the rest of the sample.

Secondly, we have omitted income units headed by a 'juvenile' as it was thought, particularly in tables concerned with income, that their inclusion would make the tables less useful. An income unit headed by a juvenile was one in which there were no dependants and the head was either under 21 years or, in the case of a full-time tertiary student, over 21 but still living at home. Whatever the economic circumstances of these juveniles, to include them in income tabulations was likely to distort our estimates of the numbers in poverty and their characteristics. In particular, if a juvenile was in poverty at the time of the survey because he was receiving juvenile rates of pay or living on a small student's allowance, it is likely that the poverty would only be temporary and would be left behind automatically as he commanded adult rates of pay. This view of the transitory nature of juvenile poverty is one that may justifiably be held in an economy that has had virtual full employment for three decades.

The group that remained when these subtractions had been made totalled 4,791 income units. When the appropriate weights were attached to each of these we estimated that there were approximately 771,000 adult income units with known incomes in Melbourne.

In Table 2·5 we have the first overall estimate of poverty in the Melbourne metropolitan area. It can be seen that over 59,000 adult income units (7·7 per cent of the total) appear to be living below the poverty line. As well, there are a further 40,000 adult income units who may be described as marginally poor, being less than 20 per cent above the rather austerely drawn poverty line. These estimates must be regarded as being of a preliminary nature only, as not all income units that have a low adjusted income are in fact in need. In various parts of this book, particularly in Chapter 4, the problems of modifying these results are discussed and, in the light of additional information, new estimates are made. These show that a smaller proportion of the aged were poor than disclosed in the first estimate and that some other cases of poverty were temporary. The proportion of the total that were in need is estimated to be 4 per cent.

TABLE 2·5

ADULT INCOME UNITS CLASSIFIED BY ADJUSTED INCOME   Unknown Incomes Omitted

	Adjusted income in $				
	0-27	27-33	33-39	39 and over	Total
	Very poor	Poor	Marginal	Not poor	
Estimated number	32,594	26,906	40,462	671,531	771,493
Percentage	4·2	3·5	5·2	87·1	100·0

The simple classification in Table 2·5 of income units according to their adjusted income needs some further explanation. The first class, less than $27, contains those income units which were more than $6 (or about 20 per cent) below the poverty line and may be thought of as 'very poor'. The class $27-$33 contains the rest of those in poverty. Those in this class have been described as 'poor' and must be added to the 'very poor' to get the total estimated to be in poverty. The class $33-$39 contains those who may be thought of as being 'marginal' in that they are less than $6 (or about 20 per cent) above the poverty line. Income units in this group seem to be quite vulnerable and in many cases only a slight change in their circumstances would result in them falling below the poverty line. The final class contains those whose adjusted income is over $39. This class is described as 'not poor' and includes income units with a wide variety of circumstances, right through to the most affluent members of the community.[5]

It should be remembered that these estimates relate to the population living in private households only and make no allowance for those in poverty who live in institutions. The estimates are also dependent on the methods of analysis and the assumptions outlined above. The use of other measures of income, other methods of adjusting income, other criteria in estimating poverty or other definitions of the poverty line would, no doubt, yield somewhat different results.

In Table 2·6 a different estimate is made, measuring the incidence of poverty after housing costs have been met. In this table the classes are set out in a fashion similar to those in the previous table. The appropriate poverty line is now set at $27, and the classes containing income units less than $6 above and below this line are shown. The total number of income units in this table is less than in the previous one, the difference arising because there were some for whom income was known but either rent, instalments or board payments were not known.

TABLE 2·6

ADULT INCOME UNITS CLASSIFIED BY ADJUSTED INCOME AFTER HOUSING COSTS

Unknown Incomes Omitted

| | Adjusted income after housing costs in $ | | | | |
| | Less than 21 | 21-27 | 27-33 | 33 and over | Total |
	Very poor	Poor	Marginal	Not poor	
Estimated number	39,365	15,468	27,601	683,659	766,093
Percentage	5·1	2·0	3·6	89·3	100·0

From Table 2·6 it can be seen that the overall incidence of poverty calculated by this criterion is slightly lower than that estimated by the adjusted income criterion, falling from 7·7 per cent to 7·1 per cent. From this it might be thought that housing costs are not an important cause of poverty in the community and, in fact, they appear to be a

[5] In all income classifications throughout the book the class intervals used have been quite precisely defined. For example, the classes used in Table 2·5 are $0 but less than $27, $27 but less than $33, $33 but less than $39, and $39 and over. These classes have been described more simply, however, at $0-$27, $27-$33, $33-$39, and $39 and over in order to make the presentation less cumbersome. This simplification is used throughout the book.

factor in the alleviation of poverty for some. A general conclusion such as this would be deceptively simple, as housing costs by no means cause all families to move upward on the poverty scale. One or two further comments on housing costs and the incidence of poverty are warranted.

Firstly, the percentage in the 'very poor' class is greater after housing costs have been met than before, rising from 4·3 per cent to 5·1 per cent. This indicates that housing costs for at least some families are high enough to reduce them to a standard of living that is very meagre.

Secondly, the effects of housing costs tend to differ between the different forms of occupancy. For example, among householders who owned or were buying their homes 6·9 per cent were in poverty according to the adjusted income criterion. This fell to 5·5 per cent when housing costs were allowed for. In general, housing costs were sufficiently low in this group of owner-occupiers to raise some families above the poverty line. This was because many of them owned their homes outright and therefore, by our definition, had no housing costs. Among the buyers there was, however, evidence of poverty resulting from extremely high instalment payments. This was particularly true among the migrants, many of whom were heavily over-committed with instalment payments. Among householders who were Housing Commission tenants there were 16 per cent in poverty on the basis of their adjusted income. After housing costs had been met this figure fell slightly to 15·7 per cent, no doubt reflecting the subsidised rents granted by the Commission in cases of hardship. Householders who rented privately fared rather worse, housing costs causing the numbers of them in poverty to increase. There were 8·8 per cent estimated to be in poverty when measured by adjusted income and this rose to 10·1 per cent after housing costs had been allowed for.

Within each of these groups there were diverse movements. The overall effect of housing costs conceals some cases of good fortune in housing but rather more cases of considerable hardship resulting from high rents or instalments that were out of proportion to the income of the householder.

People in Poverty

The results so far have all been stated in terms of an artificial concept, the income unit. As a consequence perhaps they may have lost meaning and impact and it may help to restate them in terms of people, for it is human beings, not concepts or theories, that are the ultimate concern in our study of poverty.

Our first calculations indicated that the income units, whose adjusted income showed them to be in poverty, contained about 120,000 people.[6] In other words, approximately one person in every eighteen appeared to be living below the poverty line. In this group there were approximately 42,000 dependent children. While for most purposes in a study of poverty it is sensible to ignore the income units headed by juveniles, it is of interest to record that these included a further 24,000 people whose adjusted income indicated that they were in poverty. Many, but not all, of these juveniles, while appearing to be in poverty, are not in need as they are living with relatives and are being subsidised by them. If, however, we do include them all, the total number of people in poverty would then be 144,000 or about one person in every fifteen.

TABLE 2·7

POPULATION CLASSIFIED ACCORDING TO TYPE OF PERSON AND ADJUSTED INCOME
Unknown Incomes Omitted *

Type of person		Adjusted income in $				
		0-27 Very poor	27-33 Poor	33-39 Marginal	39 and over Not poor	Total
Adults	No.	43,111	34,164	64,185	1,108,370	1,249,830
	%	3·5	2·7	5·1	88·7	100·0
Dependent children	No.	19,330	23,266	47,020	596,621	686,237
	%	2·8	3·4	6·9	86·9	100·0
People in income units headed by an adult	No.	62,441	57,430	111,205	1,704,991	1,936,067
	%	3·2	3·0	5·7	88·1	100·0
Independent juveniles	No.	19,237	5,148	12,783	103,865	141,033
	%	13·6	3·7	9·1	73·6	100·0
All people	No.	81,678	62,578	123,988	1,808,856	2,077,100
	%	3·9	3·0	6·0	87·1	100·0

*This table excludes people in income units for which adjusted income was unknown. The excluded people include 55,479 adults, 15,266 children and 6,729 juveniles and when added to the total of the above table give the estimated population of Melbourne (excluding the institutional population) of 2,154,574.

In the marginally poor group, those not more than 20 per cent above the poverty line, there were a further 111,000 people in income units

[6] These estimates are revised, particularly with respect to the aged in poverty, in subsequent chapters.

headed by an adult. Within this number there were some 47,000 children. In addition there were 13,000 juveniles who were marginally poor.

Further details of how adults, dependent children and juveniles are placed in relation to the poverty line are set out in Table 2·7.

What are the characteristics of these people living in or near poverty? How do they differ from the rest of the community? Several of the later chapters are devoted to providing quite detailed answers to such questions. The structure of households and income units—their size, and the age and sex of the head—are studied in conjunction with many other factors. The most important of these is, of course, income, but factors such as the type of accommodation, work status, occupation, country of birth and period of residence in Australia are all of importance.

In the remainder of this chapter two additional ways of looking at our data are examined as a preliminary to these more detailed studies. Firstly, income units are classified into various types of families and the incidence of poverty in each is examined. Secondly, the analysis of our data in terms of economic 'disabilities' is outlined. Estimates are made of the numbers suffering from various disabilities and the incidence of poverty in each disability group is given. Finally, some estimates are made of the relative importance of various combinations of disabilities as factors contributing to poverty.

Families

It is obvious that some types of families are more prone to poverty than others. To examine this observation further we have used the three factors which seemed most important—the age and the sex of the head of the income unit and the presence of dependent children within the income unit—and classified all adult income units into six types of families. These are families headed by an aged male, by an aged female, by a male without dependent children, by a female without dependent children, by a male with dependent children and by a female with dependent children. A comparison of these types of families is set out in Table 2·8

The first two types of families consist of those income units headed by a person of pensionable age, either male or female, irrespective of the numbers of dependants. Many of these will, of course, be single person income units, particularly in the cases where an income unit is headed by an aged female. In the case of a married couple, the male, by definition, is always regarded as the head, therefore all aged married couples are counted in the first class. The remaining types of families all consist of income units in which the head is below pensionable age. In the first two of these there are the income units in which there are no dependent children. Many of the families headed by a male will be married couples but the families headed by a female, although they may live in households with others, are, by definition, single person families. The last two groups contain the families in which there are dependent children. In almost all cases where such a family is headed by a male it is an 'intact' family; the number of cases of a father caring for dependent children without the aid of a wife is relatively few. In the final group we have the families in which a mother is bringing up a family without the aid of a male breadwinner.

TABLE 2·8

ADULT INCOME UNITS CLASSIFIED BY TYPE OF FAMILY SHOWING PERCENTAGE IN EACH
ADJUSTED INCOME CLASS   Unknown Incomes Omitted

Family headed by	Estimated number	Adjusted income in $				
		0-27 Very poor	27-33 Poor	33-39 Marginal	39 and over Not poor	All classes
Aged male	58,348	11·8	3·4	21·8	63·0	100·0
Aged female	73,309	8·3	17·8	13·1	60·8	100·0
Male without dependent children	250,266	2·0	0·9	0·6	96·5	100·0
Female without dependent children	84,595	8·3	2·9	2·8	86·0	100·0
Male with dependent children	291,770	1·8	1·9	4·3	92·0	100·0
Female with dependent children	13,205	18·3	12·1	14·1	55·5	100·0
Total income units	771,493	4·2	3·5	5·2	87·1	100·0

In Table 2·8 the varying incidence of poverty among these families can be seen. The low incidence of poverty among the families with non-aged male heads, both with and without dependent children, is a reflection of the fact that almost all adult males are able to secure employment incomes that are sufficient to keep their families out of poverty. Only when they have a large number of dependent children to support are they likely to fall below the poverty line.

The families that are most vulnerable to poverty are those headed by an aged person or a female. In particular, the circumstances of the 'fatherless families' appear markedly more difficult than those of any other family type, as among them over 30 per cent were below the poverty line and a further 14 per cent only marginally above it.

Disabilities and Poverty

Studies in other countries as well as observations in our own economy have made it clear that poverty is closely associated with certain economic 'disabilities', particularly the disabilities of old age and the absence of a male head in the family. To discover the relative importance of the various characteristics that may be associated with poverty in Melbourne we have cross-classified income units according to the disabilities suffered by the head of the income units and their adjusted income. The disabilities that were chosen as being the most relevant for this purpose were as follows.

1 Old age—income units in which the head was of pensionable age i.e. 60 and over for women, 65 and over for men

2 Lack of a male head—income units in which the head was female but there were no dependent children

3 Fatherless families—income units in which the head was female and there were one or more children

4 Large families—income units in which there were four or more dependent children

5 Recent migrants—income units in which the head arrived in Australia after 1960 and was not born in the United Kingdom, North America, New Zealand or South Africa

6 Low skill—income units in which the head normally worked at an occupation that required little or no skill

7 Sickness or accident—income units in which the head had been prevented from working for eight or more weeks in the past year

8 Unemployment—income units in which the head had been unemployed for eight or more weeks in the past year

An income unit head obviously may suffer from more than one of these disabilities. For example, an income unit headed by an aged female has the disabilities of age and lack of a male head; an unemployed migrant with a large family has three disabilities, each of which may be part of the reason for him having a low adjusted income. In recording the incidence of disabilities we have defined our classes on an inclusive basis, that is, income units like those above have been included in the totals of each of the relevant disabilities.

Table 2·9 shows the estimated number of income units having each of the disabilities, the number having none of the disabilities, and how they were distributed through the adjusted income classes. Of the 771,000 income units it is estimated that 408,000 (or 52·9 per cent) had none of the selected disabilities. Within this no-disability group nearly 97 per cent were classified as 'not poor'. This is indicative of a strong relationship between these disabilities and poverty.

TABLE 2·9

ADULT INCOME UNITS CLASSIFIED BY DISABILITIES SHOWING PERCENTAGE IN EACH
ADJUSTED INCOME CLASS   Disabilities Counted on an Inclusive Basis; Unknown Incomes Omitted

Disability	Estimated number	Adjusted income in $				
		0-27 Very poor	27-33 Poor	33-39 Marginal	39 and over Not poor	All classes
Old age	131,658	9·8	11·4	17·0	61·8	100·0
Female head without dependent children	157,788	8·2	9·8	7·6	74·4	100·0
Fatherless family	13,432	18·5	12·3	14·1	55·1	100·0
Large family	44,974	1·5	7·2	14·0	77·3	100·0
Recent migrant	38,286	13·7	0·8	2·4	83·1	100·0
Low skill	67,636	4·4	2·4	6·5	86·7	100·0
Sickness or accident	22,079	9·4	4·4	7·5	78·7	100·0
Unemployment	2,349	6·7	0·0	22·0	71·3	100·0
No disability	408,058	1·4	0·7	1·0	96·9	100·0
Total income units	771,493*	4·2	3·5	5·2	87·1	100·0

*As many income units suffer from more than one disability the addition of the estimated number suffering from each disability is greater than the total number of income units.

The estimates of the percentages in poverty in each of the disability groups provide us with some information that is of interest and is relevant to any anti-poverty programme. The most commonly occurring disabilities were the lack of a male head and old age: these occurred in 20·5 per cent and 17·1 per cent of all income units respectively. Income units with either of these disabilities had a relatively high incidence of poverty, 17 per cent of the female heads and 21 per cent of the aged falling below the poverty line.[7] Fatherless families were the group in which poverty was most noticeable: over 30 per cent were below the

[7] After more detailed investigation at Stage II the percentage of the aged in poverty is estimated to be 15·2. See Chapter 5, Table 5·1.

poverty line. However, they were a relatively small group as only $1 \cdot 7$ per cent of all income units suffered from this disability. The large families, the recent migrants and those suffering from sickness or accident all had percentages in poverty that were higher than the $7 \cdot 7$ per cent found among all income units. The association of poverty with all these disabilities warrants further examination and each of them is discussed in detail in subsequent chapters.

Low skill and unemployment, two factors that have been associated with poverty in other countries, do not appear to be important explanations of poverty in Melbourne. However, the number who were unemployed in our survey were too few for much reliance to be placed on statistics based on them and it is probable that unemployment, although affecting a very small percentage of the population, is more strongly associated with poverty than our estimates in Table $2 \cdot 9$ suggest. Unemployment is discussed further in Chapter 9. Low skill, on the other hand, which was one of the more commonly occurring disabilities, has been rejected as a significant factor causing poverty. Only $6 \cdot 8$ per cent of those with low skill appeared to be below the poverty line. In addition, there is considerable difficulty in defining low skill in a meaningful and consistent way. For these reasons the relationship between low skill and poverty is not discussed further.

In Table $2 \cdot 9$ the disability groups were defined on an inclusive basis, thus resulting in double or treble counting of any income unit that had two or three disabilities. The most important example of this is that income units headed by elderly females were counted in the totals of both the income units with the disability of old age and the income units having a female head. This overlapping of disabilities needed to be examined further. If we were to make the most effective policy recommendations, we needed to pinpoint more exactly which disabilities or combinations of disabilities were most closely associated with low adjusted income. To do this we have reclassified our income units into disability groups defined so that they are mutually exclusive. Under this arrangement each income unit is counted in one disability group only.

The seven disabilities we have considered (now omitting low skill) give rise to a very large number of exclusive disability groups. Not only are there the seven groups containing income units with each of the single disabilities only, but there are all the possible combinations of two, three or more disabilities that could occur. In fact, in our survey we found more than two dozen different combinations. To present an

analysis of so many groups would be confusing and, of course, the
numbers in many of the groups would be so small as not to be meaningful. In Table 2·10, therefore, we have presented only eleven different
groups. The first seven groups are those in which are recorded the
income units with one disability only—one group for each of the seven
disabilities. There are two groups of income units which have the two
most commonly occurring combinations of two disabilities—groups containing income units in which the heads were both aged and female, or
recent migrant and female. The group containing all other disability
combinations includes income units that had all two-disability combinations other than the two combinations just mentioned, as well as those
that had combinations of three or four disabilities. The final group contains all those income units that had none of the seven disabilities.

TABLE 2·10

ADULT INCOME UNITS CLASSIFIED BY DISABILITY SHOWING PERCENTAGE IN EACH ADJUSTED
INCOME CLASS   Disabilities Defined on a Mutually Exclusive Basis; Unknown Incomes Omitted

Disability	Estimated number	Adjusted income $				
		0-27 Very poor	27-33 Poor	33-39 Marginal	39 and over Not poor	All classes
Aged male head only	56,508	10·2	3·5	22·5	63·8	100·0
Female head only	75,934	5·9	3·3	2·4	88·4	100·0
Fatherless family only	12,776	18·4	11·3	13·8	56·5	100·0
Large family only	43,125	1·2	7·2	13·9	77·7	100·0
Recent migrant only	25,557	1·3	0·3	3·0	95·4	100·0
Sickness or accident only	16,377	4·9	5·5	8·5	81·1	100·0
Unemployment only	1,277	9·5	0·0	0·0	90·5	100·0
Aged female head only	69,540	6·9	18·6	13·8	60·7	100·0
Recent migrant, female head only	6,588	34·7	0·0	0·6	64·7	100·0
All other disability combinations	11,488	29·8	3·2	7·9	59·1	100·0
No disability	452,324	1·7	0·8	1·2	96·3	100·0
Total	771,493	4·2	3·5	5·2	87·1	100·0

A number of interesting points emerge from this table. Whereas in
Table 2·9, 21·2 per cent of the aged were below the poverty line, Table
2·10 indicates that poverty among the aged males was considerably
lower than this (13·2 per cent), but among the aged females it was

25·5 per cent. It appears, therefore, that it is not the disability of age alone that is critical but rather the combination of being aged and female. Eighteen per cent of those income units headed by a female were below the poverty line in Table 2·9. However, when we see in Table 2·10 the aged female heads separated from those females who have no other disability it is evident that poverty appears to be much more a function of old age than of a lack of a male head. Table 2·10 isolates the aged females as a group with a very high incidence of poverty and in need of help. As explained in Chapter 5, many of these aged females were helped by their families and by having low housing costs, although some remained in need.

Among the recent migrants 14·6 per cent were seen to be in poverty in Table 2·9. We may ask whether they were below the poverty line because they were recent migrants or whether it was because of other disabilities that they suffered. In Table 2·10 we see that among those income units that had only the disability of being a recent migrant, less than 2 per cent were in poverty. This suggests that poverty is more likely to result from other disabilities in combination with migration. This is also indicated by the high incidence of poverty among the income units headed by females who were recent migrants. (Many of them, however, were living with and supported by other members of their families who were above the poverty line.)

Fatherless families were the group with the highest incidence of poverty in Table 2·9, 30·8 per cent. In Table 2·10, of those families which had this disability alone, 29·7 per cent were below the poverty line. It seems that no other disability need be combined with that of being a fatherless family to cause a high incidence of poverty. This finding isolates another group which is in need of help.

Finally, the large percentage in poverty among the group having all the other disability combinations should be noted. This is a heterogenous group made up of many and varied combinations of disabilities. It is clear that many in this group need help, but because those with each specific combination of disabilities are few in number there is a danger that they will be overlooked.

All the estimates in this chapter are based on Stage I of the survey. Stage II of the survey, which is discussed in the next chapter, provided material to illuminate and modify the generalisations that have been made in this chapter. Information from both Stages is used in subsequent chapters in the more detailed discussions on the important disability groups.

3 Stage II and Food Expenditure*

To discover the nature and effects of poverty we needed to know more about low-income families than we could find out in the first interview. Stage II was designed to gather this information. More than 500 of the poor or nearly poor income units were questioned in detail about their personal backgrounds and present circumstances. Most of the questions were factual, but some opinion questions were also included. In addition, about 150 families kept a daily record of purchases of food over a fortnight. This chapter contains a brief outline of how this information was collected and a general review of the findings which emerged.

Collection of Information

Selection

Selection of income units to be reinterviewed was made after classifying all those interviewed at Stage I according to adjusted income. Nearly all those chosen were below or only just above the poverty line; a few with higher incomes were reinterviewed for comparative purposes. The sample was chosen so that it contained the same proportions of characteristics such as old age, lack of a male breadwinner, large family size and recent migration as the Stage I population from which it was drawn. Independent children living at home were not reinterviewed unless their parents were selected. In that case they were interviewed so that the family's circumstances could be seen as a whole.

The Questionnaire

The questionnaire was a substantial document containing sixty-eight major questions grouped into seven schedules. These covered family background, health, employment, housing, committed expenditure, income for the past year, and social contact. Such diverse information was needed to put income and housing costs into wider context and to provide material for a case-study approach to poverty.

The interview opened with questions on family background: where respondents were born, where they grew up, and what level of schooling they reached. A series of questions followed which asked at what age children had left or were likely to leave school and what educational expenses had been incurred in the past year.

The interviewer next turned to the health of all members of the income unit: illnesses during the year, nature and costs of health treatment, and satisfaction with domiciliary services such as council house-

* This chapter was written by Sheila Shaver.

keepers and meals on wheels. Were the present services being used? Were additional services needed? We also wanted to know about membership of voluntary health insurance, costs of contributions and refunds received. Expenditure on health care was recorded separately for general practitioner and specialist care, hospital care, nursing, dental care and chemist bills. An important subject of inquiry was the use of pensioner medical service, Repatriation Department health services and other government health services.

The employment schedule had to cover people in two situations: those usually working and those usually at home. For working people it sought details about their jobs over the past three years, the number of hours worked weekly in the present job, and for women, preferred working hours and the arrangements made for the care of children. Those who had once worked were asked why they were no longer working, whether they would like to resume and, if so, what would enable them to do so.

The housing schedule included questions regarding the number of rooms the family occupied, the extent to which they were shared and how the house or flat was heated. The type and condition of facilities for the provision of hot water, cooking and laundry were recorded. We also asked about satisfaction with housing, what dissatisfied occupants would prefer and whether the person's name was on a waiting list for Victorian Housing Commission or other accommodation. Interviewers made independent assessments of housing from the standpoint of basic structure, basic facilities, furnishings and equipment, and cleanliness and household management.

The fifth schedule dealt with committed expenditure. A large part of this concerned costs of housing for owners, buyers, tenants and boarders, and the cost of gas, electricity and other fuel. For owners and buyers the purchase price, mortgage payments or instalments, rates, insurance and repairs were collected, as well as the source of finance and interest rates. This schedule also included questions on the cost of travel to work, superannuation, insurance and hire purchase commitments. The reason for including this information was to get some idea of the level of certain expenditures which in the short run at least could not be postponed or varied should income fail.

As in Stage I, income questions were delayed to allow as much time as possible for rapport to develop between interviewer and respondent. A wide range of questions had to be asked in the sixth schedule to ensure the disclosure of all income received during the past twelve months from all sources. Firstly, a sequence of questions was directed towards establishing gross annual earnings and tax, with an alternative sequence available to take account of self-employed persons. Then followed other questions, covering income from superannuation, annuities and non-government pensions; government cash payments, including pensions, child endowment and repatriation benefits; workers' compensation; income from dividends, interest and rents; payments from family and non-family boarders; and lump sum receipts and several types of miscellaneous income including gifts and legacies. The second half of the schedule collected information on assets and debts.

Some miscellaneous information, mostly of a social nature, was collected in the final schedule. Social contact outside the home was explored in terms of the type and frequency of contacts made, and whether these were regarded as sufficient. Respondents were asked when they last had a holiday away from home and where they stayed. A group of questions investigated the sources of help to which people would turn in different kinds of crisis. We were particularly interested to know people's attitudes towards social services and how familiar they were with social service provisions. What experience had they had with social services? Did they know what was available? Finally, respondents rated their own future circumstances as better, worse or the same as at present, listed their most urgent problems and gave their opinions about what should be done to improve the welfare of people in the community.

Thus the completed questionnaires contained a vast amount of information about the circumstances of low-income persons and families. Some of this material has yet to be analysed.

The Food Expenditure Survey

Some respondents were asked to complete a diary of household expenditure on food during the fortnight following the interview. We restricted our choice of families so that the sample was reasonably homogeneous and therefore not difficult to interpret. Firstly, we excluded migrant families who had arrived in Australia in 1960 or later, in order to minimise language difficulties. (Nevertheless several diaries had to be translated from Greek and Italian and one from Russian.) Secondly, we excluded households containing more than one income unit, as it would have been difficult to decide what share of food expenditure belonged to each unit.

The interviewer left the diary and asked the respondent to record all expenditure on food. The next day, and at least three more times during the fortnight, a 'food diary recaller' came to help fill out the diary and to see that purchases of non-food items, such as matches and soap powder, were not included. Respondents were asked to enter all food purchases, including food and drink bought and consumed away from home, and to keep grocery dockets where possible. On these visits the recaller also asked about shopping habits and bulk purchasing, meals provided by or for friends and relatives, and whether the diary fortnight was typical. When the diary was complete the respondent was given $2 as some recompense for the time and trouble involved.

Interviewing and Analysis of Data

Interviewers: Interviewers skilled in casework were required and for this reason most of the fifteen employed at Stage II were qualified and experienced social workers. Some of the others were psychologists. Their preparation for the survey included pilot interviewing (which served to test the questionnaire as well as to train the interviewer), practice interviews with the final version of the questionnaire, and small group discussions to standardise approach and review commonly occurring problems. A detailed *Guide to Interviewers* was provided for reference.

Ideally the interviewer should have supervised the food diary; it would then have been possible to take advantage of the rapport already established and to avoid any repetition necessitated by the introduction of another field worker into the household. However, as the supervision of each diary required a number of visits, it was considered an uneconomic use of the interviewers' very limited time, and three food diary recallers were employed. Two of them were social workers and the third an experienced interviewer who had been a supervisor at Stage I.

Several interpreters were employed to assist interviewers. The decision whether to use an interpreter was left to individual interviewers because several of them spoke foreign languages and on some occasions a family member was able to act as interpreter.

Since it was obviously important to keep changes of circumstances between the two stages to a minimum, we tried to keep the interval between the first and second interviews as short as possible. In most cases the second stage interview was completed within three months of the first. In a few cases longer intervals, sometimes as long as eight months, were an unavoidable consequence of the small number of interviewers and the difficulty of relocating respondents.

Processing of Data: Second questionnaires and food diaries were processed in much the same way as the first questionnaire. Each completed questionnaire was checked for completeness, accuracy and consistency by interviewing supervisors. Incomplete or otherwise unsatisfactory cases were returned to the interviewer. Next, questionnaires were passed on to a team of editor-coders who transformed most of the data into numerical codes for computer processing. Each case was coded by two coders working independently, and errors and differences of interpretation were checked and resolved.

Reliability: The objective of the sampling process was to direct the second questionnaire to the poor and the near-poor. In certain disability groups small numbers of income units with higher incomes were selected for comparative purposes. The resulting sample does not attempt to represent the population of Melbourne as a whole but does represent the low income population as identified in Stage I.

TABLE 3.1

STAGE II SAMPLE AND NON-RESPONSE

Total number of income units selected	701	
Less:		
Non-sample	23	
Total number of interviews attempted		678
Less non-response:		
Refusal because of ill health	11	
Refusal for other reason	76	
No contact	34	
Deceased	10	
Deferral	11	
Incomplete	8	
Total non-response	150	
Total number of interviews completed		528

A total of 528 interviews were completed, out of 678 attempted. This over-all response rate of nearly 80 per cent was considered satisfactory, in view of the demanding nature of the interview. The various reasons why completed interviews were not obtained from all income units selected in the Stage II sample are set out in Table 3·1. The twenty-three listed as 'non-sample' cases were ones in which a change in circumstances between the two interviews made the income unit unsuitable for reinterview. For example, an old person who between Stage I and Stage II had entered an institution was not reinterviewed. Nor were families who had moved out of Melbourne. Thirty-four income units who had moved and could not be located are listed as 'no-contact'. Every effort was made to find selected respondents and many were traced successfully to their new addresses, in some cases through three or four moves. In most no-contact cases there was evidence that they had moved, but no information as to their new addresses.

'Deferral' represents respondents who indicated willingness to participate in the survey, but who for various reasons were not able to complete the interview within the survey period. Besides unfinished interviews, the group 'interview incomplete' includes several questionnaires which, although technically complete, were believed to be unreliable and were not used.

Out of a sample of 197 food diary cases selected, twenty-nine households refused to keep a diary and another four began but did not complete the diary. Seven completed diaries were not sufficiently reliable for analysis. This resulted in 157 completed records of a fortnight's food expenditure.

In order to achieve a high degree of accuracy, interviewers encouraged respondents to refer to documents such as rates notices, pay envelopes, taxation records, savings bank books and medical bills. In addition, the truthfulness and accuracy of the information collected was checked throughout interviewing and processing. Interviewers were careful to follow up any answers which seemed doubtful or inconsistent and they often referred back to such points later in the interview. Supervisors checked each incoming questionnaire carefully and suspected inaccuracies were investigated by a further call. Each questionnaire was also checked for internal consistency by computer.

The interviewer rated the reliability of the material, giving separate evaluations for respondents' understanding of questions and sincerity of response, as well as for completeness of information and accuracy. The degree of co-operation was also rated and difficulties of language, hearing or attitude were noted.

Comparisons of Incomes at Stage I and Stage II

In some cases the income shown by the Stage II questionnaire did not agree with the income figure reached in the first interview. In general, we believe the Stage II figures were more accurate because of the more comprehensive questionnaire and because Stage II interviewers were more highly trained in asking questions. Furthermore, the collection of income for an entire year minimised inaccuracies due to the collection at Stage I of income for a single week.

For analysis the 528 completed questionnaires were divided into smaller, more homogeneous groups. One of these, the aged, was large enough for statistical treatment and is discussed in Chapter 5. The other groups, notably the large families and the fatherless families, were too small to permit statistical testing of the variations in income between the two stages. Instead, a comparative study was made of the first and second questionnaire information on all those large families and fatherless families included in the second sample. Another study was made of all income units, excluding the aged, in three of the ten matched sub-samples of which the Stage I sample was composed.

These comparisons suggest that the Stage I results are broadly accurate with a slight tendency to overstate the numbers in poverty. For instance, of the thirty-one cases of fatherless families chosen for re-interview, the first questionnaire suggested that thirteen were below the poverty line. After study of the second questionnaire the estimate was eleven below the poverty line. There was a greater chance of finding people probably poor who on reconsideration might be judged to be above the poverty line than there was of finding people apparently above the poverty line who upon more evidence might be judged to be below it. Because the primary purpose of Stage II was to obtain more information about the needs of poor people and how they might be met, interviews were conducted mainly with those identified as probably poor. Thus a small reduction in the numbers below the poverty line among the cases studied in this way was not evidence that for the whole population the numbers deemed to be in poverty were too high.

In some cases the circumstances of those interviewed had changed between the two survey stages. Of the thirty-five large families inter-viewed a second time, eight had been judged to be below the poverty line according to the results of the first interview; four of these were better off and above the poverty line at the time of the second interview. Two others were reclassified, one upward and one downward, because of some detailed information including tax returns showing overtime payments. For example, one man, a taxi driver, was found to have a highly variable income. At Stage I his income appeared to be above the poverty line. Stage II results, however, showed that the weekly income collected at Stage I corresponded to an unusually favourable week. When his position was assessed for the year as a whole he was classified as below the poverty line.

Most cases were similar to this man's in that a year's income was a better measure of poverty than one week's income. But there were exceptions to this. One was the case of a widow, aged forty-eight, with two children. She had come from Italy with her husband in 1954. For most of the previous year she had been working in a textile factory, and therefore her income for the year as a whole appeared sufficient to put her above the poverty line. But just before the Stage I interview she had become unable to work because of sciatica. By the time she was reinterviewed at Stage II she had been off work two months. Weekly income as shown by Stage I thus gave a more accurate picture for this case. Despite her more fortunate circumstances earlier in the year, she was now poor and likely to remain so. She had not applied for either a widows' pension or sickness benefit. (The interviewer suggested that she apply for sickness benefit.) She was supported by her daughter aged eighteen, who was a secretary; her son of fifteen was at school with a Commonwealth Scholarship and hoped to become a chemist.

General Conclusions

The completed Stage II questionnaires provided an extensive range of information. In some cases they revealed unsuspected areas of difficulty for the poor and the near-poor. More often they provided documented evidence of problems already familiar to social workers, other welfare workers and administrators of voluntary and statutory bodies. The wide range of cases included many that have been used as case studies to give life to the statistical findings of the first questionnaire.

Many answers to survey questions were recorded in the respondents' own words. In addition, interviewers wrote a summary of each case. Extraordinarily vivid portraits of personalities and circumstances have often resulted. For example, one man described his employment history in much greater detail than the questionnaire required.

I've had more jobs than breakfasts. When I left school I started as a technician in training with the railways. They paid 35/- a fortnight so I only stayed three months.

I worked as an apprentice fibrous plasterer—well not really an apprentice, a learner. I got £13 a week and left after four years. I always worked with blokes who were on piece work. They worked hard to get big money. I was only paid wages of £13 so blow working your guts out. The jobs would be anywhere in the metropolitan area, Rosanna,

Moorabbin and Christ knows where. I had to push a bike to the job. I left after four years.

Next I worked as a freight handler at Essendon. Good job as only two shifts. Would sit on my backside sometimes waiting for a plane from Queensland with peas for the Victoria Market. The plane might be four hours late and I was getting paid sitting around. Sometimes made £50 or £60 a week. The day they started three rotating eight-hour shifts I snatched it. I wouldn't work shift work unless I was getting big money.

Then I was an orderman for a timber yard. Not enough money but it was a happy holiday for twelve months.

Then I was a mechanic cum grease-monkey at a garage for twelve months. I left to get better money with an uncle. He was a trotting trainer and got rubbed out of the game for twelve months. We chased brumbies in NSW and sent them to Melbourne for dogs' meat. Camels paid £25 bounty and donkeys £10 and there was plenty of dogs' meat in a camel. Job finished after twelve months as the uncle got his trotting licence back. Later I was a labourer in a cardboard box factory. Well, I started as a labourer on £14 and finished as foreman on £27 and plenty of overtime.

When I had enough money I bought a truck and did contract carting. In the credit squeeze of 1961 I lost the lot. Worked for a plumber digging drains for water pipes. He cut down, as the credit squeeze caught up with his work later than it hit me, so I was out of work. Went up the bush to Balranald and worked on a farm for relatives—a 2,000 acre show. I stayed there fourteen months and made £1,300. The old woman was living in Melbourne looking after the kids and she didn't like living apart so I came back to Melbourne.

I've been driving as a plant operator for three years tomorrow and I'm switching it tomorrow for a job with more money. Would like to have a farm but it would take £50,000 capital for wheat or £30,000 for grazing.

Perhaps the most striking feature which emerged from the 528 completed Stage II interviews was the diversity and complexity of situations existing among people within a restricted range of income. The broad scope of the questionnaire brought out forcefully the variety of personal circumstances prevailing within groups of apparently similar people. A family whose home is in good order can live much more comfortably on a low income than a similar family whose house is substandard. Economies which can be achieved by careful planning of expenditure are not available to those whose income is insecure or fluctuates widely. The number of factors affecting living conditions is large, and it is important to recognise that the process of generalisation inherent in the translation of survey responses into policy recommendations may obscure some of the individuality of each family's circumstances.

Incomes and Disabilities

The poor and near-poor are separated into disability groups in Table 3·2. Two groups have been omitted: sixty juveniles, and eleven income units for whom satisfactory estimates of income could not be reached. Because the figures shown in this table have not been weighted no precise conclusion can be drawn from them regarding the incidence of poverty in the population as a whole.

TABLE 3·2

INCOMES AND DISABILITIES OF STAGE II INCOME UNITS   Unweighted

	Below poverty line		Marginally above poverty line	Not in poverty	Total
	In need	Not in need because of family help			
Aged	18	61*	53	63	195**
Fatherless families	8	5	4	14	31
Female heads without dependent children	6	14	3	22	45
Large families	6	0	9	19	34
Sickness, accident or unemployment	1	1	0	0	2
No disability	16	2	17	115	150
Total	55	83	86	233	457

Income units headed by juveniles and those whose incomes were unknown have been omitted.
*Determined on basis of assets, cost of housing and assistance from families and friends.
**This figure includes a number of cases referred to in paragraph three of Appendix C.

The cases below the poverty line have been further subdivided into two groups, 'in need' and 'not in need because of family help.' In effect we have defined two kinds of poverty. The first group must be regarded as requiring action urgently. They are below a very austere poverty line and have no one upon whom they can rely. All their needs must be met out of incomes which are too small. The other group contains income units whose family and friends make up the income gap with regular supportive assistance, varying from total financial support in some cases to frequent casual gifts of food and clothing in others.

The effect of family help is to enable some people whose income is too small to live as well or almost as well as those whose incomes are adequate. By comparison with people who are without this kind of help they appear well off and for this reason we have classified them separately, but it would be a mistake to overstress the distinction. The most fundamental aspect of family help is its arbitrariness; to a large extent its availability is beyond the control of those who depend upon it. Some have families and others do not; some families have extra resources and others do not. This important determinant of living standards carries no rights, no rules determining eligibility and no guarantees of permanence. For example, a deserted wife may find that gifts of clothing for the children stop arriving because her parents have fallen ill and cannot continue to help her. A bachelor son who has been paying rates for his pensioner mother may marry and soon have a wife and children to support. Usually family help is freely given and warmly received, but for some people it may be an embarrassment to pride and independence. We believe it is entirely desirable that these eighty-three income units classified as 'not in need because of family help' be assisted by the measures we recommend for the relief of poverty in the same ways as the fifty-five units 'in need'.

The marginal group—less than 20 per cent above the poverty line—is quite large. If the poverty line had been drawn even slightly higher most of these eighty-six income units would have been classed as in poverty. A man, wife and two children with a 1966 money income of no higher than $39 per week, or a disposable income after payment for housing of not more than $33, would have fallen into this marginal class. Any measures to alleviate poverty which spilled over to this marginal group could not be regarded as wasteful.

Food Expenditure

The stringency of the poverty line showed clearly in the average food expenditure of families of different sizes. From the 157 diaries some very useful general indications emerge of the amounts which low income families spend on food. The families of man, wife and two children— similar to the standard family used in setting the poverty line—showed an average weekly expenditure on food of $21.83, which is about half the average weekly income for families in the group, or nearly two-thirds of a basic wage plus child endowment income of $33. It works out at $5.46 a head. Per head figures were somewhat higher for single persons and declined to $3.68 per head for families of seven persons.

That such low levels of food expenditure cut deeply into income is a compelling demonstration of the existence of poverty in the community. For comparison one may note that for the population as a whole food expenditure represents one-fifth of personal disposable income. From the diaries we find that 41 per cent of these low-income families spent more than two-fifths, or twice as large a proportion of their income on food. As one would expect, there are many cases among the aged in which food expenditure takes a large proportion of a small income.

In 1967 the dietitian of a major Melbourne public hospital estimated the minimum weekly food cost of a single elderly person as $4.40. The range of average food expenditures for various sizes of household taken from the survey diaries was quite compatible with this figure. Some families spent more, as might be expected considering the greater nutritional requirements of younger, more active people and the fact that the hospital estimate assumed an ability to plan well and to shop every day. Larger families tended to spend less per head because of economies of scale possible in cooking for a larger number of persons.

Although the main purpose of the food diaries was to measure total expenditure on food, they also provide an indication of the quality of diet. One such indication is the expenditure on protein foods such as milk, eggs, cheese, fish, meat and bacon. There were a number of cases in which expenditure on these foods was less than one dollar per person per week, which seemed on the face of it to indicate a poor quality diet. Several of these, however, proved on closer investigation to be special cases involving people who had received substantial gifts of food from friends or had meals out with them. On the other hand there were two families, each with five young children, whose expenditures per head on protein foods were only 89 cents and 99 cents a week and who bought large quantities of bread and other starchy foods. Neither of these families was poor or even nearly poor: food expenditure was a small proportion of their income even measured after payment for housing. There were also cases of elderly widows who spent very little on protein foods. One, spending 22 cents a week on such foods, was reported as subsisting mainly on fruit, bread, jam and peanut butter. But again her adjusted income was above the poverty line. It cannot therefore be claimed that these poor quality diets were due to inadequate incomes. What can be claimed is that the generally low levels of food expenditure shown in the diaries in many cases absorbed an unduly large proportion of income.

4 Low Income, Poverty and Need*

For most people in normal circumstances, whether they were age pensioners or men and women in regular employment, one week's income provided a good indication of whether or not they were poor. But for some people the income of the previous week was not normal. The most important of such cases were those who for one reason or another had had no money income in the previous week. For many of them it was a question of timing—they normally received a money income but in that particular week they had not done so. But there were also some who were not normally in receipt of any money income of their own in any week. All these people were, of course, below our poverty line, and yet it was clear that some of them at least were not 'in need'.

Because we wanted to recommend policies directed to reducing poverty, we had to be sure that our necessarily arbitrary definition of poverty did not result in an over-statement of the problem. Consequently a detailed study was made of each income unit with a weekly income of less than $3; information was taken from second questionnaires when available, as well as from first questionnaires. This study showed that the variety of human experience leads to a large number of groups of people with no appreciable income in one particular week. These groups are set out in Tables 4·1, 4·2 and 4·3. In each of these cases we made the best judgment possible on the evidence as to whether the people concerned were 'in need', considering their reason for having such a low income.

We have regarded low income, poverty and need as three separate concepts. 'Low income', of itself, was not an adequate criterion for defining poverty, as it did not take into account the number of persons for whom that income had to provide. Thus our definition of 'poverty' considered the previous week's income in the context of family size and composition. Our definition of 'need' took into account many other circumstances which bear on low income, such as its likely duration, its cause, and other resources which could be called upon such as assets and assistance from family and friends. This chapter concerns a group of income units with low incomes in the week of the survey, all of them well below the poverty line, and considers what proportion are in need and what policies are relevant to them.

* This chapter was written jointly by Ronald F. Henderson and Sheila Shaver.

People Who Normally Have No Income

Our definition of an income unit assumes, firstly, that only wives and dependent children may have no income of their own and be supported by the husband or father, and secondly, that all other persons can be classified by their own money income. This is generally true for this community, but some modification must be made for particular circumstances.

A number of households consisted of recent migrants of working age who had living with them one or more parents who were not gainfully occupied and so did not have an income of their own. These parents emerged in our analysis as separate income units with no income. To judge whether they were in need we added them on as dependants to the family and recalculated standard costs against family income on that basis. Also some women who were separate income units engaged on home duties and without an income were treated in the same way—for example, a woman keeping house for her brother.

Two groups of people, most of them elderly, were living on capital with some help from members of their families, so they, too, had no income in the strict sense of the term. Some of them were running down savings to be eligible for a pension when they reached the retiring age. One example of those who had retired slightly before pension age was a man of sixty-three who had left his job as a cleaner when he was changed to a night shift. He was dependent on his sister and some savings until he became old enough to receive the age pension. Another was a man of sixty-four who received $60 a year bank interest from his savings and who had living with him an unmarried son paying him $12 a week board. One married couple, too, were living on private savings which were almost exhausted; the husband was fifty-seven. Their unmarried son was paying $10 a week board.

Most of those living on savings or being supported by a family member were judged not to be in need; several of them were widows living with a son or a daughter and being supported by them. Migrant parents living with an adult son or daughter, although similar in several respects, were not quite in the same category since, should family support fail, they would not be eligible for a pension by right until they had resided in Australia for ten years. In all these cases we made the best judgment we could on the available evidence as to whether their means of support were sufficient to keep the family unit of which they were a part above the poverty line. The majority of them were not in need; however, some of those people engaged in caring for a sick parent or relative were in a precarious situation. On the death of the parent or relative such a person might be left without either any income or any experience or training for gainful employment. A scheme for the provision of facilities for training widow pensioners was instituted in late 1968 and early in 1970 a similar scheme for other women was forecast. It is important that information describing these training facilities be disseminated actively so that it does get through to the people who need it. Many of the people concerned, by the very nature of their occupation of caring at home for a sick person, are not in a good position to collect information concerning facilities available. In one of the cases in the survey the person concerned was apparently eligible for a special benefit of $8.25 (now $10.00) for caring for an invalid mother on an age pension but was unaware of its availability.

TABLE 4·1

ADULT INCOME UNITS NOT NORMALLY RECEIVING MONEY INCOMES

Unweighted Numbers of Income Units with Incomes of Less than $3

Reason	Total	May be in need	Not in need
Migrant parent of pension age	16	1	15
Aged migrant not supported by children	2	2	0
Migrant parent below pension age	10	1	9
Caring for sick parent or other relative	4	2	2
Other home duties	4	0	4
Living on savings or supported by family member	27	4	23
Retired slightly before pension age	6	5	1
Income in kind received from church or other organisation	2	0	2
Total	71	15	56

Nearly two-thirds of all income units with incomes under $3 were women and many of these, as we have said, although they had no significant income of their own, were not in immediate need because they were in effect part of a larger group which had sufficient income to share among its members.

It would be possible to refuse to pay an age pension to people who have children capable of supporting them, or to any widow who had a brother or sister capable of supporting her. But that is not the policy in

Australia. Australian policy treats old people, widows, invalids and the disabled as income units, and social service benefits are determined to secure for each of them a certain minimum income. Surely this is right. In a survey such as ours we are enquiring into the adequacy of the minimum provided for people in different situations. If the minimum is inadequate for some group such as widows with dependent children living on their own, it is no argument against raising it that some widows are fortunate enough to be supported by relatives. There is a sense in which they are 'poor'—although not 'in need'. Moreover, as pointed out above, the support of family or friends may not be permanent. A spinster may spend her life up to the age of fifty-five looking after her parents and supported financially by them. She may then be left with inadequate income and no experience in earning. An aged widower or widow may not be 'in need' because he or she is living on savings, but later the savings may be exhausted.

People Whose Incomes are Temporarily Low

There was a small group of cases in which low income was clearly likely to be only temporary. These are shown in Table 4·2. They include a young woman from New Zealand having a working holiday in Australia, and a builder spending a week adding to his own house.

TABLE 4·2

ADULT INCOME UNITS WHOSE LOW INCOMES WERE TEMPORARY OR INCORRECTLY RECORDED
Unweighted Numbers of Income Units with Incomes of Less than $3

Reason	Not in need
Unpaid holiday	8
Changing jobs	7
Self-employed and income irregular	2
Income incorrectly recorded	4
Total	21

Further small categories of people with temporary low incomes are shown in Table 4·3. They include people awaiting compensation for sickness or accident, some unemployed and some waiting to be eligible for a pension. In most cases their low incomes are temporary in the sense that these particular individuals will be better off within the next few weeks. But at any point of time there will be a number of individuals and families in poverty for these reasons. It is, therefore, proper to ask what can be done to reduce the size of this pool of poverty into which some slide down as others climb out.

TABLE 4·3

ADULT INCOME UNITS WITH TEMPORARILY LOW INCOMES WHO MAY BE IN NEED

Unweighted Numbers of Income Units with Incomes of Less than $3

Reason	Total	May be in need	Not in need
Sickness or accident, temporary	7	6	1
Sickness or accident, unlikely to resume work	5	5	0
Unemployed	7	7	0
Application made for age pension but not yet awarded	5	5	0
Deserted wife whose six-month waiting period for pension had not yet elapsed and not receiving other assistance	2	2	0
Awaiting workers' compensation	1	1	0
Migrant just arrived in Australia and not yet employed	3	3	0
Total	30	29	1

The pool of temporary poverty can be reduced by shortening the waiting time before receipt of sickness and unemployment benefits. A scheme has recently been proposed in New Zealand by a Royal Commission[1] which 'would provide immediate compensation without proof of fault for every injured person, regardless of his or her fault and whether the accident occurred in the factory, on the highway or in the home.' The principle on which this scheme is based is that it is the responsibility of the community to maintain the income of those prevented from working and earning by an accident. As the Commission points out, it is logical to extend this to maintenance of income to all those prevented from earning by sickness.

The New Zealand scheme is for benefits related to income, but this is not a necessary feature of it. The essential aspect is that payment of benefit should start promptly, without the delays which must arise if investigation and legal action have to be taken to ascertain the cause of the accident or illness.

Some time, of course, must be taken by inquiry into eligibility for benefits, whether unemployment, sickness, age pension, widows' pension

[1] *Compensation for Personal Injury in New Zealand, Report of the Royal Commission of Inquiry*, Government Printer, Wellington, December 1967, p. 26

or payment to a deserted wife. The greater the emphasis on ensuring that no undeserving cases slip through to receive benefit, the longer that time will be. The greater the emphasis on prevention of poverty and real hardship, even at the risk of making some payments to those who do not deserve them, the shorter the waiting time for benefit will become. It will help towards shortening the waiting period if the administration is imbued with determination to prevent hardship through loss of earnings. We have come a long way from the old British Poor Law's emphasis on making sure it is less attractive to be on benefit than to be gainfully occupied and financially independent. But some traces of this attitude still remain. At the time of the survey, for instance, in Queensland a deserted wife with two children would have been entitled to only $7.35 a week for six months before becoming eligible for a widows' pension. In 1968 the *States Grants (Deserted Wives) Act* raised this to $20, a level still substantially below our poverty line. In Victoria in June 1968 a deserted wife was entitled to receive during the first six months of her desertion a special benefit from the Commonwealth of only $8.25 per week for herself and $1.50 for each child. Even with a State supplement a widow with two children would still have had an income of at most only $22.25 a week, again a sum well below the poverty line.

'Unemployment benefit is payable from the seventh day after the day on which the claimant became unemployed; or from the seventh day after the day on which the claim was lodged; whichever is the later.'[2] The effect of this provision is that if people who expect to find another job quickly fail to lodge a claim immediately they become unemployed, they suffer a waiting period of more than a week without income. Is this provision really in the spirit of an administration trying to prevent hardship through loss of earnings? Is it really necessary to prevent widespread abuse?

A similar query can be raised on sickness benefit. This 'is payable from the seventh day after the day on which the claimant became incapacitated for work.'[3] Why should it not be payable from the day after that on which he ceased to earn? If it is argued that most people are paid for a week's work after they have completed it, then one can reply that the gap in income is merely transferred to the first week in which work is resumed. Provisions aimed at income maintenance should surely be such as to eliminate the gap in income.

[2] Commonwealth Department of Social Services, *Commonwealth Social Services*, Commonwealth Government Printing Office, Canberra, October 1964, p. 10
[3] *Commonwealth Social Services*, p. 10

Numbers in Poverty and in Need

The figures presented in Tables 4·1, 4·2 and 4·3 represent two per cent of all adult income units when the appropriate weights have been applied. The group which may be in need represents 0·5 per cent, or about one quarter of all those with incomes of under $3.

We can use this and some other information to adjust our first estimate of those 'in poverty'—7·7 per cent of all adult income units—downward to 4 per cent 'in need'. The other information which we must use consists of the outcome of a case-by-case examination of those below the poverty line who had none of the disability characteristics associated with poverty, described in some detail in the last section of Chapter 9, and the Stage II sample of the aged, treated fully in Chapter 5.

About half of those below the poverty line who had no disabilities were in real distress. The other half were mainly persons whose low incomes were either temporary or in some way voluntary. For example, some had left a job and were about to begin another. Some others had taken unpaid leave.

Thus there were some cases with income below the poverty line in the week of the survey who were clearly not 'in need'; others such as some of the sick were much more doubtful. There were also some who were above the poverty line but suffered from high housing costs which reduced their disposable income, and others who were below the poverty line but probably not in need because their housing costs were low.

There is considerable overlap between income units with little or no money income, those with low income but no disability, and some of the aged. In terms of absolute numbers the effect of removing from the total estimate of the number in poverty those whose low incomes do not reflect economic deprivation is quite small. The difference in the proportions 'in poverty' and 'in need' arises principally because of the stringency of the criteria used. In view of the hardship which often accompanies even a short cessation of income and in view of the strains of economic dependence sometimes experienced by those who have no incomes of their own, we must not draw the conclusion that only those now 'in need' should receive additional benefits.

5 The Aged*

Analysis of results from the first questionnaire showed a large proportion of the aged apparently below or not far above the poverty line. However, the aged are likely to differ from the rest of the population in several respects relevant to their poverty status. It was only from the second questionnaire that we could expect to get reasonably complete information about them.

Many of the aged have more than one source of income. Those in receipt of pensions may have in addition some part-time earnings, some property income, some superannuation. Because of the means test they may be cautious in a short interview about revealing additional income. Yet even a small addition is of tremendous importance at the margin of poverty where the aged would find themselves if they were dependent solely on the pension.

Most of the aged are home-owners and will have finished paying off their mortgages. Some have spare accommodation vacated by their children which they can let. Some have designed their houses to include a unit to be let. Those who are tenants have often been in the same house for a long time and are paying relatively low rents. Net housing costs for the aged are, on the average, less than for the population as a whole. Housing costs incurred by owner-occupiers for rates, repairs and insurance were not included.

Some have accumulated assets by their own saving or from legacies or retirement grants on which they can draw to eke out their income or to meet an emergency. For many their age and increasingly dependent condition is likely to call forth some help from family, friends and church or other charitable organisations.

Information about all these aspects was collected on the second questionnaire. The response from aged income units was sufficient to enable us to analyse their poverty status through a more refined classification relevant to their condition.[1]

* This chapter was written by R. I. Downing.

[1] Appendix C discusses some technical and definitional aspects of this poverty classification.

In addition to the new and more reliable information collected at the second stage of the enquiry, we inevitably encountered also some cases whose circumstances had changed in the few months that had elapsed since the first enquiry. There was little net effect on the poverty classification from these changes, some being for the better and some for the worse. The most appealing case was that of a couple who had the good fortune to lose their pension between the two enquiries, for the eminently satisfactory reason that they had won $20,000 in Tattersall's lottery. Another couple, recorded in the first survey as having an income of only

The Poverty Classification of the Aged

Tables $5 \cdot 1$, $5 \cdot 2$ and $5 \cdot 3$ show the poverty classification for the aged. We find some $84 \cdot 8$ per cent of the aged above the poverty line although $10 \cdot 6$ per cent were less than \$6 above and are described as 'in marginal poverty'.

TABLE 5·1

THE CONDITION OF THE AGED IN MELBOURNE, 1966

	Estimated number of income units	%
Above marginal poverty	105,300	74·2
In marginal poverty	15,100	10·6
In poverty	21,600	15·2
Total aged income units	142,000	100.0

TABLE 5·2

THE CONDITION OF THE AGED POOR

	Estimated number of income units	%
In poverty but not in need —by cheapness of accommodation	9,200	6·5
—by annuity-worth of assets	4,100	2·9
—by help from family and others	5,000	3·5
In poverty and in need	3,300	2·3
Total aged income units in poverty	21,600	15·2

The remaining $15 \cdot 2$ per cent of aged income units are described as being 'in poverty' because they either had inadequate income or were meeting housing costs so high as to impoverish them. However, of this group, $6 \cdot 5$ per cent who had low incomes were saved from need by the cheapness of their accommodation. In many cases, as discussed below,

---

\$7 a week, turned out to have \$18,000 in the bank, the remains of a windfall from the same source. Winning Tatt's kept these couples well above the poverty line, but this finding leads us to no useful recommendation.

Changes in the poverty classification arising from changes of information and of circumstance are fully analysed in Appendix C paragraph 6.

their housing was of poor quality; their income after housing costs was sufficient to put them above the poverty line only in respect of their needs other than for housing.

A further 2·9 per cent had assets of a value sufficient to save them from need if they were willing to use them in accordance with the austere rules laid down for the valuation of assets by the Commonwealth Department of Social Services, as discussed below. And a further 3·5 per cent were saved from need only by the help they received from their family and friends, or from charitable organisations. The remaining 2·3 per cent of aged income units have been classed as being poor and in need, with inadequate incomes, accommodation, assets and family help.

TABLE 5·3

POVERTY CLASSIFICATION OF AGED PERSONS

	%
Above marginal poverty	76·2
In marginal poverty	9·5
In poverty but not in need —by accommodation	5·1
—by assets	3·8
—by family help	3·4
In poverty and in need	2·0
Total	100·0

Of the 142,000 aged income units estimated to be represented by the sample, 43,000 were married couples, giving a total aged population of 185,000 people. The small change in the poverty classification of people set out in the Table 5.3, compared with the earlier classification of income units, arises from the fact that married couples, as discussed later, had rather better incomes and more assets than did single aged people.

Determinants of Poverty Status

The poverty classification for the aged has been derived from information about their incomes, their housing costs, their assets and any help they receive from their families and other sources. Each of these determinants of the poverty status of the aged needs further comment.

Incomes

(i) Pensioners and Non-pensioners: Aged income units fall into two broad groups—the 87,200 or 61·4 per cent who receive Government pensions (usually age pensions, but some service and war widows' pensions) and the other 54,800 or 38·6 per cent who have no pensions. In Table 5·4, column A shows, as is to be expected, that the bulk of those in poverty are in the pensioner group, of whom 3·4 per cent are in need compared with only 0·4 per cent of non-pensioners. Of the 18·1 per cent of pensioners who are below the poverty line, 10·1 per cent are saved from need by the cheapness of their accommodation.

In the non-pensioner group, of the 10·8 per cent below the poverty line, 7·4 per cent are kept out of need by help from their families. These are mainly migrants' parents who have arrived under guarantees of family support and do not become eligible for the age pension until they have been in Australia for ten years. In some cases family circumstances make them eligible for a compassionate allowance from the Commonwealth Department of Social Services. Most of these migrants' parents have little or no income of their own and are kept out of need, if at all, only by the help they receive from their families.

(ii) Size of Household, Sex and Marital Status: The adequacy of aged people's incomes is greatly affected by the circumstances of the individual. Married couples and single people living with others are able to share overhead expenses and so reduce living costs per head. Single females have lower standard costs than single males, reflecting presumably both smaller physical needs and greater capacity for economical household management.

Yet the age pension, on which the bulk of aged income units depend as their main source of income, is the same for all single pensioners regardless of their sex and their living conditions; and the single rate is only 56·6 per cent of the married-couple rate, whereas our standard cost formula suggests that something nearer to 70 per cent would be more appropriate.

Column B in Table 5·4 shows that the proportion in poverty and in need falls sharply as the number of persons in the household increases; in households of three or more persons, family help keeps out of need virtually all those in poverty by income. Column C in Table 5·4 shows that 4·9 per cent of single males are in poverty and in need; of single females, 2·7 per cent; and of married couples, 0·8 per cent.

TABLE 5·4

POVERTY CLASSIFICATION OF AGED INCOME UNITS

	A. By source of income	
	Pensioners	Non-pensioners
Estimated number of income units	87,200	54,800
	%	%
Above marginal poverty	66·6	86·3
In marginal poverty	15·3	2·9
Above poverty line	81·9	89·2
In poverty but not in need —by accommodation	10·1	0·2
—by assets	3·1	2·8
—by family help	1·5	7·4
In poverty and in need	3·4	0·4
Total	100.0	100.0

(iii) Income Additional to Pension: In defence of the level at which age pension rates have been set in Australia it has sometimes been argued, though not frequently in recent times, that the pension has never been intended to provide an adequate living income, but rather to supplement what provision people had themselves made for their retirement.

Tables 5·5 to 5·8 analyse some aspects of income, in addition to the pension, received by full-rate age pensioners represented in the Stage II sample. Table 5·5 reveals how difficult it is to base policies on generalisations about social conditions. Nearly half of this limited sample of the aged population had additional income of $3 a week or more, the average additional income being about $7.50 a week. But 23·5 per cent had nothing, a further 6 per cent had less than $1 a week and 23·3 per cent had between $1 and $3 a week. Of this last group, 4·2 per cent had only the Supplementary Assistance of $2 a week, which is paid to single-rate pensioners who have to pay rent and who have little or no income other than the pension. It is particularly important, in interpreting Table 5·5, to recall that our sample excluded altogether aged income units residing in institutions and overnight shelters, among whom additional income would be unusual. It must also be remembered that

B. By size of household			C. By sex and marital status		
One person	Two persons	Three or more persons	Single males	Single females	Married couples
40,000	59,000	43,000	44,000	78,000	20,000
%	%	%	%	%	%
61·6	71·5	89·7	80·9	68·9	82·6
10·5	18·0	0·6	7·1	13·5	5·9
72·1	89·5	90·3	88·0	82·4	88·5
21·5	0·2	0·5	5·4	9·5	0·5
2·6	5·2	—	0·4	1·4	6·9
—	2·2	9·1	1·3	4·0	3·3
3·8	2·9	0·1	4·9	2·7	0·8
100·0	100·0	100·0	100·0	100·0	100·0

the Stage II sample was drawn from the section of the original sample presumed likely to be in poverty.

The most important sources of additional income are property income and part-time earnings or receipts from boarders. These part-time earnings are often within the range of $7 to $14 a week, and usually are enough to keep the recipients above the poverty line. This source of supplementary income, however, will fail as age increases and health and strength deteriorate. In particular, a number of respondents who were paying high rents were kept out of poverty only by part-time earnings additional to the pension. Other respondents who had been in this situation were approaching or had reached the end of their part-time earning capacity and were in despair as to how they could carry on with only the pension. Their position was aggravated by the fact that it was usually poor health which forced them to stop earning, but which brought also the prospect of higher expenses and increasing dependence on help from others.

Table 5·6 shows the distribution of additional income by sex and marital status. The average additional income was $4.60 a week for single males, $3.80 for females and $5 for married couples.

TABLE 5·5

SOURCES AND AMOUNTS OF WEEKLY INCOME ADDITIONAL TO PENSION *

Stage II Full-rate Age Pensioner Income Units

Source of additional income	Less than $1 a week	$1 to $3 a week	$3 or more a week	Total
	%	%	%	%
None	23·5	—	—	23·5
Supplementary Assistance	—	4·2	—	4·2
Superannuation	0·4	2·2	7·3	9·9
Earnings or boarders	1·3	3·9	14·2	19·4
Property	0·4	7·2	14·7	22·3
Family help	3·7	3·7	—	7·4
Combination	—	2·1	11·2	13·3
Total	29·3	23·3	47·4	100·0

*Detailed information about income additional to the pension was available for the 45,000 age pensioner income units represented in the second sample. The data in Tables 5.5 to 5.8 refer to only those 40,000 income units who received full-rate pensions and so had additional income amounting to less than the limit beyond which the pension was reduced ($10 a week for single pensioners, $17 a week for married couples).

TABLE 5·6

ADDITIONAL INCOME, SEX AND MARITAL STATUS

Stage II Full-rate Age Pensioner Income Units

	Less than $1 a week	$1 to $3 a week	$3 or more a week	Total
	%	%	%	%
Single males	11·5	25·7	62·8	100
Single females	33·1	25·8	41·1	100
Married couples	26·3	17·5	56·2	100

Table 5·7 shows that a large proportion of full-rate pensioners with additional income of less than $1 per week owned their own houses and a few more enjoyed free housing. The proportion of owners falls as additional income rises, with a corresponding increase in the proportion of those who pay for their own housing.

The poverty classification of this group of full-rate age pensioners, shown in Table 5·8, is much as would be expected. The proportion above the poverty line rises as additional income rises. A great many of those below the poverty line and with little additional income are kept out of need only by the cheapness of their accommodation; some rely on family help. The proportion in poverty and in need is kept up even for those with larger additional incomes by cases of high rent or instalments, as discussed below.

TABLE 5·7

ADDITIONAL INCOME AND PAYMENT-STATUS FOR HOUSING*

Stage II Full-rate Age Pensioner Income Units

	Less than $1 a week	$1 to $3 a week	$3 or more a week	Total
	%	%	%	%
Own housing	83·3	54·5	42·8	57·4
Free housing	4·8	19·3	3·6	7·6
Paying for housing	11·9	26·2	53·6	35·0
	100·0	100·0	100·0	100·0

*The Commonwealth Department of Social Services has published some figures on pensioners' assessed means. That table is, however, so differently constructed as to be not at all comparable with the figures derived from our survey.

TABLE 5·8

ADDITIONAL INCOME AND POVERTY CLASSIFICATION

Stage II Full-rate Age Pensioner Income Units

	Less than $1 a week	$1 to $3 a week	$3 and over a week	Total
	%	%	%	%
Above marginal poverty	10·2	33·5	51·7	35·3
In marginal poverty	32·4	24·0	25·1	27·0
Above poverty line	42·6	57·5	76·8	62·3
In poverty but not in need —by accommodation	39·9	33·1	4·4	21·5
—by assets	—	—	13·2	6·3
—by family help	10·6	—	0·3	3·2
In poverty and in need	6·9	9·4	5·3	6·7
Total	100·0	100·0	100·0	100·0

(iv) Attitudes to the Pension and the Means Test: In only two of the replies to the second questionnaire was there any direct evidence of embarrassment about accepting a government pension. One woman, aged seventy-seven, living comfortably with her daughters and obviously well looked after, had no income and only $1,600 in assets; she refused to ask for the pension, although she said she would like more independence. The interviewer commented as follows:

An old lady of considerable character, she appears to be over-protected by her daughters. They do not like her going out alone (she does this without telling them) and they are slowly taking over the running of the house and the cooking. She feels slightly resentful about this as it is tending to show up her absolute dependence on them. They support her in the idea that it would be beneath her dignity to be a pensioner: in fact they seem to be even more opposed to it than she is.

Another woman who was drawing the pension refused, nevertheless, to use any of the fringe benefits, such as the pensioner medical service and the travel concessions, as she was ashamed of being on the pension —to have 'gone so low'—and did not want people to know.

Interviewers recorded comments from a large number of pensioner-respondents to the effect that they would like to earn some money in order to supplement the pension, but were prevented by the means test. These comments usually came, however, from pensioners who had no income apart from the pension, or a small supplementary income still well below the means test limit. One must conclude that here the real factor preventing part-time earning, as was made explicit by many other respondents, was that they were no longer well enough to work even part-time; and, to a less extent, that suitable part-time work was not easily available, especially for older people. More convincing were the few, especially migrants who had been here long enough to get the pension, who did not understand the rules well enough and were frightened that earning any extra money at all would bring them into trouble with the Department of Social Services. One woman, this time an Australian pensioner, who had a grandson of thirteen living with and wholly dependent on her, did not even claim child endowment for him because she was afraid that this might bring her into difficulties with the Department. Another couple classed as poor and in need because their sole resources consisted of $6,000 in the bank, would have been entitled to draw the full married-couple pension and would then have been well above the poverty line. They had no embarrassment about going on to the pension and intended to do so at some time in the future, but they were quite content for the time being to live on their assets and were proud of their independence.

While many people had evidently arranged, or were in the course of arranging, their affairs so as to bring their assessable assets down just to the limit which would permit them to draw full pension, others seemed to lack an adequate understanding of the rules. Some said they had used up *all* their assets in order to qualify for the pension; some were in the course of doing so although their assets as reported to us were already well below the qualifying level.

In fact, and as is confirmed by the replies of many respondents, the Department of Social Services is zealous in its attempts to help aged people to get their full rights. It appears, nevertheless, that there is a substantial problem of communication still to be overcome. That there is a problem appears to be confirmed by the fact that, on occasions when the means test has been liberalised, some new applicants turn out to have been eligible at least for part-pension under the previous rules. This may be due either to ignorance, or to reluctance to submit to the means test; it may also be that, under the old rules, the part-pension for which they would have been eligible was too small to bother about. In any case, it is doubtful whether ignorance about pension entitlements extends to aged people with little or no means. Their plight would inevitably bring them into contact with people who could advise them of their rights.

In general, those who were in receipt of reduced pensions because their other resources exceeded the means-test limits, or who had arranged their affairs so as to fit within those limits and draw full pension, seemed well satisfied with their situations—and certainly were well above our poverty line. Those who complained about the means test were usually well below the level of resources where it could impinge on them and appeared, as suggested above, to be channelling on to the means test their complaints about getting old, their failing health, the scarcity of work-opportunities and the inadequacy of the basic pension rate.

The introduction in 1969 of the tapered means test, under which pensioners have their pensions reduced by only one-half, instead of the whole, of their means as assessed in excess of the limit which permits payment of a maximum rate pension, should remove the basis for most

of the objections to the means test. It will, however, have no effect whatever in reducing poverty, as any pensioner affected by the means test
would have been already well above marginal poverty.

(v) Recommendations on Pension-rate: (a) *Single and married-couple
pension rates*. The Australian age pension system already differentiates
between aged persons according to whether they are married or single;
according to the amount of any means other than the pension in excess
of the limits provided under the means test; and according to whether
those with little or no additional means are obliged to pay rent. There
would be a case for finer differentiation, particularly according to sex
and size of household and according to additional means within the
means-test limits. On the whole we believe, mainly for political and
social reasons, that no further differentiation should be introduced.

*We recommend that the single pension-rate should be raised to at
least 60 per cent of the married couple rate*. With the married-couple
rate set for 1969-70 at $26.50 a week, the single rate should be $16,
not the $15 at which it was set. This recommendation would raise total
expenditure on age pensions by about 4·8 per cent.

The wife of an age pensioner is not eligible for an age pension unless
she is aged sixty years or more. A younger wife with a child less than
sixteen years old, an eligible student child or a husband permanently
incapacitated, can receive an allowance which, however, is only $7 a
week, in contrast to the present differential between married-couple and
single rates of $11.50. Yet provided she satifies the means test, her need
can be no less than that of a woman eligible by age for a pension. Indeed,
as some cases in our survey demonstrate, the wife may have been forced
to give up lucrative employment in order to stay home to look after her
incapacitated husband. Moreover, non-pensioner wives who cannot
satisfy the conditions for the allowance are likely to be in poverty unless
they have been working and continue to do so: they are unlikely to be of
an age at which it would be reasonable to expect them to start working.

*We therefore recommend that the allowance for a wife, aged less than
sixty, of an age pensioner should be increased to the full difference
between the married-couple and single pensioners' rates, and should be
made available to all non-pensioner wives of age pensioners, subject
only to the normal operation of the means test*.

We estimate that this would involve an increase in expenditure on
age pensions of 0·7 per cent. If this recommendation is thought too
generous, then we suggest that the increased allowance should at least

be made available on an age-qualification similar to that for Class B widows—that is, for non-pensioner wives aged fifty or more, or aged forty-five or more if they have until then had a dependent child.

(b) *The pension rate and average earnings.* We believe that poverty is a relative concept and, therefore, that the poverty line should move up in step with average earnings in the community. It follows that if pensioners are to be kept above the poverty line the basic pension rate, which is all or nearly all the income available to a substantial proportion of the aged, should also move up in step with average earnings.

Table 5·9 shows the basic pension rate (since 1963, the weighted average of the single and married rates) as a percentage of average earnings.

TABLE 5·9

BASIC AGE PENSION RATE AS PERCENTAGE OF AVERAGE EARNINGS

Period*	Percentage
1946 to 1952	26·0
1952 to 1958	22·6
1958 to 1964	22·7
1964 to 1967	22·1
1967 to 1970	20·9

*Each year's pension rate, as announced in the Budget Speech in the September quarter, is related to average earnings in the financial year ending on the previous 30th June.

The ratio of the pension rate to average earnings was fairly stable, at about 22·7 per cent, throughout the twelve-year period from 1952 to 1964. This level was substantially lower than the 26 per cent of the period 1946 to 1952. Since 1964 the ratio has been falling to average 22·1 per cent in the three years 1964 to 1967, and 20·9 per cent in the latest three years to 1970. This trend inevitably puts an increasing proportion of pensioners below a poverty line which rises, as we think it should, in step with average earnings.

The earlier recommendation to increase the single rate by $1 would raise the latest ratio of the basic pension rate to average earnings from 20.9 per cent to 21.8 per cent. *We recommend further that the basic pension rate should be raised each year in step with the average earnings index.*

With average earnings expected to rise between 1968-69 and 1969-70 by some 5 to 6 per cent this recommendation would imply that the

married-couple rate should be set in the 1970 Budget Speech at about
$28.00 and the single rate at $17.00.

Housing

From Stage I evidence it appears that more than half the aged in private
houses were living on their own—33,000 married couples, 34,000 single
women and 6,000 single men. That so many people can afford to live
on their own is evidence of the wealth of the community; that they
choose to do so is evidence of the extent to which the old concept of
the three-generation family has been superseded.

The practical importance of this pattern, however, lies in the large
numbers for whom help may be needed as their health deteriorates or
they become frail with age—help with domestic chores or shopping,
meals on wheels or nursing, help to carry on in their own homes or help
to move if they cannot carry on.

Table 5·10 shows the poverty classification of all aged income units
subdivided according to their housing costs. Among aged income units,
56·7 per cent own their own houses, free of mortgage or debt, compared
with 27·4 per cent in the population of Melbourne as a whole and 21·0
per cent for income units other than the aged. A further 14·8 per cent
have rent-free housing, usually those living with their families or in
houses owned by their families but sometimes caretakers or house-
keepers. These two groups include most of those kept out of need by
cheapness of accommodation and by family help, and very few are left
in need.

Those paying less than $5 a week in rent or instalments are also
largely free of poverty and need. But the supply of privately owned
accommodation at such low rents is shrinking, since it is completely
uneconomic for landlords to use valuable land in this way. Moreover
in some cases the quality of this cheap housing is badly substandard.
The judgment of the Victorian Housing Commission should be noted.[2]

The demand for accommodation in many suburbs for the section of the
community so deserving of our help is greater than the supply and many
elderly citizens still live in substandard housing conditions. The problem of housing Victoria's elderly citizens is increasing year by year.

Most old people are adequately housed. A small minority solely
dependent on the pension who have to find accommodation for them-

[2] Annual Report of Victorian Housing Commission, 1966-67

selves are in grave trouble since decent privately owned accommodation is not available at a rent which they can afford to pay. At the time of the survey in 1966 a single pensioner could probably not afford to pay more than $5 a week and a married couple more than $7 a week. The provision of subsidised low cost housing for the aged poor is therefore urgent. But it needs to be emphasised that this is a manageable problem, since such a large proportion of old people own their own homes or are living with others.

There are 16·7 per cent of aged income units who are paying rents of $5 a week or more, with the average rent over $12 a week. Evidently many of those paying these rents can afford them. But it is in this group, inevitably, that the bulk of those poor and in need are found; and of them, only one-third receive the Supplementary Assistance, which is confined to single-rate pensioners who are tenants with little or no income other than the pension.

TABLE 5·10

POVERTY AND HOUSING COSTS OF THE AGED

All Aged Income Units

	Owner, no mortgage	Rent-free	Rent or instalment			Total
			Under $3	$3 to $5	$5 and over	
	%	%	%	%	%	%
Above marginal poverty	41·8	10·4	6·4	4·1	11·5	74·2
In marginal poverty	8·3	0·2	0·3	0·5	1·3	10·6
In poverty, but not in need —by accommodation	4·6	1·5	0·3	0·1	—	6·5
—by assets	1·0	—	—	—	1·9	2·9
—by family help	0·8	2·6	—	—	0·1	3·5
In poverty and in need	0·2	0·1	—	0·1	1·9	2·3
Total	56·7	14·8	7·0	4·8	16·7	100·0

Ownership of a house free of debt is, naturally, a major factor in keeping the aged out of need in our poverty classification. However in allowing for the cost of housing no provision has been made for the cost to owners of rates, taxes, insurance and minimum essential repairs which are met, for tenants, by their landlords. We have accordingly recalculated the poverty-classification after reducing the income of owners by $2 a week, which replies to the second questionnaire suggest is a bare minimum allowance for housing costs incurred by owners. On this basis, the proportion of the aged in need and in poverty would rise by 0·3 per cent, from 2·3 to 2·6 per cent; about half this increase is on account of owners without mortgage and half on account of buyers by instalments. The proportion of those in poverty but not in need on account of assets would rise by 0·2 per cent. The proportion in marginal poverty would fall by 0·4 per cent, and of those in poverty but not in need by the cheapness of their accommodation by 0·1 per cent.

TABLE 5·11

POVERTY AND HOUSING COSTS OF THE AGED

All Aged Income Units, Income Reduced in Each Case by $2 per Week for Costs of Housing Incurred by Owners

	%
Above marginal poverty	74·2
In marginal poverty	10·2
In poverty, but not in need —by accommodation	6·4
—by assets	3·1
—by family help	3·5
In poverty and in need	2·6
Total	100·0

Recommendation on Supplementary Assistance: Replies to the second questionnaire suggest that most pensioners eligible to receive Supplementary Assistance towards their rent do so. It helps all those who do receive it and is probably enough to keep out of need the fortunate few paying rents of a few dollars a week. It is inadequate for the many paying more.

A notable defect in the provision for Supplementary Assistance is its exclusion of married couples who pay rent. The few couples in this category who pay rent and have little income additional to the pension are as much in need of the assistance as are single-rate pensioners. In the United Kingdom, assistance towards the cost of rent is determined individually for pensioners, according to the amount of rent they actually pay. Appropriate administrative machinery for such graded assistance does not exist in Australia and social attitudes may not be sympathetic to its establishment.

We have considered the desirability of suggesting some special assistance for those with little or no income other than the pension and who have to pay rates and insurance on houses they own and, especially, for those still paying instalments to purchase their homes. We believe, on the whole, that these problems should not be met by the extension of Supplementary Assistance to home owners.

We do, however, recommend that local government authorities should be encouraged, where appropriate by assistance from Government funds, to extend universally the option which exists in some places for aged home owners to defer payment of rates, which then become a charge against their estates after their death.

Assistance with maintenance and repairs to the houses and gardens of old people is a valuable voluntary activity which deserves to be more widely practised. It offers scope for active young people to lend a hand and be of service to the community. The knowledge that such help is available would relieve the anxiety felt by many lonely elderly people as to whether they can cope with these problems.

Supplementary Assistance to pensioners who are tenants should be designed, then, to help them meet housing costs in excess of those incurred by home-owners. It is impossible, without introducing some form of national assistance, to help tenants meet the very high rents which some of them choose or are obliged to pay. This problem can, in the end, be solved only by the building of much more accommodation for the aged by the Housing Commission which is then in a position to grant rent rebates to those eligible by the lowness of their income.

We recommend that the amount of Supplementary Assistance for rent-payers should be increased to $4 a week and that married couples should be eligible for this grant as well as single-rate pensioners.

This amount would be reduced by the amount of income additional to the pension. We estimate this would involve an increase of expenditure on age pensions by about $3 \cdot 3$ per cent.

Two groups who, our survey suggests, do not always claim Supplementary Assistance even though they may be eligible for it are migrants and family boarders. This underlines the need for wide and continuing publicity for the benefits that are available. In particular, there is some evidence to suggest that aged migrants who have been here long enough to qualify for a pension are so glad to have it and so frightened of the possibility of losing it, that they do not ask in addition for Supplementary Assistance for which they are eligible.

The Condition of Housing: We have said earlier that ownership of a house or low rent payments may keep an aged person out of need, but may also mean poor housing conditions. This applies even to those paying rents of $5 a week, which is already beyond the means of age pensioners with little or no additional income. Interviewers' comments are revealing.

A cold, cobwebby little bungalow (rent, $2.30 per week), the door the main source of ventilation, a dirty chenille bedspread tacked outside the door, probably to keep out the wind; damp and smelly, floor lumpy— linoleum appeared to be on bare earth.

She has kitchen facilities on an outside landing but there is no piped water. The owner's son brings buckets of water to her. She does not generally cook for herself as she does not have the use of either a stove or a refrigerator (rent, $5 a week).

A bungalow in a decrepit Fitzroy rooming-house (rent, $5 a week). Two out of five louvre window panes are missing, the door doesn't close properly and can't be locked. There are no sheets on the bed, and the furniture consists of a bed, a dressing table and a wardrobe held up by the dressing table. He sits on the bed or on the stairs. He has no heating, no refrigerator, no radio or television. He shares the kitchen, bathroom, laundry and two toilets with eight or nine other people.

Lives in a hundred-year-old house which he owns. The only means of heating is lighting the gas stove. When interviewer arrived at 11 a.m., he was in bed 'keeping warm'.

Aged people who rent Housing Commission houses or flats and are eligible for rent rebates are the fortunate ones—we found none of these tenants in need. The recent decision by the Commission to accept single males as tenants will greatly help those who succeed in getting such accommodation. However, it is not easy to get Commission flats and houses, especially in areas where people want to live.

A married couple, paying $15.50 a week rent for a good house, 'would like a cheaper place but have not applied to the Housing Commission as they feel it is "hopeless".' An 88-year-old spinster, paying $7 a week for a bed-sitting room and kitchenette in fair condition, 'has had her name on the waiting list for a Housing Commission flat for a single person, but after many years on the list she was told she was too old and that more flats were built for married couples than for single persons.' 'A 74-year-old spinster pays $8 a week for a room in an old house. She shares sitting room, kitchen, bathroom, lavatory and laundry with three other people. She would like a flat of her own and was on the Housing Commission waiting list for six or eight years. She was offered a Commission flat in Carlton but she refused it because it was not on the ground floor and because she didn't want to leave East Malvern where all her friends are.'

Some aged respondents are living in houses too large for them or in very poor condition, but they are not anxious to move. 'It's old and inconvenient, but it'll have to do me till I die,' said the occupant of a house (rent, $5.75 a week) described by the interviewer as 'poor housing overall: in need of repair and maintenance inside and out; damp and cracked walls.' A widow, living on in the house which she owned and in which she had brought up seven children, said: 'Sometimes I feel a smaller place would be better. It's big to look after—the gardening is not good for my arthritis. But the grandchildren can stay here which is good. A pensioner's flat might be better but I haven't gone into it. I'd really like just to drift along.'

Another frail old woman, with little remaining ability to manage her affairs, was paying $13 a week for a flat; she refused to leave, although offered accommodation in an old people's home, because she had lived in the flat happily with her husband who had died there in her arms.

Cases such as these suggest the need for provision, especially through local initiative, for helping people to do up old homes they don't want to leave, and possibly for helping them to get someone else to live in spare accommodation, perhaps making it more convenient to do so by spending a bit on subdivision and improved facilities.

Assets

Information about assets was collected only from respondents to the second questionnaire. The ownership of assets was significant (in the sense that it improved the respondent's situation by more than 10 per cent) for about 18 per cent of those respondents, although it kept out of need only about 7 per cent of them (equal to $2 \cdot 9$ per cent of all aged respondents). The rest were already out of need by income or by cheapness of accommodation.

There is, however, ample evidence from the survey that small asset-owners do not, in general, manage their affairs so as to derive the greatest benefit from those assets. They derive little or no income from them. Many refuse to draw on them to supplement the pension, but keep them untouched in case they need money for house-repairs or hospital bills.

Those who draw on their assets in order to supplement their pension report their anxiety that their assets are running down and that they will be left with nothing unless they are fortunate enough to die soon. A respondent who received $5,200 retirement gratuity when he went on the pension had drawn steadily on it to supplement his pension—a supplement badly needed as his rent was $8 a week. Five years later, at seventy-two, he had only $770 left. Another, aged eighty, had had savings of $3,800 nine years before but had used them all up to supplement his pension, just when because of his age and increasing dependence he was most in need of extra income.

It is well-known that the Commonwealth Department of Social Services is helpful in advising applicants for pensions how to arrange their affairs so as to qualify for maximum Government assistance. But there was evidence in the survey of people with assets being ignorant about the means test rules or badly advised by private sources. They did indeed become eligible for the pension but only by spending or losing all or an unnecessarily large proportion of their assets.

In valuing assets for the purpose of determining poverty status, we have followed, with some misgivings, the rules laid down by the Commonwealth Department of Social Services (see Appendix C, paragraph 7). For people who by their actual income are below the poverty line, we have deducted any property income and have added back, instead, 10 per cent of the value of their assets in excess of the amounts ignored by those rules.

One difficulty encountered in assessing the value of assets was to decide whether the owner had access to them. Property such as a flat which is an integral part of a house owned and occupied by the respondent, or a house marked for demolition, may be unsaleable even though it may represent a substantial asset. In such cases, we have ignored the value of the asset and included as part of income only any rent actually received. In another kind of case, a married pensioner couple are paying a rent of $13.70 a week and have no income other than their pension. By this information, they should be classed as 'in poverty and in need'. But the wife owns a house worth $7,200, as a result of which the couple is classed as 'not in need by the annuity-worth of assets'. However, the house is lived in by the wife's daughter by a previous marriage. The daughter's husband is earning a good wage. But the wife will not ask for rent as she is 'too soft-hearted'. She and her second husband realise that if they could live in this house they would solve their own rent problem. They recently applied to the Salvation Army for low-rent housing, but found they would have to pay $5,400 for a flat which would revert to the Salvation Army on their death, and also they would have to pay for the upkeep of the flat. They are on the waiting list for a Housing Commission flat but think they have no hope of getting one because of the length of the list.

In a case like this, there are clearly grounds for ignoring the asset and classing the people as in need. On the other hand, however, can one conscientiously argue that this is a case of need justifying a demand for an appropriate Government policy, when the wife has it in her own hands to improve their situation? Even then, one has to add that the situation is no doubt complicated by the daughter's presumable attitude to her mother's second marriage, and to her own right to occupancy of her mother's house.

We are not happy about the ability of aged people to manage their assets to best advantage; nor about the rules we have followed in our valuation of assets for those who would, without them, be below the poverty line. In the end, however, it has seemed to us best to keep in line with the not altogether illogical departmental rules which underlie the determination of eligibility for pension. While we consider it wise to regard with some reserve the class described as 'not in need because of assets-valuation', it should be added that in all except a negligible proportion of the population the additional income attributed through revaluation of assets lifted the respondents clear even of marginal poverty.

Assets and Preparation for Retirement: The poverty classification of the aged demonstrates that preparations for retirement in the form of accumulated savings and superannuation rights are highly effective in keeping people out of poverty. Yet distressingly few of the aged enjoy such reserves; and distressingly few of the present working population are accumulating them. The following table shows how many of the working population of Melbourne in 1966 were contributors to superannuation schemes or insurance policies. We have no information about the amounts of their contributions but it can be assumed that, in general, contributors to superannuation schemes are building up a larger and more certain provision for their retirement than are contributors to often small insurance policies.

Of males at work, only one-third are in superannuation schemes and, of females, only 13 per cent. Membership of superannuation schemes is higher for those with higher incomes.

In this context, it is worth noting that some people have accumulated surprisingly few assets. One couple had reared only one child who left school and started working at age fourteen. The husband had worked all his life and the wife had worked for thirty-one years. They had never bought a house and were living in a Housing Commission flat which cost them, after allowing for their rental rebate, $3 a week plus $1 for heating. Their total joint assets amounted to $100.

TABLE 5·12

POPULATION AT WORK: CONTRIBUTORS AND NON-CONTRIBUTORS TO
SUPERANNUATION SCHEMES AND INSURANCE POLICIES

Actual weekly income	Numbers of workers	Non-contributors	Contributors	
			Superannuation or superannuation and insurance	Insurance only
	'000	%	%	%
Males				
Less than $39	68·3	78·2	15·1	6·7
$39 to $79	305·9	51·9	32·5	15·6
$80 or more	160·1	29·1	44·0	26·9
Total	534·3	48·4	33·7	17·9
Females				
Less than $39	49·0	83·8	10·2	6·0
$39 or more	25·7	70·0	18·8	11·2
Total	74·7	79·0	13·2	7·8
Total working population	609·0	52·1	31·2	16·7

Another couple had never had any children, both husband and wife had worked all their lives, suffering neither unemployment nor ill-health; they had bought a house in 1957 for $3,900, on a deposit of $600, and were still paying it off in instalments of $8 a week. Their total assets, apart from their equity in the house, consisted of 80 cents in the bank.

A woman, single, was classed by us as in need because her only income was the pension plus Supplementary Assistance and out of that she had to pay $7 a week rent for an unfurnished bed-sitting-room and kitchenette. She had worked all her life from fifteen until she retired at age eighty-seven, yet her sole assets were $120 in the bank.

One second-stage respondent, living alone and paying $3 a week rent, with the pension plus the Supplementary Assistance her only income, said she regretted now that she had not contributed to her employer's superannuation scheme when she was young and earning good wages. Another, supplementing his and his wife's age pensions with part-time earnings of $14 a week, but paying rent of $15.50 a week, said he had been in two superannuation schemes but had lost his accumulated benefits in each of them because of changing his jobs. He had never saved nor made any other provision for his retirement.

These cases remind us that there are plenty of people in our fully-employed and well-paid working population who would have been well able to contribute to superannuation schemes had such schemes been available to them. They underline the need for a national superannuation scheme (which would automatically preserve benefits throughout all changes of employment) to ensure adequate incomes for a dignified and comfortable retirement.[3]

Family Help

The other main source of information relevant to the poverty classification was collected in response to questions about help received from family and friends.

Of the second-stage population, 37·7 per cent were recorded as receiving the equivalent of $2 or more a week in help of this kind, 2·5 per cent as receiving smaller amounts and 59·8 per cent as receiving no help. The help, though often marginal, was sufficient in 8·4 per cent of the second-stage cases (equivalent to 3·5 per cent of all aged respondents), to lift the respondent out of need.

The most substantial help was rent-free or low-rent accommodation usually with family or friends. In many other cases, independent children lived with the aged respondent and gave substantial help with living expenses. Altogether, nearly 30 per cent of the second-stage respondents either lived with their independent children or had them still living with them. This was not always a happy arrangement. In one case, a mother

[3] See R. I. Downing, 'National Superannuation: Means Test and Contributions', in *The Economic Record*, Vol. 44, No. 108, December 1968, pp. 407 ff. The author outlines in some detail a proposal for a national superannuation scheme with generous retirement benefits financed by contributions graduated in relation to income. The extension of such a scheme to cover all aspects of social security, including widows' and invalid pensions, health and medical benefits, unemployment and sickness benefits and accident compensation, is also proposed.

paying $13 a week rent was taking from her daughter, who lived with her, $25 a week, virtually her whole earnings. She had a bad relationship with her other children, who had already left home.

There were many other forms of help: regular or occasional gifts of cash, food and services; contributions towards rent, instalments, rates, taxes, insurance and repairs; regular visits more or less frequently, evidently greatly appreciated; and care of the aged respondents in their own homes for one or several days a week. In some cases, help from churches or from organisations like Legacy was making it possible for aged people to avoid finding themselves in need.

One old lady was aged eighty-seven, quite deaf, almost blind with cataracts, had plaster casts on both legs and eczema on her hands. The interviewer reported:

The interview was possible only through her stepson, who lives elsewhere but visits her every evening, except at the weekends, for dinner. He cannot recall her being in bed for a day or longer. She does her own shopping, cooking, housework and laundry and visits the doctor twice a week. She is tall, spare in body, quite cheerful and, despite the outside temperature of 86 degrees and all her disabilities, had been burning off rubbish. The stepson pays for gas, electricity, fuel, telephone, rates and repairs but said he could not ask the respondent how much money she had in the bank or her pension rate. This evidently is where her independence shows. Stepson would pay for any help she needed and could get, preferably through the council.

Migrant Parents: The most important contribution by families was made to recently-arrived parents of migrants, with no or virtually no income of their own. These people turned out usually, but not always, to be reasonably well looked after by their families who had arranged their entry-permits under maintenance guarantees. In all such cases we calculated an adjusted family income to test whether the addition of dependent parents to the supporting income unit still left the family above the poverty line. In nearly all cases where the revised adjusted income was inadequate, however, it turned out that a compassionate allowance had been granted by the Department of Social Services. There were one or two unfortunate exceptions, but it was not clear in these cases that application for the allowance had been made and refused.

In some cases, especially where support of a parent-in-law rather than a parent was involved, the support was given grudgingly and was felt by the recipient to be so given. In more cases, the recipients clearly avoided as far as possible expenditures such as for clothing and medical attention, which would involve their families in cash outlays; the parents usually felt they gave in services enough to offset the accommodation and food they received. In general, the situation of these migrant parents with no income of their own was unenviable.

We recommend that an allowance at the rate of one-half of the age pension should be paid to elderly migrants eligible by age but not by length of residence, the allowance to be reduced by half the amount of income which they receive from any source.

There were a few cases of help in the opposite direction, with the aged person contributing to the maintenance of younger people, sometimes impoverishing themselves in the process. These situations arose either from younger children with regular earnings contributing less than the cost of their food, or from older children apparently unable to earn regularly and still dependent on their aged parent or parents for support. One pensioner supported wholly a 13-year-old grandson and had living with her also an 18-year-old son who earned $24 a week and paid her only $3 a week for his board. Another pensioner couple were too poor, especially because of medical expenses, to keep up repayments of the money borrowed from friends to enable them to buy their house, and yet they received no regular board from their middle-aged son who lived with them and worked only intermittently. The respondent concluded: 'We get old and sick. Every day I pray that I shall die.' Another woman who spent her life looking after a sick father, an invalid husband and a sick brother, now all deceased, was on the pension with no other income and looked after yet another brother who paid her nothing for his keep. He stopped working when he was aged 58, and decided to live on his savings ($40) and his sister's pension. He said his sister was very good to him. His sister said she had always spoiled him, and things would improve when he became eligible for the age pension in two years' time.

There were many cases of pensioners who handed over their whole pension to their family. In most of these cases, it was clear that the pensioners were unable because of age to look after their own affairs and were perfectly well looked after by their families. In a few cases, however, it appeared that the pensioner became virtually 'a family prisoner'. One woman in this position complained that she was left alone all day and most nights, that nothing was provided for her apart from meals, that she wanted to go to a home for aged people where she could have company, but that her family would not let her do so because of the disgrace they thought it would bring on them.

The availability of family help obviously varies greatly according to the personalities and to the financial and economic situation of both the aged people and their families and friends. It is often a less certain, a less durable and a less dignified source of sustenance than income and assets under a person's own control. More than half (62·3 per cent) of the income units responding at Stage II received little or no family help. It is not a source, therefore, for which any substantial allowance should be made in devising general policies for the avoidance of need among the aged.

Mental Attitudes and Physical Health

This chapter on the aged has been concerned with objective and measurable criteria of income, housing costs, assets and family help. But what people are able to do with these resources depends very much on their own attitudes and on their physical health.

Some aged people are well adapted to making the best of their situation. One respondent has come to be referred to by us as 'the cheerful invalid'. He has the pension and Supplementary Assistance and pays $5 a week for a room in a large rooming house of not very good standard. He takes full advantage of services provided by the local council, has his lunch each day for 12 cents and his hair trimmed once a fortnight for 20 cents. He is certainly poor and in need by any objective test but is philosophically and cheerfully making the best of his difficult situation. Another single male pensioner is still a bit of a dandy, making very much the best of himself and his life, his only regret that his sex life is behind him. A couple, the man aged eighty-one and the wife sixty-five, have married recently, and say they live happily on love—supplemented by assets the amount of which they refused to disclose. There are plenty of sprightly old ladies, neat, contented and managing well.

But there are also, among the interviewers' reports, many more sad stories of widows simply unable to manage their affairs after their husbands have died, heavily dependent on their children, if they have any, and on charitable organisations. Many of the single males, living in rooms, are quite unable to make the best of their situation. Some of the earlier migrants, even though qualified for the pension, have clearly never made the adjustments to life in a new country and carry their failure into their old age.

Loneliness was mentioned quite often as a fact of age, but not nearly as often as was expected. Those with families and friends on the whole seemed to see as much of them as they wanted. Those without seemed to accept their comparative loneliness as something they could cope with. The general impression was rather of people wanting to be independent and resenting only the increasing financial and physical difficulties of remaining so.

One woman, a widow, never lacked for company. She had been left by her husband a legacy which included a couple of murderers whom he'd been helping after their release from gaol—and she had gone on cheerfully, carrying on his good work with several more. Another, having survived her own *de facto* husband, had twelve illegitimate brothers and sisters scattered all over Australia and happily visited them all. Yet another, married at fourteen and widowed at fifteen, was only grateful to have been on her own ever since.

The darkest side of the picture revolves very much around ill-health. A woman of fifty is forced to give up work in order to look after her 80-year-old blind pensioner husband, but she can get only the quite inadequate wife's allowance because she is not yet sixty. Her husband suffers from her resentment. A woman completely crippled by arthritis and unable to move, is dependent for everything on a cousin, assisted by daily visits from the district nurse. Two frail old sisters struggle to look after their senile and incontinent 80-year-old brother. Diabetics complain that they cannot afford the expensive diet they need to keep alive.

And dominating nearly every reply where health problems are not already acute is the fear of failing health and what it threatens for the future—loss of earnings, loss of independence, the fear of being forced into an institution because of disabilities which, marginal in themselves, may be crippling if no help is available.

Conclusion and Summary of Recommendations

Few of the aged have incomes, assets or housing conditions which permit them to pass their retirement in comfort and dignity. Nothing short of a national superannuation scheme is likely ever to remedy this situation for the great bulk of the population.

Thanks to the not too ungenerous basic pension rate and means test provisions, and to Supplementary Assistance, serious poverty and need is confined essentially to those like migrants' parents who are not yet eligible for the pension and are inadequately looked after by their families, and to the not insignificant number of pensioners who have to pay rents in excess of $2 or $3 a week. To meet these problems there is need for a much greater provision of accommodation for the aged by the Housing Commission, which is able to grant rent rebates according to its tenants' incomes; an increase in the rate of Supplementary Assistance and its extension to cover married-couple tenants; an extension of and increase in the allowance for non-pensioner wives of age pensioners; and the introduction of an allowance for migrants' parents ineligible by length of residence for the age pension.

Few pensioners are in a situation where an increase in the pension rate of several dollars a week would be regarded as a national extravagance. It would permit a few more urgent needs to be met and still not make most pensioners even comfortably off. We confine ourselves, however, to what we regard as an absolutely minimum recommendation. The single-rate pension should be raised to at least 60 per cent of the married-couple rate and pension-rates generally should be raised each year in step with the index of average earnings.

The estimated cost of these recommendations is derisory. If applied in 1968-69, they would have required additional expenditure of only some $40 million, representing about 8 per cent of total expenditure on age pensions in that year. We are embarrassed that the climate of opinion in this rich country encourages us, if we are to be realistic and to expect to be listened to, to ask for no more.

6 Families without Fathers*

Far more important than counting the poor is the identification of groups in the community that have the highest risk of poverty. As has been seen in Chapter 4, the group at greatest risk are the families without fathers. We should make special efforts to combat poverty among these families, for not only do they suffer the deprivations of being poor, but their problems are compounded by the lack of a husband and father.

Governments and social welfare agencies can do little to fill the gap of the missing father. They should, however, spare no effort to see that the economic deprivation of these families is reduced as much and as quickly as possible. The cost of eliminating poverty among them is not large since their numbers are relatively small. Lack of resources, public or private, cannot be used as an argument for denying them adequate income nor for delay in providing it. The diversion of resources to their use will, moreover, be an investment for the future.

On the basis of the Stage I interviews there were estimated to be nearly 15,000 fatherless families in Melbourne. Of those for whom income was known, it was estimated that over 30 per cent (about 4,000 families) had an adjusted income of less than $33 per week and were in poverty. Apart from this high incidence of poverty, the most disturbing feature of these estimates is that in these 4,000 families there were about 8,750 dependent children. A further 14 per cent of families (1,800 families with 3,200 children) had an adjusted weekly income that exceeded the poverty line by less than $6. When one recognises the problems facing fatherless families it is obvious that the position of those in this marginal group is precarious as they may easily fall below the poverty line.

It is, perhaps, of some comfort to find that the incidence of poverty in this group is less when the estimate is made in terms of income after housing costs have been met. On this basis it is estimated that about 22 per cent of the fatherless families are in poverty. A further 14 per cent are in the marginally poor category, having an adjusted income after housing costs of less than $33 per week.

However, although it appears that for many families within this group housing arrangements alleviate rather than aggravate poverty, the incidence of poverty among them is still substantially higher than in almost any other group in the community. In individual families, too, we do find situations that are far different from this general picture: some families could manage reasonably well but for the fact that their present accommodation is so costly that it brings them below the poverty line.

* This chapter was written by R. J. A. Harper.

Second stage interviews were conducted with thirty-four fatherless families. In some of the interviews, it is true, additional sources of income were revealed. There were also many cases in which the circumstances of the family had changed in some way since the first interview; sometimes for the better but in some cases for the worse. Any assessment based on income in one week only, as was the case in the first interviews, was likely to differ from one based on more detailed interviews which attempted to collect information on income over a whole year. In some cases the view over the longer period revealed a better economic position; in others it showed up additional weaknesses in the families' finances. In all cases the longer interview made it apparent that these families were confronted by many more problems, both economic and non-economic, than would be revealed in a brief interview. Problems concerning housing, health, delinquency, debt, education, employment and loneliness could now be understood better and put into perspective.

On balance there is not much evidence to suggest that the estimates of the percentages in poverty based on the earlier interviews are an overstatement. Because these second interviews were relatively small in number and because, in general, they do not appear to indicate any major modifications to the results of the first stage, no attempt is made to give quantitative estimates based on them. They were very valuable, however, in providing human interest and personal details. Without these case studies, the statistical analysis would be impersonal and lacking in impact.

It is worth mentioning some of the general impressions that these second stage interviews create.

Variety

The first is that these fatherless families in or near poverty are not a homogeneous group. The outstanding impression given by the women who head these families is one of variety: variety in their education, in their social backgrounds, in their experiences and in their ability to cope with their common problem of bringing up children without the help of a father.

Some had obviously been happily married and the death of the father had been a tragic and shattering blow; for others the death or desertion of the father had been something of a relief. In several families the situation before separation or desertion had been quite intolerable, with alcoholism and cruelty often mentioned as the cause of the breakdown of the marriage. In one case the relationship had deteriorated to such an extent that the wife had attempted to murder her husband.

Some mothers were poorly educated—sometimes in other countries —or not very intelligent, and the experiences they had been through had drained them of what little ability they might have had to cope with their current problems. They were depressed and apathetic and their families were disintegrating. Many mothers, some with quite poor educational backgrounds, found in response to the new calls made on them added resources of character and ingenuity that enabled them to manage their affairs with considerable efficiency and keep their families happy and tightly-knit units. A few were very capable and had been well educated, even to the tertiary level, and they were able to draw on their training to help build a new life for themselves and their families. Their attitude was one of hopeful anticipation of the future.

Some were well-housed at manageable costs; others, badly housed and paying high rents. In their employment the same variety existed. Some were happily employed in congenial occupations which added greatly to their social as well as economic well-being. Others worked at menial tasks in a disgruntled and unhappy fashion. Many, of course, did not work at all and among these there were quite a few who regretted the idleness that was 'forced' on them by the means test, the responsibility of caring for their children, or their inability to find suitable work.

Our interviews all served to show the difficulties and perhaps the dangers of generalising without knowledge of individual families. Each family is, after all, a unique entity.

Health

A second vivid impression gained from studying these questionnaires is that of the importance of health problems in the lives of these families. In discussions of family problems with a woman recently widowed this is understandable, as the terminal illness of her husband had frequently dominated the lives of all members of the family both emotionally and financially. As well as suffering the emotional impact of the illness and death, a family has often to face drastic changes in economic circumstances. Earnings diminish as the father becomes too ill to work and then cease altogether; assets are sold in order to maintain a semblance of past standards and some measure of comfort for the sick; finally, debts mount up as medical and hospital costs add to the unpaid bills arising out of every day living. The eventual relative security of the widows' pension and the pensioner medical scheme brings little solace, as these provide no compensation for the losses the family has suffered and no resources to settle accumulated debts.

This is graphically illustrated by the case of a migrant widow with three young children. The family's assets had all been used up during her husband's illness and there was still an accumulation of debts when he died. While in receipt of the widows' pension she attempted to pay off some of the debts by working, and in doing so exceeded the allowed income under the means test. As a consequence her pension was reduced until she had paid back the amounts of pension to which she had not been entitled. She has now ceased to work.

Apart from these problems associated with recent widowhood it is very clear that the incidence of health problems among the fatherless families is high. Whether the illnesses of the mother and children result from the additional strains to which they are subjected is difficult to say. There do, however, seem to be an unduly high proportion who suffer from mental illness, nervous disorders and psychiatric problems as well as the usual run of physical ailments. When such situations are coupled with low income it is often difficult to see what promise the future can hold for these families. Their depression and apathy, where they exist, are easily understood. The optimism and hope which many of them display can only be admired and wondered at.

Just one case will suffice to illustrate the combination of illness and adversity that strikes some families.

A widow of thirty with three children had recently lost her husband after a lengthy illness. Of the three children, the eldest, a seven-year-old girl, had been sent to the country and had lived with relatives for the previous year. The second child, who had just started kindergarten, was not strong and was in need of an eye operation to correct a congenital defect. The third child, who suffered from a serious skin complaint, had spent much of her short life in hospital. At eighteen months she had not started crawling and because of the seriousness of her condition the doctors did not know how long she would live. The mother had also spent six weeks of the previous year in hospital being treated for depression.

The husband did not work for at least the last twelve months of his life and for part of that time the family had to live on sickness benefits and a State welfare allowance. One hospital bill alone amounted to $1,200 and to meet this and other expenses they sold their house. Because of the $1,800 that came from this sale the State welfare allowance ceased and now, although the family live entirely on the widows' pension, the remaining cash they have in the bank makes them ineligible for Supplementary Assistance. They now pay a rent of $15.00 per week and because of the condition of the youngest child there is no possibility of the mother working.

In spite of the great strain imposed on her, the mother is managing. She receives help from Red Cross and other organisations and she looks forward to the day when a Housing Commission flat will become available and she will have accommodation at a rent she can afford.

Outside Help

The third general impression that needs to be recorded is that many of these families who fell below the poverty line and would have been in dire need were managing because of the help from their relatives and friends. Time and time again the comment was made: 'We could not continue but for the help that the family give us.' Sometimes it was help with housing—the family being taken in by parents, or relatives coming to live with the family to share the costs of housing; sometimes it was help with clothing for the children, boxes of groceries or school books; sometimes it was help with child-minding while mothers worked. In all these cases it was the moral support as well as the material aid that made such a difference. The fact that somebody cared, somebody was interested, somebody was there as a back stop, was clearly of crucial importance. There seems ample evidence that a system of cash social service benefits is not all that is required to ensure the welfare of families at the lower end of the income scale.

The role of the voluntary agencies should also be mentioned in this context. From the frequency with which organisations like the Brotherhood of St Laurence, the Society of St Vincent de Paul and Legacy were mentioned it is certain that they provide help, advice and understanding that are absolutely essential to many families. They fill a need in the community and provide a service that would be difficult to provide in any other way.

Although family, friends and welfare organisations have this great importance in the lives of so many families, it is still true that there are families completely lacking all these sources of support. Perhaps friends and relatives have been alienated, perhaps left behind in other countries or perhaps they have just drifted away. Sometimes there is reluctance, even aversion to accepting charity from organisations. Whatever the reason, the result is a tightly-knit but lonely family whose members rely almost entirely on each other. The mother carries tremendous burdens in these situations and if she becomes ill or unable to cope, these burdens are borne by whatever children are old enough to bear them.

This sort of situation can be illustrated by the case of a deserted wife aged forty-nine and her two teenage school children. Their pension income placed them well below the poverty line. The mother had been very dependent, financially and otherwise, on an older son who had recently been killed in a car accident. The mother was now apathetic and depressed and receiving psychiatric treatment. This family had no relatives, no friends and virtually no outside contacts. The mother claimed she was 'past the age of visiting outside' and when asked where they would go for help in any crisis replied: 'If I had any problems I would go to the doctor if he was not too busy.'

Situations such as these are not confined to the fatherless families: the aged are even more likely to be isolated in this way. Whoever the people are, the quality of their life is far lower than even their low incomes suggest. The existence of these deprived families is widely acknowledged, but to identify them in the community and provide them with the aid they need in a manner which they will find acceptable is far from easy.

Household Composition

In looking at the fatherless families in the survey we recognise that the structure and size of the households in which such families live have an important bearing not only on their social contacts and integration with the rest of the community but also on their economic circumstances and the economic opportunities that are open to them. Three rather different groups can be distinguished. Firstly, there are the families consisting of mothers with dependent children only who live on their own—a group whose social and economic problems usually appear to be greatest. Secondly, there are the families in which there are independent children as well as dependent children, but whose household is confined to this nuclear family. Usually the existence of such older children provides a wider range of social contacts as well as a source of additional income to the family. Finally, there are the families living in households containing other adults, either relatives, friends or boarders—a situation which provides further opportunities for additions to the household income and for additional economies in housekeeping.

These three groups of fatherless families occur in roughly equal proportions in the community. As is to be expected there is a considerably higher incidence of poverty in the first group, the third group suffering least. There is, however, some evidence to suggest that the second group includes those most likely to be in poverty after housing costs have been met.

Marital Status

The marital status of the mothers in these families is of some relevance when considering both their social and economic problems. Only about half of these women are widows and of the rest the largest group consists of the deserted wives. Other causes of the family being without a father are divorce, voluntary separation or the absence of the husband in prison or a mental hospital for a lengthy period. In addition there are unmarried mothers who are attempting to raise their children themselves rather than place them in an institution or make them available for adoption.

The widow is much more likely to receive the sympathy and assistance of her relatives and friends and, indeed, the community in general. Families in the other categories mentioned are often somewhat reluctant to acknowledge their exact situation; it is therefore less likely that what assistance is available will be offered to them speedily. The community tends to be prejudiced against them, and relatives and former friends are often critical or unhelpful. The effect is to isolate these families to their further detriment.

Financially, the marital status of the mother is important. As noted already, the events which precede widowhood are often very damaging to the economic security of the family. In some cases insurance, super-annuation or workers' compensation payments are available to help restore the family's finances after the death of the father. However, these seem to be the exception rather than the rule and among the poorer families any amounts received in this way tend to be quite small.

Marriages that have ended in divorce or voluntary separation produce a variety of financial situations. In some cases the mother and children are adequately provided for by a maintenance allowance from the father. In many cases, however, the whereabouts of the father is unknown or he is completely incapable of making any contribution. Even if there is any maintenance order, it cannot always be enforced.

Deserted families and the families of prisoners and mental patients are likely to fare still worse. The events which lead to the father's depar-ture are so often associated with financial difficulties that usually the family is left with few assets, a pile of bills and the threat of repossessions because of unpaid hire purchase commitments. The situation differs from that of the widow's family in that there is neither an insurance policy nor superannuation to help out and friends and relatives are usually much less likely to give financial assistance. One example illustrates the plight of such families.

A deserted wife had two daughters, aged fourteen and eleven, and a son of one year. She had been deserted when she became pregnant, as an additional child, coupled with the other financial problems and debts, was more than the father was prepared to tolerate. The wife was left to face these problems and the birth of her son with practically no income because, as a deserted wife, she could not qualify for at least six months for a widows' pension. At the time of the interview the family's circumstances had improved. Their weekly income consisted of the widows' pension ($21.50), child endowment ($3), an allowance from the Social Welfare Department ($3) and a grant of $78 per annum from the Education Department, made because of their necessitous circumstances. They were fortunate, too, in that they had a Housing Commission flat on which they were allowed a rental rebate, their rent being only $3.20 per week. The additional allowances and the low rent put them just above the poverty line, but the mother claimed that there were many things they simply could not afford like overcoats, new bed linen, replacement of the children's shoes and wood for heating in the winter. Sometimes they just ran out of money—fortnightly payments made it difficult to ensure that money lasted for the second week—and it was distressing for both mother and children when money could not be found for the extras required at school. Their situation was further complicated by the baby being sick. The mother, a tired, worn woman of forty, had been advised by her doctor that she needed a hysterectomy, but that was impossible as she had no one to care for the children while she was in hospital. She would have liked to divorce her husband but she was unlikely ever to be able to afford to do so.

Many of these fatherless families eventually become recipients of Class A widows' pensions.[1] But here again the deserted wife is at a dis-

---

[1] Pensions are paid to three different classes of widows, of which the first only is relevant to fatherless families.
Class A—A widow with one or more children in her care.
Class B—A widow at least fifty years old without a child; or a widow at least forty-five years old whose Class A pension has stopped because she no longer has a child in her care.
Class C—A widow under fifty years of age without children, who finds herself in needy circumstances within the twenty-six weeks following her husband's death. If such a widow is pregnant, payment continues until the birth when she may qualify for a Class A pension.
The standard rates of pension for Class A and Class B widows, and the mothers' and children's allowances paid to the former at the time of the survey, together with those appropriate in mid-1970, are set out in Chapter 1, Table 1·2. Rates for Class C widows were, at both times, the same as those for Class B widows.

advantage when compared with the widow. Provided she is not made ineligible by the operation of the means test the widow's entitlement dates from the death of her husband. However, the deserted wife has to establish that she is in fact deserted, has been so for six months and has taken reasonable action to obtain maintenance from her husband. Only then does she become entitled to a widows' pension. At the time of the survey a deserted wife in Victoria was eligible during this waiting period to receive a Commonwealth special benefit of only $8.25 per week for herself, plus $1.50 for each child. This was sometimes supplemented by grants made by the Victorian Social Welfare Department on the basis of individual need. In other States no Commonwealth benefit was paid, but grants of varying amounts were made out of State funds.

This varying and anomalous treatment of deserted wives led the Commonwealth Government in the Budget Speech of August 1967 to offer grants to the States of half the amount paid by them to deserted wives, provided the payments did not exceed the Class A widows' pension.[2] This has raised the level of income of the deserted wives and also assisted State revenues in the States that were previously making all the payments from their own funds. But unfortunately for deserted wives in Victoria, the Victorian Government did not immediately accept the Commonwealth offer. The explanation of its reaction lay in the history of Commonwealth-State financial relations. It was said that a matter of State rights was involved. Such rights, however, provided little comfort to deserted wives and children as they waited in need through the six months necessary to qualify for the widows' pension.

In the Victorian Budget Speech of September 1969, the Premier, Sir Henry Bolte, indicated that this situation had been reviewed and that Victoria would now fall into line with the other States and accept the two-year-old offer of the Commonwealth. He also added, however, that Victoria would come into line on other matters. Victoria would 'progressively vacate the field of assistance' in the case of families which were in receipt of full pensions and the responsibility for whom had thus been accepted by the Commonwealth. This decision, which again appears to use Commonwealth-State rights and responsibilities as the criteria for decisions on welfare matters, will remove a source of additional income from families, who, like the one described above, are in necessitous circumstances.

[2] This offer was embodied in the Commonwealth *States Grants (Deserted Wives) Act,* 1968

Any discussion of the marital status of mothers of fatherless families would not be complete without some further reference to unmarried mothers. Actually the survey produced little direct evidence of their problems. It is likely that any unmarried mothers who were interviewed described themselves as widows or deserted wives. Be that as it may, it is true that in Victoria there have been about 4,000 ex-nuptial births each year in the last few years, and among these is a substantial number of mothers who have decided to keep their children and provide for them from their own resources. In this endeavour they have received only minimal and brief assistance from the public purse. In Victoria an unmarried mother could, at the time of the survey, receive a sickness benefit for six weeks before and for six weeks after the birth of the baby. From then on she had to make her own arrangements for caring for the baby and providing an income to support them both. In most other States the unmarried mother received almost the equivalent of the widows' pension from the State Government. The position of the un-married mother has recently improved in Victoria as she is now covered by the provisions of the Commonwealth *States Grants (Deserted Wives) Act*.[3]

Pensions

It must be recognised, of course, that not all the fatherless families are dependent on government pensions. There are some families that have quite adequate incomes from earnings, property, private pensions or annuities. Nevertheless, estimates from the survey indicate that in approximately half the families a Commonwealth pension was the main or sole source of income. Of those who received pensions about 70 per cent received a widows' pension, about 25 per cent had a war widows' pension and there were instances of the aged pension, invalid pension and unemployment, sickness and special benefits being received.

In terms of poverty these pensioners may be thought of as falling into two groups—the war widows and the rest. According to our definition of poverty no recipient of the war widows' pension was below the poverty line. Their pension is more generous and it is not subject to any means test. Consequently their economic position in general is far

[3] Although this Act provides that those eligible may be paid a pension equivalent to the Class A widows' pension it should be noted that the Victorian Social Welfare Department is applying a much more stringent means test than that applied by the Commonwealth to an applicant for the widows' pension.

superior to that of other pensioners. It is to the other pensioners, particularly the widow pensioners, that we need to direct our attention. Our survey data revealed that for most of these the pension and child endowment were their only sources of income. If there was any other income it was usually of little consequence. Few pensioners had assets, although some did own or partly-own their homes.

This situation is substantiated by the statement made by Mr Whitlam, Leader of the Opposition in the Commonwealth Parliament, on 19 March 1969 that '76 per cent of all Class A widows have incomes of not more than $52 per year, 81 per cent have property valued at not more than $400 and only 35 per cent own or are acquiring a home.'[4] The figures quoted were taken directly from a survey of pensioners in New South Wales conducted by the Commonwealth Department of Social Services in February 1965. It seems that there has been little improvement in these circumstances since 1965. A similar survey conducted in New South Wales and Victoria by the Department in March 1969 revealed that $83 \cdot 8$ per cent of Class A widow pensioners had 'means as assessed' of not more than $52 per year and that only $37 \cdot 5$ per cent owned, partly-owned or had an interest in the home in which they lived.[5]

It seems, then, that those fatherless families receiving the widows' pension (or the age or invalid pension) are likely to be entirely dependent on it. It is therefore very relevant to consider the circumstances of families of varying size that have to live on an income consisting of the pension and child endowment only. Details of the actual and the adjusted incomes of a number of families of different size and age structure are set out in Table 6·1. The adjustment is based on the method detailed in Chapter 2. The June 1966 incomes are those appropriate to the pensions being paid at the time of our survey: these should be compared with the poverty line income of $33. To bring the picture up to date the incomes of the same families are set out as they would be in June 1970, taking account of all the pension and child endowment changes introduced prior to or in the Commonwealth Budget of August 1969. The adjusted incomes here should be related to a poverty line income of about $42.40.[6]

---

[4] *Commonwealth Parliamentary Debates*, House of Representatives, March 19, 1969, p. 640

[5] *Social Services 1968-69*, Twenty-eighth Report of the Director-General of Social Services, Canberra 1969, p. 71

[6] For explanation of the up-dating of the poverty line see Chapter 2.

TABLE 6·1

THE CLASS A WIDOW PENSIONER AND THE POVERTY LINE

Family comprising mother plus	June 1966		June 1970	
	Pension plus child endowment	Adjusted income	Pension plus child endowment	Adjusted income
	$ per week	$ per week	$ per week	$ per week
One child under 6 years	18.00	31.90	24.00	42.53
One child between 6 and 15 years	18.00	29·28	22·00	35.79
Two children under 6 years	20.50	30.22	28.50	42.01
One under 6, one 6 to 15 years	20.50	28.13	28.50	39.10
Two children 6 to 15 years	20.50	26.30	26.50	34.00
Three children 6 to 15 years	23.50	25.41	31.50	34.07
Poverty line income		33.00		42.40

From these calculations it appears that the position of these families has noticeably improved since our survey was carried out in 1966. In all cases their situation has improved in relation to the poverty line. However, it is only in families in which there is a child under six years that their cash social service income puts them above the poverty line. While the 1969 legislation has made a notable contribution to helping these families it does introduce one unfortunate aspect. The mothers' allowance of $6 is paid only when there is a child under six years (or an invalid child requiring full-time care). In all other cases the mothers' allowance is $4. This means that there is a fall in pension entitlement when the youngest child turns six, a time when with the beginning of school life the expenses of the family are likely to rise. It may be that the philosophy behind this is that it is desirable for a mother to work when all her children are at school. Be that as it may, a pension reduction is surely an unfortunate and rather negative way of encouraging such mothers to enter the work force.

Comparison with Intact Families

One way of appreciating the difference that it makes to the quality of a family's life to be without a male parent is to compare the characteristics and experiences of the fatherless families with those of the intact families. By 'intact' in this context we mean families consisting of both

mother and father and their dependent children. Growing up in a family
with both parents is, of course, the common experience of the vast
majority of children. This is not only because two-parent families in the
community outnumber fatherless families (the ratio being about 20 to
1) but also because, as Table 6·2 indicates, the number of dependent
children in the fatherless families is smaller.

TABLE 6·2

PERCENTAGE OF FAMILIES OF VARIOUS SIZES

Size of family	Intact families	Fatherless families
	%	%
One child	30	50
Two children	34	27
Three children	21	22
Four or more children	15	1
	100	100

At any point in time it is fortunately relatively rare for dependent
children in the community to be without a male parent. Nevertheless,
our estimates for Melbourne in 1966 indicated that more than 26,000
children were growing up in fatherless families. This represented about
4 per cent of all dependent children. However, the very fact of growing
up as one of such a small but different minority does itself represent
some handicap quite apart from the more obvious economic and emotional handicaps involved.

Poverty and Family Size

The difference in the incidence of poverty between intact and fatherless
families has already been discussed and need not be laboured. Among
the fatherless families just over 30 per cent of those with known incomes
were estimated to be in poverty. By contrast, only 3·8 per cent of the
intact families had adjusted incomes below the poverty line of $33. A
further 14 per cent of the fatherless families were judged to be marginally poor; of the intact families only 4·3 per cent were in this category.
In both groups the incidence of poverty tended to be higher the larger
the number of dependent children in the family. Table 6·3 illustrates
this and highlights the very high risk of poverty among fatherless families with more than one child.

TABLE 6·3

PERCENTAGE OF FAMILIES OF VARIOUS SIZES IN POVERTY

Size of family	Intact families	Fatherless families
	%	%
One child	0·6	17·6
Two children	3·3	46·2
Three or more children	6·7	46·5
All families	3·8	30·9

Housing

Income differences are reflected in the manner in which families are housed. Among the intact families about 98 per cent are householders —that is, they either own, are buying or are renting their accommodation. For an intact family to live as boarders in the household of another family is rare. But about 18 per cent of fatherless families are living as boarders in the households of others. It is true that in almost all cases they are boarding in the homes of relatives. Nevertheless, whatever compensations this may offer, one element of freedom which is highly prized in our community—the opportunity to live as a family in one's own home—is lost.

The housing situations of intact and fatherless families are different in other respects too. Whereas about 80 per cent of the intact families either own or are buying their homes, among the fatherless families only about 45 per cent of householders do so. Tenancy is far more common among the fatherless families than in any other group in the community and this means that these families who, on the whole, are poorly equipped to deal with economic problems are the ones most affected by the shortage in Melbourne of dwellings available for rent at low cost.

It is encouraging to see the very considerable impact of the Victorian Housing Commission on the welfare of these families. The Commission provides accommodation for a very much larger proportion of fatherless family households than of intact family households. Thus, although the Commission is subject to criticism from many directions and on many counts, it should be given credit for making a very important contribution to the housing of the most needy families in the community.

Nevertheless, some 30 per cent of fatherless family households and 15 per cent of intact family households are living in privately rented accommodation, sometimes substandard, frequently costly, occasionally both.

The survey clearly indicated a need for further expansion of the work of the Housing Commission or some alternative government action to provide suitable low-cost housing for families.

The following examples illustrate the situations that confront families when they have to seek rented accommodation.

A 30-year-old deserted wife with two school-age daughters rented two rooms and shared a bathroom, toilet and laundry with eight people. The furniture and facilities were quite primitive. For this she paid $8 per week out of her total income of $21 per week.

Another deserted wife had been living with her three children in one room, sharing a kitchen and bathroom, and paying $10 per week until she obtained a Housing Commission flat. She then paid rent of $6.30 for a three bedroom self-contained flat.

One would expect from what has been said that the cost of housing would have the effect of increasing the percentage of families in poverty. This is true for the intact families, of whom only $3 \cdot 8$ per cent were in poverty on the basis of adjusted income before payment of housing costs, as against $5 \cdot 7$ per cent in terms of adjusted income after housing costs have been met. However, among the fatherless families the position was reversed. Earlier we saw that 30 per cent were in poverty on the basis of adjusted income only. This percentage falls to $22 \cdot 6$ when we take account of their housing costs. This is a somewhat surprising result. However, it gives no cause for complacency and it should be remembered that although fewer appear to be in poverty according to this measure, among those who are in poverty are many who are in extreme difficulty. The fall in the percentage is due almost entirely to the help given by the Housing Commission in providing low-cost housing, particularly to families with three or more children. Other factors helping some of these families to rise above the poverty line are that some are able to find cheap accommodation by living with relatives and others are able to reduce their housing costs by taking in boarders.

Health Insurance

As was mentioned earlier in the chapter, ill-health and the worries it brings loom large in the lives of the fatherless families. It is therefore interesting to see the extent to which they are covered by some type of insurance to help them meet their hospital and medical expenses. Because of the relatively large number of pensioners in this group about

30 per cent of the fatherless families are covered by the pensioner medical scheme or by the Repatriation Department and are thus fully covered for most expenses connected with illness. A further 45 per cent have some private insurance cover, but in many cases the cover is minimal and the payment of premiums presents a constant problem. In some cases families have been unable to keep up their contributions and their health insurance fund membership has lapsed. As a consequence, at least 25 per cent of all the fatherless families in our Stage I interviews had no health insurance cover at all, as against about 17 per cent without cover among intact families. In this latter group, however, the motivation to insure was greater (82 per cent belonged to some fund) as very few of these families were eligible for benefits under pensioner or repatriation schemes.

These figures are for the groups as a whole. It is true that some of the families who have no insurance cover may be rich and/or healthy and their lack of insurance may cause them no distress. However there was evidence in the survey that many of those in the greatest need were uninsured. For example, among twenty-four large intact families interviewed at Stage I and found to be in poverty, nine had no cover at all; of thirty-eight poverty-stricken families headed by females, thirteen were without cover. One wonders what happens to the sick members of these families. Do they receive adequate medical care? Or do they go without because of the burden of cost involved in treatment?

Interviews revealed cases of families who were struggling to pay medical and hospital expenses of hundreds of dollars out of pitiably low incomes. Just one of these will suffice by way of illustration.

A deserted wife with two young children, one of whom was severely asthmatic, stated that she 'could not afford the contribution for health insurance.' She had unpaid hospital and specialist accounts of over $200. Her annual income, including child endowment, was $862.

The Commonwealth Government's Subsidised Medical Service introduced in 1970 to provide free health insurance for low-income families (see Chapter 10) should help to reduce the costs of illness. Because the income limit for eligibility does not vary with the size of the family and because it has been set so low (the limit for free insurance being only 20 cents above the minimum adult male weekly wage rate in Victoria) very few intact families will be eligible for this assistance. It is, however, likely to be helpful to some of the fatherless families although, even for them, it should be remembered that it will reduce but not eliminate the costs of medical and hospital care.

Employment of Mothers

One final point of comparison between intact and fatherless families can be made by studying the proportion of working mothers in each group. The proportion of female heads of families who work is not substantially greater than the proportion of working wives with dependent children—37·8 per cent, as against 30·9 per cent (see Table 6·4).

There is, however, a considerable difference in the breakdown between part-time and full-time work. Of the wives who worked, almost half worked only part-time, whereas of the female heads of families who worked only about one in twenty worked less than a thirty-five-hour week.

TABLE 6·4

WORK STATUS OF MOTHERS WITH DEPENDENT CHILDREN

Percentages

	Work full-time	Work part-time	At home	Total
Wives	16·6	14·3	69·1	100·0
Female heads	35·8	2·0	62·2	100·0
All mothers	17·5	13·7	68·8	100·0

It seems, then, that the mother who is a family head is not much more likely to go out to work than other mothers, but if she does so she is almost certain to work full-time. Obviously, if she has the need and opportunity to work at all there are reasons why she decides in favour of full-time work. The working wife, not being the mainstay of the family finances, is in a better position to balance the financial benefits from work against the convenience of extra time in the home and may choose to work the hours she finds most suitable. By contrast, if the woman who is head of a family decides to support her family by her own earnings, her financial needs are likely to be far greater and full-time work becomes almost a necessity.

It was fairly apparent in the interviews with many non-working mothers who were widow pensioners that the operation of the means test had a considerable influence on their decision not to work. At the time of the survey the maximum rate of a widows' pension was reduced by the amount by which her 'means as assessed' exceeded $520 (per annum). If a pensioner worked part-time and earned less than $10 per week (assuming she had no assessable property) her pension was left intact but her absolute net gain for having given up part of her leisure was likely to be small. Her gross earnings would not provide an accurate indication of her gains from working as she would have to meet many additional expenses associated with going to work. If she worked longer hours and earned more than $10 per week she was faced with the loss of her pension at the rate of one dollar for every additional dollar of income. That is to say she suffered what amounted to a tax of 100 per cent on this part of her income.

Admittedly when there are dependent children a higher earnings income is allowed before pension loss takes place[7], but in these circumstances the existence of the children often introduces additional costs into working. In particular the costs of minding and caring for pre-school children or for looking after children after school are often prohibitively high for the average worker. If a Class A widow pensioner decided to work full-time to be completely independent she was likely to find herself very little better off financially, although she would have had to make considerable physical and mental efforts to cope with a job and care for her family. The additional expenses of taxation, health insurance, travel to work, child minding, more expensive clothing, meals away from home etc. would reduce her net income from work very considerably. As well as this she would lose the security of the pension and its associate fringe benefits, such as concessional fares, rent rebates from the Housing Commission and, most particularly, the pensioner health scheme which is so important in protecting the family from financial strain in time of sickness or accident to herself or children. The risks and effort involved in becoming independent seem to be a sufficient deterrent to work unless the earning capacity of the widow is very high.

It is difficult to say whether women who are the sole support of their children are sufficiently well-informed and rational to make the appropriate decision about whether or not they would improve their circumstances by working. Certainly many of them made it clear during their survey interviews that they felt that the operation of the means test did

---

[7] At the time of the survey, for example, a Class A widow pensioner with no assessable property above $4,500 in value and no other income, could earn $10 a week plus up to an additional $1 a week in respect of each child without her pension being affected. This additional $1 was raised to $3 in September 1966 and to $4 in September 1969.

deter them from working. Comments like the following were indicative of this feeling.

I resigned my full-time job to get the security and benefits of the widows' pension.

It is a farce: if you earn something on top of the pension you lose as much or more.

I'm not interested in part-time work—that would only knock down the pension.

I could only return to work by giving up the pension. Then if I am sick I have to stop work and I have nothing.

Some of these comments reflect a lack of knowledge about the exact operation of the means test and how pensions are assessed and such erroneous views could perhaps be overcome by better publicity of the facts. Nevertheless these attitudes were the prevailing ones at the time of the survey and no doubt still prevailed in September 1968 when the Commonwealth Department of Social Services launched its training scheme for widow pensioners in an attempt to encourage widows to re-enter the work force.

The penal tax of 100 per cent no longer applies. As a result of the introduction of the tapered means test in 1969, only 50 cents are deducted from the pension for every dollar in excess of the allowed income. This is a considerable move forward and will mean a substantial increase in income for those pensioners who are already working and should have the effect of inducing more to enter the work force. There are, however, one or two additional ways in which these mothers could be assisted to undertake paid employment.

A number of specific expenses should be allowed as deductions from income in determining the 'means as assessed' of the widow pensioner. Costs of travel to work, child-minding expenses and income tax paid on earnings could well be regarded as unavoidable expenses associated with working and deducted from gross earnings.

Eligibility for the pensioner medical service should be retained without means test to cover all families in which there are dependent children in the care of a working widow, deserted wife or unmarried mother. This would cost the government little, and would remove the enormous financial burdens that confront the few whose families are hit by serious illness, but whose earned income has put them outside the present scope of the pensioner medical scheme.

Recommended Pension Increases

It is apparent that a substantial proportion of mothers of fatherless families will choose to, or, for a variety of reasons, will be forced to stay at home rather than go out to work. We believe that the widows' pension should provide them with an alternative income that is sufficient for them to keep their families above the poverty line.

Consequently we recommend that the Class A widows' pension should be raised to $17·00 per week. We also recommend that the mothers' allowance be $6·00 in all cases. A mothers' allowance of $6·00 is at present paid only to pensioners with a child under six years (or to those with a handicapped child), in all other cases the allowance is $4.00. As the costs of supporting a child tend to rise as the child grows, especially at the beginning of school life, we find this differentiation difficult to justify.

We have not argued for increased allowances for children because of the substantial increases in child endowment that we are recommending ($1.00 for the first child, $1.50 for the second, $3.50 for the third and $4.50 for the fourth and subsequent children). Should our proposals on child endowment be unsuccessful, however, some further increases in the children's allowances would have to be made.

These additional payments, coupled with a rise in Supplementary Assistance from $2 to $4, are, we feel, the minimum that are required to ensure that the families of widow pensioners do not grow up in poverty.

7　Large Families*

Large families—those with four or more dependent children—are quite likely to be poor. When we compared the adjusted incomes of large families with those of families with only three dependent children we found 7 per cent of the large families in the range just below the poverty line ($27-$33), as compared with 3 per cent of the families with three children (see Table 7·1). There was also a substantial group of large families only just above the poverty line.

TABLE 7·1

LARGE FAMILIES: INCOME OF HEAD AND POVERTY

Adult Income Units

Income	Actual income of head		Adjusted income of income unit	
	Man, wife and three children	Man, wife and four or more children	Man, wife and three children	Man, wife and four or more children
$	%	%	%	%
0 to 27	2·0	1·4	2·4	1·4
27 to 33	2·8	3·5	3·1	7·0
33 to 39	2·9	1·0	3·4	13·9
39 to 49	17·5	18·8	16·3	15·4
49 and over	74·8	75·2	74·8	62·3
Total*	100·0	100·0	100·0	100·0
Total number of income units	61,258	44,669	61,258	44,669

* Any inconsistency between figures and totals is due to rounding.

The heads of large families earned just as much as those with smaller ones; the families were in or near poverty because their needs were greater. Of eleven large families interviewed in Stage II in which the head was earning less than $49 a week, ten were in poverty.

A typical family with four children just above the poverty line might have father's income $45, child endowment $4.50, total $49.50. Suppose they spent $4 a head on food (a total of $24) and $10 on rent; this only leaves $11 for all other expenditure, or $1.83 per person per week.

One actual survey case was a family of man, wife and four children. He earned $43.70, so that with child endowment his total income was $48.20. They were tenants of the Housing Commission and paid only

* This chapter was written by Ronald F. Henderson.

$8.80 rent. Our food diaries suggested that families of this size spent on average $25.56 a week on food, or $4.26 per head. If they spent that amount they would have $13.84 for everything else—$2.31 per head.

Another case is that of a family with four children who, although they owned their house outright, were still poor. (Their adjusted income was $27.40.) The father earned $35.30 per week, so that with child endowment their actual income was $39.80. They spent $3.65 per head each week on food, leaving $17.90 (just under $3 a head) for all other expenditure including rates (which amounted to $1.30 a week) and house maintenance.

We compared large families with other householders who had no disabilities (Table 7·2). The proportion of large families with low money incomes was rather smaller. But because these incomes had to support a greater number of children, more of these large families were poor—8·7 per cent below the poverty line as compared with 2·3 per cent of the others. Again, more large families were just above the poverty line. Fourteen per cent were in the adjusted income range of $33 to $39, as compared with 1·3 per cent of the others. It seems that nine out of ten of the large families with a money income of less than $59 were below or just above the poverty line.

TABLE 7·2

POVERTY AMONG LARGE FAMILIES AND INCOME UNITS WITH NO DISABILITY

Householders Only

Adjusted income	Large families	No disability
$	%	%
0 to 27	1·5	1·6
27 to 33	7·2	0·7
33 to 39	14·0	1·3
39 and over	77·3	96·4
Total	100·0	100·0
Total number of income units	43,046	405,426

Some light can be thrown on the nature of the cases in the poor and marginal groups by illustrations from second questionnaires and food diaries.

One marginally poor large family consisted of a man and wife and four children at home ranging in age from eleven to four years. Another baby was expected very soon so the wife was unable to earn. Their eldest daughter, aged thirteen, was away in a convent at the time of the interview but would soon return to help when the baby was born. Their income including child endowment was $56.80. They had left a Housing Commission house after becoming in arrears with the rent, and were renting from a private landlord. They paid $15 a week for poor, cramped accommodation. Expenditure on food was $21.69 per week—$3.62 per head—just over half their income after payment of rent. When they had paid for a week's food and rent the family had $3.35 per head available for all other expenditure. They were not insured for hospital or medical benefits because, they said, it was 'too expensive—about a dollar a week. We have to be pretty ill before we can afford a doctor. We won't be able to pay for this baby and they tell us the hospital sues people now!'

Another large family was well below the poverty line because the husband, a shopkeeper, was trying to run his own business with his wife's part-time unpaid help. Their income was only $39.70 (adjusted income $24.70), and they had five children ranging from three to thirteen years old. They had been able to afford a large deposit for purchase of their house eleven years before, so had only $6 a week to pay towards buying it. Food expenditure was $19.01 a week ($2.72 per head), and so absorbed nearly half their total income. Disposable income after payment for food and housing was only $2.10 per head. They were receiving some gifts from friends and relatives.

Another family with five children ranging from nine years to seven months old was paying a high rent of $14.00 out of an income of $62.40. Their adjusted income was $43.00, but their adjusted income after payment of rent was $32.20, bringing them into the category of 'marginally poor'. In this case the husband did not want his wife to go out to work until the children were older. Their expenditure on food was $23.76 per week, half their income after rent, and only $3.39 per person. So they had a similar amount available for all other expenditure.

Thus it is clear that the current rates of child endowment are insufficient to provide an adequate income for the family of four or more dependent children, when added to a single low wage of $45 to $50.

Housing Costs for Large Families

The examples above also reveal the importance of housing costs to large families. A market rent of $14 or $15 a week takes a big slice out of any income of less than $50. But because large families need more space and may not be attractive tenants, such rents have to be paid, as Elaine

Martin has already pointed out in her study *High Rents and Low Incomes*.[1] The accommodation obtained in some cases is badly sub-standard. For instance, the family mentioned above with a daughter temporarily away, four children at home and another baby expected, were paying $15 rent, for a house described by the interviewer thus:

The front door opens directly on to the street. The total width of the house is approximately ten feet. Entering the front door you are in the children's bedroom, which has to be negotiated to go to any part of the house. This bedroom is not divided by a passageway. It contains a double and single bed where normally five children sleep. A passageway then continues to the living room past bedroom number two, where the parents sleep. The living room is about ten feet by eight feet and contains a wood-burning cooking stove. This stove provides the only means of keeping warm in the house. Part of the living room is taken up by the stairs which lead to the landlord's flat.

TABLE 7·3

LARGE FAMILIES:
POVERTY AS MEASURED BY ADJUSTED INCOME AND BY ADJUSTED INCOME AFTER
HOUSING COSTS
Householders Only

Measured by:	Below poverty line		Marginally above poverty line	
	Number	%	Number	%
Adjusted income	3,743	8·7	6,023	14·0
Adjusted income after housing costs	4,523	10·5	7,056	16·4

If poverty is measured on the basis of adjusted income after payment of cost of housing, slightly more large families were below the poverty line, or only just above it, than when judged by adjusted income only (Table 7·3). This confirms the importance of housing costs for large families. They need either more cheap housing or more child endowment.

The Victorian Housing Commission has made an important contribution to the welfare of many large families by the provision of houses for purchase on moderate terms. Families with three or four children comprise a much larger proportion of purchasers from and tenants of the Housing Commission than of the population as a whole.

[1] Elaine M. Martin, *High Rents and Low Incomes*, a research project of The Brotherhood of St Laurence, Melbourne, 1964

The stage at which a large family is most likely to be poor is, of course, while the children are all young and before any of them is old enough to go to work and earn an income. Of such families with incomes between $39 and $40, nearly three-quarters of those paying rent or instalments (i.e. excluding outright owners and rent-free tenants) were paying between $6 and $9 a week. Some, but not all, of these were buying through or renting from the Housing Commission. It is satisfactory that so many were able to find such cheap housing, but it should be added that many of these would have contracts for rental or house purchase entered into some years previously when housing was cheaper. Other evidence suggests that those with four children who have to find accommodation now, such as recent migrants, are unlikely to obtain it as cheaply as this. Of large families throughout the complete range of incomes studied only 16 per cent of those paying for their housing were paying as little as $6 to $9, and of those with an income of $49 to $59 a week rather less than a quarter were paying this amount. When we measure poverty by adjusted income after payment for housing we find that 8 per cent of large families were below the poverty line on the basis, and were paying between $9 and $21 a week for their housing. This is perhaps the clearest indication of the significance of high housing costs as a cause of poverty among large families.

At the next stage in the family life cycle, when there is at least one independent child earning, large families are often still poor; of the forty-one actual (unweighted) cases, eight were below the poverty line measured by adjusted income after payment for housing, and nine when measured by adjusted income only.

Short-Term Poverty Among Large Families

Since in Stage I we were measuring income of the previous week, we wondered whether a significant proportion of the large families below the poverty line were so recorded because for one reason or another they had reduced earnings in that particular week. A question on reduced earnings was included, and from this we learned that a quarter of the poor large families did have reduced earnings in that week. The numbers are not large enough for further statistical analysis of the causes of reduced earnings to be worthwhile for this particular group. Inspection of a number of these individual cases shows that they included several suffering from accidents and receiving workers' compensation, a labourer out of a job, a meat packer out of work because of an industrial dispute and a self-employed metal polisher with low earnings because of lack of work that week.

An analysis of causes of reduced earnings for the whole population is given in Chapter 4 above. Measures to maintain the income of those out of work because of sickness, accident or unemployment will, of course, help large families as well as others. But the three-quarters of the poor large families who were below the poverty line when receiving their normal weekly income need help in other ways.

Measures for Relief of Poverty in Large Families

The obvious remedy for poverty among large families is an increase in rates of child endowment. Moreover it is payments for the third and subsequent children that need to be raised. Child endowment payments have not been increased as fast as incomes have risen in Australia in recent years. In 1950-51 they constituted $1 \cdot 28$ per cent of gross national expenditure; by 1968-69 they were $0 \cdot 7$ per cent of gross national expenditure.

It is suggested that child endowment should be increased to $3.50 per week for the third child and to $4.50 a week for the fourth and each subsequent child.[2]

This would bring the income of a family with four children and earnings of $45 up to $52.52 net of tax.[3] This is 30 cents above the income that such a family would have needed to be out of poverty at June 1969. Without such an increase in child endowment they would need a further $4.45 to bring them out of poverty; so the effect of this proposal would be to fill the poverty gap for such families.

The poverty gap for a six-child family with earnings of $45 a week was $7.46 in June 1969. This would be filled by the increases proposed, and the family brought $2.04 above the poverty line. The cost of such an increase in child endowment would have been about $108 million in 1968-69.

One way of financing such expenditure would be to substitute higher child endowment payments for the concessional deductions for children now allowed before assessing taxable income.

[2] In order to calculate the exact amount of the increases in child endowment required it is necessary to calculate the actual (unadjusted) incomes for various sizes of families which, when adjusted, will be equal to the poverty line.

[3] Detailed calculations of the effects of proposed increases of child endowment on income net of tax for families with four and six children are shown in Appendix D.

Because rich people pay high marginal rates of income tax, these concessional deductions are much more valuable to them than to the poor. Thus this change would benefit the poor large families at the expense of the rich.

In order to give some compensation to families with one or two children, child endowment for each of the first two children might also be increased by 50 cents each per week at a cost of $71 million.

This would produce a scale of child endowment as shown in Table 7·4.

TABLE 7·4

EXISTING AND RECOMMENDED RATES OF CHILD ENDOWMENT

	Existing	Proposed	Increase
	$	$	$
Child 1	0.50	1.00	0.50
Child 2	1.00	1.50	0.50
Child 3	1.50	3.50	2·00
Child 4 and subsequent	1.75*	4.50	2.75*

*This increases by 25 cents a week for each subsequent child at present, so the flat rate of $4.50 for the fourth and each subsequent child which we propose represents a smaller increase for the subsequent children.

Small increases are proposed for the first and second children to make up for the withdrawal of the concessional deductions. Large increases are proposed for third and subsequent children to lift large families out of poverty.

Under this scheme some extra burden of taxation would fall on the low income earner. But the net income after tax of the man with four children earning $45 a week would still be raised from $47.77 to $51.19. The poverty gap for this family would be reduced from $4.45 to $1.03.

In June 1969 a family of man, wife and six dependent children (four under six years old) would have been in poverty if their income had been less than $60.31 including child endowment. The 1969 position if earnings are $45 is that net income after tax including child endowment is $52.85—$7.46 below the poverty line. The proposed increase in child endowment as a substitute for concessional deductions would be a great help to these families. For their income would be raised to $60.19— only 12 cents less than is required to lift them out of poverty.

Increases of 50 cents each for the first and second children would cost $71 million. Thus the cost of all the proposed increases in child endowment for children up to sixteen years of age would be about $179 million a year. It is estimated that the savings to the Treasury from the abolition of tax deductions for children would have been $160 million in 1968-69. So the cost of these combined proposals would have been $19 million in that year.[4]

These proposals make no provision for an increased child endowment for student children aged 16 to 21. The evidence of the survey is not sufficient for discussion of the position of tertiary students; but it suggests that $5 \cdot 8$ per cent of secondary students over fifteen were in income units below the poverty line. So for relief of poverty there would be a gain in raising the child endowment payments for each secondary school child over sixteen years of age from $1.50 to, say, $3.50. In general, any measure which makes it easier for children of poor families to receive further education is a valuable investment in human capital for the community. On these grounds, as well as other evidence of poverty among tertiary students, it would be desirable to extend the increase in child endowment to them also at a combined cost of some $21 million.

Another method of directing assistance to poor large families but not to rich ones would be to treat child endowment payments as an addition to the taxable income of the father. If this were done with the above schedule of rates of child endowment, families with four children whose head was earning $45 a week would be brought up almost to the poverty line, and those with six children just above it. But the amount of additional taxation received by the Treasury from this would be only about $50 million. So the net cost to the community would be greater—$129 million ($179 million less $50 million). Furthermore it seems preferable to continue paying child endowment to mothers, to encourage them to spend it on the children.

In 1970 wages and prices will be somewhat higher than in 1969. It is probable, however, that the increases in child endowment proposed above, if implemented in the 1970 budget, would prove to be of the right order of magnitude to alleviate the worst of the poverty among large families.

---

[4] Because money incomes rise each year and people pay higher rates of tax, the cost to the Treasury of the tax concessions for dependent children becomes greater. It will soon exceed the $179 million cost of additional child endowment.

Children in Poverty

In certain respects the housing situation of all intact families is good. Only 2·2 per cent of intact families were 'doubled up', that is living with parents or other relatives or as professional boarders. Over 90 per cent of the intact families with three or more dependent children were living in detached houses. Fortunately, few children were being brought up in 'rooms': 3·5 per cent of families with one child and 1·2 per cent of families with two or three children.

In this book we have chosen the income unit as the basis of our discussion because it is to the income unit that additional income must be given to relieve poverty. However, in order to realise the human and social consequences of poverty and the urgency of its relief, we should also consider the numbers of persons involved. The estimated numbers of children in poverty and only marginally above the poverty line are set out in Tables 7·5 and 7·6. More than 42,000 children were poor and another 47,000 were only marginally above the poverty line.

TABLE 7·5

ESTIMATED NUMBERS OF CHILDREN AND PERCENTAGE OF CHILDREN IN POVERTY *
FOR EACH FAMILY SIZE AND COMPOSITION

Family size and composition	Total number of children	Percentages of children of each family size	
		In poverty	Marginally above poverty line
Intact families			
1 child	86,360	0·6	1·1
2 children	197,822	3·3	3·1
3 children	183,831	5·4	3·4
4 children	136,496	7·7	11·5
5 or more children	58,280	10·4	23·2
Fatherless families			
1 child	7,167	17·6	6·5
2 children	5,282	46·2	21·5
3 or more children	10,998	46·8	24·6
Total, all children	686,236	6·2	6·9

*Adjusted income. Children whose parents' income was unknown have been omitted.

In the intact families the percentage of children in poverty is low until we reach families with four children. Of such families about one-fifth are poor or marginally poor. But the proportion of children of fatherless families in poverty is much higher—47 per cent of the families with three or more children are below the poverty line and a further 25 per cent only marginally above it. This underlines the urgency of measures to increase pensions and allowances for civilian widows and deserted wives who have several dependent children. At the same time it demonstrates that the cost of such measures would be small because the absolute numbers of children in such one-parent families are not large. Most of the children in and near poverty as shown in Table 7·6 were in intact families. Although there were a considerable number of families with two or three children, the largest single group were those in families with four dependent children.

TABLE 7·6

PERCENTAGES OF CHILDREN OF EACH FAMILY SIZE AND COMPOSITION

Family size and composition	Percentages of children of each family size		
	Total	In poverty*	Marginally above poverty line
Intact families			
1 child	12·6	1·3	2·1
2 children	28·8	15·6	13·2
3 children	26·8	23·4	13·5
4 children	19·9	24·8	33·4
5 or more children	8·5	14·2	28·7
Fatherless families			
1 child	1·0	3·0	1·0
2 children	0·8	5·7	2·4
3 or more children	1·6	12·1	5·7
Total, all children**	100·0	100·0	100·0

*Adjusted income. Children whose parents' income was unknown have been omitted.
**Any inconsistency between figures and totals is due to rounding.

8   Migrants*

The term 'migrant' covers a wide spectrum of people, if, as in this chapter, it is used to describe all settlers born outside Australia and New Zealand.[1] It includes all sorts of people from the top executive or the highly skilled worker to the unskilled peasant, barely literate in his own language and with no experience of an industrialised society. General statements about migrant conditions are therefore not of much value. We must look at different ethnic groups and the length of their residence in Australia if we are to understand what is happening to migrants in our society.

It is not surprising, therefore, that the preliminary analysis of Stage I showed that for all recent migrants the incidence of poverty was not significantly higher than for the population as a whole. It is only when the analysis is carried further, separating out different nationalities and periods of residence, that it is possible to identify the poor. It becomes clear that although many migrants have prospered in Australia, some groups have a high percentage in poverty.

The survey was made at a good time to provide this kind of information. The twenty years preceding it had been the greatest period of sustained migration in the history of Australia. From mid-1947 until mid-1966 over two million migrants arrived in Australia, and to them were born 600,000 children. So that by mid-1966 one in five of the population was a post-war migrant or the child of one.

Melbourne received a good share of this influx and this was reflected by the numbers recorded in the survey. Of the 5,842 income units interviewed in Stage I, 2,086 were migrants. Of these 528 were British, 366 were Italian and 455 Greek. Most other European nationalities were found in the survey, but these are the only groups large enough to subdivide further by period of residence, and so make it possible to observe the changes which take place as migrants settle into their new life. In this chapter we shall therefore concentrate on British, Italian and Greek migrants and make some reference to Dutch and Germans by way of comparison. We shall look briefly at the general social background and in more detail at incomes, housing, health and social services.

* The analysis of this group and writing of the chapter are the work of Jean McCaughey. We are grateful for the financial support from the Social Science Research Council which helped make possible the detailed study of migrants contained in this chapter.

[1] Elsewhere in this book 'recent migrants' means non-British settlers who arrived in Australia between 1960 and 1966. British settlers and the non-British who arrived before 1960 are treated as part of the Australian population.

General Social Background

Predictably, the survey showed that many migrants live in the city and inner suburbs; for example, in Fitzroy and Collingwood they comprise more than half the total population. These are mostly Southern Europeans, especially Italians and Greeks. But although there is considerable overlapping of these ethnic communities, the spread is somewhat different. Both have big concentrations in the central area, but the Italians move out to the suburbs to the north and west such as Preston, Brunswick, Sunshine and Footscray, whereas the Greeks move to the east and south, to Richmond, Prahran, Port Melbourne, South Melbourne.

There is some evidence that one group may displace another. For example, in Richmond and Prahran there is a clear contrast between those who arrived before and after 1955. Of the pre-1955 arrivals there are twice as many Italians as Greeks, but since 1955 the Greeks have moved in, in a big way, and the Italians have gone elsewhere. In fact, almost one-quarter of all the Greeks who have arrived since 1955 live in Richmond and Prahran, and only 2 per cent of the Italians of the same period. This movement is borne out by the most recent arrivals. We estimate that over 1,000 Greek income units who have arrived since 1964 are living in these areas, compared with a negligible number of Italians.

The pattern of settlement of British migrants is quite different. Very few live in the inner suburbs, except in St Kilda, where almost 13 per cent of those who arrived between 1960 and 1966 are living, probably because of the high proportion of flats. Nor are they heavily concentrated in certain areas. They are spread fairly evenly through the comfortably-off suburbs, mainly to the south and east. There are also considerable numbers in new housing estates on the outskirts of the city and in areas such as Dandenong, where industry is expanding rapidly.

There are also very few Dutch or Germans in the inner suburbs. Both are spread widely, but many Germans live in St Kilda (19·3 per cent of the total German population and 39 per cent of those who have come since 1960), whereas the Dutch are more concentrated in the semi-rural areas on the eastern side of the city (28 per cent of all the Dutch live there).

Another way of looking at the distribution of the migrant population is to compare the percentages in certain areas with the percentage in the whole population. Such a comparison shows that whereas the Italians are about 4 per cent of the total population, they constitute about 12 per cent in Carlton, Fitzroy and Collingwood and 10 per cent in the northern suburbs. The Greeks are about 3 per cent of the whole population, about 20 per cent in Richmond and Prahran and 14 per cent in Port Melbourne and South Melbourne.

A breakdown into periods of residence confirms the view that one ethnic group may displace another. For example, in Richmond the Greeks who arrived before 1955 are less than 1 per cent of the population, whereas those who arrived between 1960 and 1966 constitute over 15 per cent. In the same two periods the number of Italians living in Prahran diminished markedly, although the total numbers of Greeks and Italians arriving in Melbourne in this period were much the same.

Turning from where migrants live to how they live we find similar contrasts between different ethnic groups and between recent and established migrants of the same nationality. Those who have recently arrived, especially the Italians and Greeks, tend to live with relatives. In fact about half the Italian and a quarter of the Greek income units who arrived in Melbourne after 1959 live with relatives, and this does not include independent children living with their parents. This pattern is partly explained by the fact that many of these migrants have been sponsored by relatives who have undertaken to provide accommodation for them. British and Northern European migrants provide a contrast. We found no Dutch income units living with relatives, and a relatively small number of British and Germans, though somewhat more than is the case with Australians.

In all groups this tendency to share accommodation changed dramatically with length of residence, and among those who had been in Australia for five to ten years the number living with relatives had dropped to negligible proportions.

There were surprisingly few boarders who were not relatives, even among recent migrants. (It must be remembered that registered lodging houses were excluded from the survey.) The Greeks had most—12·6 per cent of all 1965-66 arrivals were boarders not related to the householder or his wife. But even when the period of residence is extended to 1960-66, there were negligible numbers of Italian, German and Dutch income units in this category.

Almost all the Greeks were recorded as paying no board. They were probably newly-arrived migrants who were known to the householder, staying with him until they found employment and somewhere to live. This is supported by the fact that the percentage of such boarders falls from 12·6 per cent to less than 1 per cent for longer established migrants who had arrived between 1960 and 1964.

The Greeks move around more than the Italians. Almost half the Greeks who had arrived in the preceding year had already moved once and a further 10 per cent had moved twice. The British are also very mobile—over 10 per cent had moved once and a further 28 per cent twice in their first year.

Many single independent children live with their parents, though of course, many of the recent migrants do not have independent children. The amount of board paid varies widely. Of those who had arrived since 1954, more than 40 per cent British and more than 50 per cent Italian and Greek independent children under twenty-one were paying more than $10 per week board. This practice contrasts with that of the Dutch, who have the highest percentage of independent children living at home. Almost 90 per cent of them pay less than $5 per week. Only 7·3 per cent of Australian children pay more than $10 per week.

A further element in the pattern is supplied by the sort of accommodation in which migrants live. All recent arrivals except the Dutch had a high proportion living in rooms and sharing domestic facilities—high, that is, when compared with the rest of the population. This was especially true of the Southern Europeans. Almost half of the Greek arrivals since 1964 were in rooms and even the British of the same period had almost 10 per cent in rooms, compared with 3·9 per cent of the whole population. Again this changes with length of residence. In five to ten years most migrants have moved into flats or houses. For example, the percentage of Greeks in rooms falls from 48·2 per cent to 6 per cent over ten years. It is interesting to note that none of the Dutch income units interviewed in the survey were living in rooms or shared domestic facilities.

We found very few Southern Europeans in flats, but a relatively high proportion of British, German and Dutch. This probably accounts for the concentrations of British and German migrants in St Kilda. At the time of the survey more blocks of flats had been built there than in any other suburb.

All this evidence taken from the survey builds up a picture of some of the migrant groups in Melbourne. Greeks and Italians and other Southern Europeans create their own communities in the inner suburbs and move out into more or less clearly defined areas where their compatriots have settled. They buy big old houses, bring out their relatives and provide them with accommodation when they first arrive. The Italians are more likely to provide only for their own families, the Greeks for friends and neighbours as well. In the early years they tend to live in large composite households, frequently taking over part of a house, sharing kitchens and bathrooms with other families. The British and Northern Europeans, on the other hand, do not form communities. They usually rent a house or flat and are widely distributed through the more affluent suburbs.

The contrast between newly arrived migrants and those who have been here for five to ten years suggests that most do succeed in establishing themselves in their new country. Some evidence of this has already been given, more will be presented in the more detailed study of the economic conditions of migrants in the community.

Occupations and Earnings

The need to enlarge the work force has been one of the problems confronting Australia in the post-war period and this need has been met mainly by large-scale immigration. Between the census years 1947 and 1966 the work force increased by $1 \cdot 7$ million, of whom over one million were post-1947 migrants.

The policy of successive Australian Governments has been to encourage migration of workers, especially the skilled workers from Britain and Northern Europe, by offering assisted passages to migrants and their families. At the same time, they have permitted large numbers of predominantly unskilled workers to migrate from Southern Europe, mostly unassisted. Between 1947 and 1968, 84 per cent of the British, $67 \cdot 5$ per cent of the Northern Europeans, but only $24 \cdot 5$ per cent of the Southern Europeans were provided with Government-assisted passages. Those who were not Government-assisted were sponsored by relatives, business firms or voluntary agencies, who undertook to find accommodation and employment for the prospective settlers, and often provided or lent the passage money.

This contrast between predominantly skilled workers from Northern Europe and predominantly unskilled labourers from Southern Europe is reflected in the findings of the survey. As shown in Table $8 \cdot 1$, about one-third of the British and Northern Europeans are unskilled, compared with more than two-thirds of the Italians and Greeks.

It is worth noting that the length of residence does not make much difference to the less skilled workers. Those who begin in unskilled jobs tend to remain in them. Even if we go back further to settlers who arrived between 1949 and 1954, over 80 per cent of the Italians and over 70 per cent of the Greeks are still in the lower skilled occupations.

TABLE 8·1

OCCUPATIONAL SKILLS OF VARIOUS MIGRANT GROUPS

All Working Income Units

Country of origin and period of arrival	Estimated total number of working income units	Professional and administrative	Clerical, sales, craftsmen, farmers	Operative, service, labourers
		%	%	%
Australia	541,980	23·7	47·7	28·7
United Kingdom				
1955–59	10,997	21·9	45·8	32·2
1960–66	19,760	13·8	52·8	33·4
Italy				
1955–59	9,679	0·2	33·6	66·7
1960–66	7,674	2·5	29·0	68·5
Greece				
1955–59	8,031	1·2	28·0	70·8
1960–66	13,998	0·1	27·8	72·0
Netherlands all	12,200	6·8	65·7	27·5
Germany all	12,527	26·0	57·2	16·8
Other countries	135,827	22·6	46·6	30·7
Total population	772,673	21·2	45·7	33·1

There are likely to be some skilled tradesmen included in the semi- and unskilled class because their qualifications are not accepted in Australia. We had cases of Italians who had migrated with the impression that they would be able to work as skilled tradesmen here, only to find that their skills were not recognised. The Commonwealth Government's decision to set up a committee to inquire into recognition of equivalent overseas professional, technical and trade qualifications is to be welcomed.

Whatever their level of skill, almost all these settlers have been absorbed into the work force, and there has been very little unemployment among migrants.

There is also a contrast in the earning capacities of Northern and Southern Europeans. At one extreme are the Germans—all those interviewed were earning more than $39 per week—and the Dutch, with only 4·5 per cent earning less than $39 per week. At the other extreme are the Greeks, of whom over 50 per cent were in the low earning category. Table 8·2 shows the percentage of low wage-earners among adult male workers. At the time the survey was done the basic wage was $30.70 per week, so a range of $27 to $39 per week seems a reasonable definition of low wages for males.

TABLE 8·2

ADULT MALE WORKERS EARNING $27 TO $39 PER WEEK

Country of origin and period of arrival	Estimated total numbers	%
Australia	374,452	6·9
United Kingdom		
1955–59	9,730	12·4
1960–66	16,080	9·8
Italy		
1955–59	8,657	40·1
1960–66	5,723	24·8
Greece		
1955–59	7,594	29·0
1960–66	9,737	50·4
Netherlands		
1955–66	3,250	4·5
Germany		
1955–66	3,876	0
Other countries	125,416	10·6
Total population	564,515	9·9

The Italians and Greeks in the low earning category are not necessarily poor. These are unadjusted figures, and if the low wage-earner is single, or has few dependants, or if his wife goes out to work the family may be well above the poverty line. However such low earning migrant groups are vulnerable. They cannot afford high housing costs and misfortune such as sickness or unemployment can be disastrous.

The survey shows that most of the women wage-earners are wives and not heads of income units. We estimate that there are almost a quarter of a million working wives in Melbourne, more than a third of whom are the wives of migrants. Those most likely to be working are the British, followed by Australians, Dutch, Germans and Greeks. The Italians have the smallest proportion of working wives, especially the more recent arrivals. There is often a conflict between the need to augment the family income in order to save the deposit on a house, and the desirability of the mother being at home to care for the children. There were several cases of migrant families, especially Italian ones, in which the needs of the children came first. Sometimes the presence of the grandmother resolved the conflict satisfactorily.

The amounts earned by wives also varied considerably. Many of the British and Northern Europeans, like the Australians, belonged to families in which the combined earnings of husband and wife were more than $80, and so were not recorded. This contrasts with the Greek and Italian wives, most of whom were earning from $15 to $27.

There were not many working migrant women who were heads of income units. We estimate that out of a total of almost 80,000 adult working women who were heads of income units in Melbourne, 11,000 were migrants. The largest groups were British, Italian and Greek. Almost all the British were women who had come to Australia before 1955, whereas most of the Italians and Greeks had arrived since 1960. Between 1960 and 1966 relatively large numbers of single Italian and Greek women came to Australia and many of them settled in Melbourne. In fact, of the adults who arrived in this period $10 \cdot 9$ per cent of the Italian and $17 \cdot 4$ of the Greek income units were single women, compared with $1 \cdot 5$ per cent of British and $4 \cdot 5$ per cent of all other migrants.

Incomes and Poverty

The survey set out to discover which groups in our society are likely to be poor and the analysis of the data brought to light pockets of poverty among migrants. But even in the poorest groups over 80 per cent of all adult income units had adjusted incomes of over $39 a week.

All groups of recent migrants had a higher proportion of poor people than the population as a whole. The British fared best, with $9 \cdot 2$ per cent below the poverty line; the Italians and Greeks were worst off, with $15 \cdot 3$ per cent and $16 \cdot 2$ per cent respectively, compared with $7 \cdot 7$ per cent of the population as a whole. If the marginally poor are included, almost 20 per cent of recently arrived Greeks and over 17 per cent of recently arrived Italians were poor or marginally so, compared with $12 \cdot 9$ per cent of the population as a whole.

TABLE 8·3

MIGRANTS IN POVERTY BY ADJUSTED INCOME
Adult Income Units

Country of origin and period of arrival	Estimated total adult income units	Adjusted income		
		Less than $33 Poor	$33—$39 Marginal	Less than $39 Poor and marginal
		%	%	%
United Kingdom				
1955–59	10,340	10·4	4·0	14·4
1960–66	18,595	9·2	4·1	13·3
Italy				
1955–59	9,422	16·2	2·5	18·7
1960–66	9,878	15·3	2·1	17·4
Greece				
1955–59	7,870	4·2	4·7	8·9
1960–66	13,680	16·2	3·5	19·7
Other countries				
1955–59	17,128	4·1	6·0	10·1
1960–66	16,403	11·1	1·4	12·5
Australians and migrants before 1955	668,173	7·3	5·5	12·8
Total population	771,489	7·7	5·2	12·9

On further analysis, a considerable proportion of these people were in the $0-$3 income group, i.e. they were income units who were not earning in the particular week selected by the survey. There are many reasons for this and in all groups such people account for a proportion of those in poverty (see Chapter 4). Thus, many of those in poverty were those who were not earning. For some this was a temporary misfortune, but for others it was a more or less permanent state.

Elderly Migrant Parents in Poverty: The largest group of migrants with no income consists of the elderly parents of migrants, who are allowed to come to Australia only if their families sign a maintenance guarantee. They do not qualify for assisted passages, nor are they eligible for the age pension until they have been here for ten years. Most of them are unable to work because of language and other difficulties. An interviewer in Stage II says about one such Greek couple: 'I think these people have used all the existing resources to find a job, but with no success.' In most cases they are well cared for by their families, but the fact remains that they have nothing of their own and are entirely dependent on their children.

Many of the families involved are Southern Europeans, and the cost of bringing out parents is likely to be a burden if they are poor. The families must pay their fares to Australia and support them entirely when they arrive, and this may become an increasing problem as the health of the old people deteriorates. Such elderly migrants are not eligible for the pensioner medical service and voluntary health insurance may be unknown to them or too costly. This is more fully discussed in Chapter 10. The following case illustrates some of these problems.

Two brothers migrated to Australia from Sicily in 1961. In 1963 they had saved enough to pay the deposit on an old house in an inner suburb and pay the fares of their mother and younger brother to Australia. When the two older brothers married in 1964 the mother was left with the youngest brother, aged sixteen, who earned $15 a week. The mother walked from factory to factory trying to find work but was told she was too old: at this time she was fifty-three. In 1965 she became ill and for the next year was in and out of hospital and had a series of operations. The youngest boy left home in 1966 and ceased to communicate with the family. The two older brothers had to pay the mother's medical expenses amounting to $650 in 1965, the balance being paid by health insurance. At the time of the interview the old lady was in a private hospital, paying fees of $44 per week, of which only $24 were paid by insurance. She applied for a special benefit in early 1966, but did not receive it because her son had signed a maintenance guarantee and the family circumstances were regarded as adequate.

Another case was that of a Greek widow of sixty-five who came to Australia in 1966. Her son had to borrow $330 for her fare and she was entirely dependent on him. She told the interviewer that she was ashamed to say she needed clothing and other things because she had no money. When asked what were her most urgent problems, she said she felt a burden on the family. The interviewer comments: 'This woman feels badly about her complete dependence on her family. Many elderly migrants must have similar feelings. It creates problems in the family, who have mixed feelings about having brought their elderly relatives to Australia. This old woman feels very insecure, as before her she sees only old age and sickness, which will prove expensive.'

Many other cases could be quoted which show that considerable hardship is involved for some of the poor families. A compassionate allowance can be made if need is proved, but this is not generally known, and three cases were recorded in the survey in which an application for such an allowance was not successful. It would be better to give these elderly parents a small allowance so that they could make a small contribution to the household and have something left for personal expenses such as clothes and fares. They are not a large group—we estimate about 5,000 in Melbourne—and it would not be very costly.

We recommend (1) that elderly migrants should be eligible for an allowance of half the age pension, subject to a means test of personal income, until they qualify for the age pension; (2) that the residence qualification for the age pension should be reduced from ten to five years; and (3) that elderly migrants should be eligible for subsidised hospital and medical insurance.

It is sometimes argued that elderly migrants should not be allowed into Australia if they become a charge on our social services. Such an argument underestimates the importance of family ties to many Italian and Greek families, who feel they must bring their parents out to join them. The measures we recommend might ensure that fewer workers would return to their own country; they would certainly ease a considerable burden for many Greek and Italian families.

Analysis of the incomes of non-householders provides more evidence of this sort of migrant poverty. Table 8·4 shows the percentage of adult householders who are poor or marginally poor. If the adults who are not householders are included, as in Table 8·3, it makes very little difference to the figures for the British migrants or for the total population, whereas for the recent Italians and Greeks, the percentage in poverty and marginally so is almost doubled. Thus many of the poor are non-householders, i.e. relatives living with the family or boarders not related to the householder. A considerable proportion of these are elderly parents or newly-arrived migrants who have not yet found satisfactory employment.

For most migrants who are employed and earning, income is adequate for what might be regarded as normal needs.

Income after Payment for Housing

The relatively favourable position of migrants in terms of adjusted income changes significantly when allowance is made for the cost of housing. The general situation is indicated by a comparison of two groups of adult householders: those with no disability, and those with only the disability of being non-British migrants. Measured by adjusted income they were much the same, but by adjusted income after payment for housing 18·7 per cent of the migrants were poor or marginally poor compared with 7·3 per cent of the 'no disability' group. This general pattern is confirmed by further analysis.

TABLE 8·4

MIGRANTS: POOR AND MARGINALLY POOR:
ADJUSTED INCOME AND ADJUSTED INCOME AFTER HOUSING COSTS

Adult Householders Only

Country of origin and period of arrival	Adjusted income Less than $39 Poor and marginally poor	Adjusted income after payment for housing Less than $33 Poor and marginally poor
	%	%
United Kingdom		
1955–59	14·8	10·9
1960–66	12·4	17·1
Italy		
1955–59	19·2	24·4
1960–66	8·6	29·3
Greece		
1955–59	9·1	22·7
1960–66	8·1	22·9
Other countries		
1955–59	11·5	13·7
1960–66	6·5	12·5
Australians and migrants before 1955	13·7	10·2
Total population	13·4	11·2

The percentages in poverty by adjusted income, and by adjusted income after payment for housing are set out in Table 8·4. This table shows that whereas for the total population the percentage of poor and marginally poor falls from 13·4 to 11·2 when housing is taken into account, for all recent migrants it rises significantly and for recent Greeks and Italians it is roughly three times as high. So that more than one in four Italian and more than one in five Greek householders who arrived in Australia after 1960 is poor or marginally so after payment for housing.

Analysis of housing costs recorded in the survey shows that they were much lower for Australians than for migrants because more Australians had completed the purchase of their houses and more had started to buy at least ten years previously, when the cost of houses and land was much lower. Only 10·6 per cent of the Australian-born were paying $15 per week or more, compared with 46·3 per cent of British and 39·7 per cent of Italian migrants who had arrived between 1960 and 1966. Many of these migrants were paying $15-$21 per week.

Many cases in Stage II illustrate the problem of high housing costs. For example:

An Italian migrant who had worked on the Suez Canal until it closed came to Australia in 1956. In 1963 he went back to Italy to find a wife, and on return to Melbourne bought an old house in poor condition in a northern suburb. The purchase price was $9,600, and they paid $1,800 deposit. The previous owner, a real estate agent, would only offer them a short-term loan, and they had to pay $160 per month to repay it. The husband's wages were $42 a week, which would have been enough to keep them above the poverty line judged only by income, but when housing costs were deducted they were desperately poor. They were only able to manage because the wife worked until the baby was born in 1964, and about this time a brother came to live with them who contributed $20 a week to the housing costs. At the time of the survey, they were negotiating a long-term loan with the Commonwealth Savings Bank which would enable them to wind up the mortgage. But for these years they had been in extreme poverty because of their housing costs.

Another case illustrates several points which have been made in this chapter.

A large composite Greek family live together as one household, consisting of husband and wife and child; the mother of the wife, who is entirely dependent on them; a cousin who is working but can only contribute $3 per week to the household expenses because she is still repaying her fare; and another cousin who arrived only a few weeks ago and has not found a job. The householder arrived in Australia in 1964 and bought an old house in poor condition in an inner suburb in the following year. The purchase price was $6,750 and they paid a deposit of $800. They have a short-term loan at 7½ per cent on which they pay $30 per week. The husband earns $40 per week, the wife works full-time and earns $24. Their income, including the board which they receive, is therefore $67 per week, out of which they pay $30 for housing. If we estimate food expenditure at $4 per head, this leaves $13 for all other expenses for six people. The interviewer says they cannot afford to buy even such necessities as clothes and cooking utensils. Their situation has been made more difficult by illness. They told the interviewer that they had been insured but had let the payments lapse for financial reasons. It is not surprising that their reply to the question: 'What are your most urgent problems?' was 'Payment of house mortgage. When that is done, things will be better.'

There is a great deal of evidence in the survey of poverty caused by high housing costs, both in the percentage of migrants found to be in poverty in Stage I and also in the case studies of many migrant families in Stage II. In some cases this was in part due to the householder's desire to pay off the loan as quickly as possible, so that repayments made were sometimes higher than required by the terms of the loan. In the next section the problem of housing will be examined, and the reasons why it is so often a cause of migrant poverty discussed.

Housing

Migrants who bring capital with them or who are in highly paid occupations have a choice of housing open to them, but those who arrive with little or no money and are low wage earners are likely to find housing one of their greatest problems. Their immediate needs on arrival are met in one of two ways.

(i) Those who have migrated as assisted passage nominees of the Australian government are eligible for temporary accommodation in migrant hostels. In the past these were army-type huts with minimum standards of privacy and comfort, but in the last two years the government has carried out an extensive rebuilding programme. All the old hostels are being replaced by modern buildings with motel-type accommodation which provides adequate comfort for the short time migrants are expected to stay in them. In spite of government subsidies, hostel charges are high for low wage earners with families to support. For example, in 1969 a family with two children paid about $28.50 per week for board in a new hostel, which left little for travel to work and personal expenses out of a minimum weekly wage of $39. For the very poor there were reductions in the tariff so that a family of this size would have at least $9.50 per week left after payment for board. It would be hard to save on such an income.

The Immigration Department provides some self-contained flats in the outer suburbs for rental to migrants who have lived for not more than three months in a hostel and who have at least $500 in the bank. The flats are available for up to six months at rents slightly below market value. They provide an excellent opportunity for those who plan to buy a house to look around and save the necessary deposit, but they do not help the low wage earners without capital. The Housing Commission, the chief provider of low income housing, does not help these low earning migrants because of the long waiting period for flats and houses. They must find private rental accommodation, and here their difficulties begin.

(ii) Those who migrate unassisted by the Government must be sponsored by organisations or private individuals who guarantee them accommodation and employment. This category includes the great majority of Italians and Greeks. Between 1947 and 1968 three-quarters of the Southern Europeans came out unassisted, compared with less than one-quarter of the British and Northern Europeans.

These sponsored migrants have the advantage of having a job, a place to live and a family to help them find their feet in a new country. On the other hand, many begin their new life in debt because they have to repay their passage money. They often move in with relatives in houses which are already overcrowded and are still being paid off. There were many such cases found in the survey of which one example is given.

Two Greek brothers came to Melbourne in 1964. They were sponsored by their elder brother and went to live with him and his wife and two children. Before they arrived he had bought an old house in an inner suburb. The purchase price was $12,000, and although he had managed to save enough to pay a deposit of $2,600, he did not get a long-term loan. The weekly repayment rate was $20, and with earnings of $41.10, he would have been below the poverty line had not his brothers shared the housing costs. In 1965 one of the younger brothers married and brought his wife to live in the house, and in 1966 they had a child. In 1966 the three brothers also shared the cost of bringing out their elderly parents who were entirely dependent on them. So at the time of the survey, ten people were living in a three-bedroom house. Because they were prepared to live in overcrowded conditions they would be able to pay off this house and doubtless they would continue to live like this until they had saved the deposit for another house. The process would take longer because they had elderly parents to support. The interviewer said 'This man seems overwhelmed by all his dependants.'

The survey provides information about the ways in which various migrant groups resolved their immediate and long-term housing problems. In this analysis they are divided into non-householders, i.e. those who are boarding with relatives or outside the family, and householders who are buying or renting accommodation.

Non-householders

All recent migrant groups have a high percentage of non-householders, or boarders. This is not surprising, as many of them belong to the unassisted passage group described above. The analysis of non-householders, and the relative percentages of householders, are set out in

TABLE 8·5

TYPE OF OCCUPANCY FOR NON-HOUSEHOLDERS

All Income Units: Percentages

Country of origin and period of arrival	Estimated total number of income units	House-holders	Non-householders			Total
			Indept. children living at home	Relatives	Non-family boarders	
Australia	685,523	66·5	28·0	4·0	1·4	100·0
United Kingdom						
1955–59	13,027	81·0	18·1	6·9	0	100·0
1960–66	22,261	66·7	14·4	13·1	2·8	100·0
Italy						
1955–59	10,556	82·9	15·2	1·7	0	100·0
1960–66	10,619	47·0	5·2	47·6	0·2	100·0
Greece						
1955–59	8,207	78·1	18·3	3·6	0	100·0
1960–66	16,164	57·6	15·9	22·0	4·5	100·0
Netherlands	12,238	67·4	31·6	0	1·0	100·0
Germany	13,682	81·7	6·2	6·2	7·3	100·0
Other countries	166,457	76·6	15·3	5·7	2·4	100·0
Total population*	958,734	68·9	24·2	5·2	1·6	100·0

*Any inconsistencies between component figures and totals are due to rounding.

Table 8·5. Of those who arrived between 1960 and 1966, 13·1 per cent of the British, 47·6 per cent of the Italians and 22 per cent of the Greeks are boarding with relatives, compared with 5·2 per cent of the population as a whole. A further breakdown shows that the percentage of Southern Europeans who are boarders is even higher for the most recent arrivals. For example, of the Greeks who arrived in 1965-66, 35 per cent are boarding with relatives and a further 12·6 per cent are boarding outside the family.

Table 8·5 shows also how markedly this situation changes with length of residence. A comparison of the 1960-66 arrivals with those of 1955-59 indicates that the percentage of family boarders drops from 47·6 to 1·7 for the Italians, from 22 to 3·6 for the Greeks, and from 13·1 to 6·9 for the British. Boarders not related to the family disappear altogether.

It is sometimes said that Greeks and Italians like to live in large composite households—that they do so from choice, not from necessity. But from these figures it seems clear that, whatever their feelings when they first arrive in Australia, most of them move into homes of their own as quickly as possible. Table 8·5 shows that of those who had arrived after 1960, 66·7 per cent of British, 47 per cent of Italians and 57·6 per cent of Greeks had already become householders by 1966.

Householders

Tenancy: For most migrants this first home of their own is likely to be rented. The survey showed that of the adult householders who had arrived in the previous eighteen months 100 per cent of the Greeks and over 90 per cent of the British and Italians were tenants. The report of the Immigration Planning Council[2] states that 85 per cent of those who leave migrant hostels go into rented accommodation.

Tenancy means different things for different migrant groups. For many British and Northern Europeans it means a self-contained flat in a middle class suburb, and this is within the reach only of high wage earners. For many Italians and Greeks it means renting a few rooms in an old house, often sharing kitchen and bathroom facilities. Thus, of the householders who had arrived after 1960, 32·1 per cent of the British were living in flats compared with 1·1 per cent of Greeks; 13·5 per cent of the British were in rooms compared with 43·4 per cent of the Greeks.

A further breakdown of the tenancy figures shows that at the time

[2] *Australia's Immigration Programmes for the Period 1968 to 1973*. A Report to the Minister for Immigration by The Immigration Planning Council, p. 56

of the survey the Housing Commission was not meeting the needs of migrants, especially the Southern Europeans. Some Dutch and British were in Housing Commission flats, but few in comparison with those in private tenancy; of the British arrivals since 1960, 3·4 per cent were in Commission flats compared with 69·3 per cent in private tenancy. And of the 576 Greek and Italian income units interviewed only one was a tenant of the Housing Commission. This was partly due to ignorance, and also to the long waiting lists which make the Housing Commission unable to meet the immediate needs of migrants.

This is all the more serious because there is an acute shortage of rented accommodation at rates which many migrants can afford to pay. The report of the Immigration Planning Council referred to above states that the prevailing rent level for migrants leaving Commonwealth migrant hostels was in the $15-$20 range. There were many cases in the survey of hardship caused by high rents. For example:

A Lebanese family, consisting of husband and wife and four small children, came to Melbourne in 1965. They rented a two-bedroom house in poor condition. It was dark and damp, had no hot water service or laundry, and the cooking facilities were poor. They were paying $18 per week rent. The husband was earning $46 per week plus overtime when he could get it. His wife did not work because her health was poor and she had the children to care for. They wanted to get a house of their own, but found it very difficult to save with their present housing costs.

These prevailing high rents make the migrant feel the urgency of getting out into a house of his own, and at the same time make it very difficult for him to save the necessary deposit. As one respondent said: 'Money paid for rent just disappears. You never see it again.'

The survey showed that the percentages in tenancy fell steadily with length of residence (see Table 8·6). A comparison between the 1960-66 arrivals and those for 1955-59 shows a decrease from 75·3 to 27 per cent of the British, from 40·5 to 15·9 per cent of the Italians, and from 57·9 to 22·4 per cent of the Greeks. So that when they have lived in Australia for about ten years the percentage of migrants in tenancy is about the same as for the population as a whole.

House Purchase: There was a corresponding increase with length of residence in the percentage of householders who were owners or buyers. Almost all the 1965-66 arrivals were tenants, as stated above; but of the 1960-66 arrivals 42 per cent of the Greeks and 59·6 of the Italians were already buying their own houses, and for the 1955-59 arrivals the

percentage had risen to 77·6 of the Greeks, 84·1 of the Italians and
73 per cent of the British. These high figures for home ownership are
all the more remarkable because many of the migrants concerned are
low wage earners.

TABLE 8·6

TYPE OF OCCUPANCY FOR ALL HOUSEHOLDERS

Country of origin and period of arrival	Owners and buyers	Tenants	Estimated total number of householders
	%	%	
Australia	74·2	25·8	456,202
United Kingdom			
1955–59	73·0	27·0	10,551
1960–66	24·7	75·3	15,522
Italy			
1955–59	84·1	15·9	8,759
1960–66	59·6	40·5	4,997
Greece			
1955–59	77·6	22·4	6,414
1960–66	42·0	57·9	9,309
Netherlands all	60·7	39·3	8,251
Germany all	41·4	58·5	11,175
Other countries	70·0	30·0	128,805
Total population	72·4	27·6	659,985

Very few except the British and Dutch were buying through the
Housing Commission, and those who were had mostly been in Australia
for five to ten years. Here again, the long waiting period and the location
of much Housing Commission housing in the outer suburbs deter the
Southern Europeans. Many British migrants were found in areas like
Dandenong, where the Housing Commission provided housing for a
rapidly expanding industrial centre.

The first aim of many migrants is to save the deposit on a house. Then
they must compete for a loan in a market where the demand always
exceeds the resources available to meet it. Their best chance of a long-
term, low-interest loan from a first-class lender such as the State Savings

Bank is to buy a new house in the outer suburbs. These houses cost $10,000 or more, and the maximum loan available may be several thousand dollars short of the amount needed to fill the gap between the deposit and the purchase price. Borrowers are forced to take out a second mortgage, usually short-term at high rates of interest, and the combined repayments may bring them into poverty. The following cases show how disastrous this can be.

An Italian family with three children under the age of ten was buying a house in a new housing estate at a purchase price of $10,700. They had a loan from the State Savings Bank on which they paid $13 per week, but they also had a three-year loan from the builder, and on this they had to pay $8 a week. An elder son who had been helping to pay off the house was killed in a car accident and since his death they had not paid anything on the second mortgage, and the builder was threatening to sue. The husband earned $34 a week and the wife was unable to work because of poor health and language difficulty. At the time of the interview they had only $14 in the bank.

Another Italian family with three children was paying $22 a week on a loan of $7,800 over seven years. Their weekly income was $43, and after payment for housing they only had $21 left for all other expenses.

Most Greeks and Italians prefer to buy old houses in the inner suburbs, and for this kind of purchase it is very difficult to get a long-term loan from a savings bank. Many migrants take out private loans, and in a highly competitive market this frequently means short-term loans involving repayments taking far too high a proportion of their disposable income. There were many cases of this kind in Stage II of the survey. Thus high repayment rates for buyers and the high rents paid by many tenants make it clear why so many migrants are put into poverty by their housing costs.

Only one more case of the many which could be quoted will be added to show what some migrants can achieve, though at the price of much hardship.

An Italian family with two children was buying a house in an inner suburb. The parents came to Australia in 1959 and married soon afterwards with no savings. They rented rooms and although the husband earned only $34 a week, with whatever overtime he could get, by 1965 they had saved enough to put down a deposit of $3,180 on a house, the purchase price of which was $6,310. They had a mortgage for the remainder, repayable over 26 years at 8 per cent. They were paying

$7.20 per week—much less than they would have had to pay to rent even a few rooms. The house was in very dilapidated condition when they bought it and they were renovating it very skilfully themselves. They had already spent $100 on structural repairs and urgently needed another $100 for materials for further repairs. This family lived on the barest necessities for years to buy their home. They had no laundry facilities, no floor coverings except in the kitchen, and practically no furniture. Every penny went into the house, but after ten years of hard work and deprivation, they would have a good home and their position would be easier.

The hard work and skill of many migrants, especially the Italians, have helped to transform some of the inner city areas of Melbourne. Twenty years ago, Carlton looked dingy and depressed. Now, very largely due to the work of Italians, many of the old houses have been restored to something of their former charm, and it is an attractive suburb with a style of its own. Ironically enough, this has made it popular with Australians as well, and many business and professional people now compete for the old terrace houses. This raises the price and often puts them beyond the reach of migrants. This trend and the clearance of large areas for redevelopment by the Housing Commission, make it increasingly difficult for migrants to find accommodation in the inner suburban areas in which they like to live.

The difficulties of securing good loans, especially for buying old houses, are not peculiar to migrants. They are common to all low income groups, but migrants are at a greater disadvantage than others. They have not had the opportunity Australians may have had to save over a long period. They are not eligible for Commonwealth Government Home Savings Grants until they have lived in Australia for three years. Also, negotiating the best loan requires some understanding of our institutions, which is far more difficult for a Greek or Italian who knows little English and comes from a simple village background. To mitigate these difficulties several banks provide excellent migrant housing advisory services, but too often all they can offer is advice, because the conditions for obtaining loans are hard for many migrants to fulfil.

The State Savings Bank, the biggest source of housing loans in Victoria, will lend money for old as well as new houses, but on considerably less favourable terms. To be eligible, an applicant must have maintained a substantial account—about $1,000—for a year, though this may be waived in the case of migrants who open an account immediately on arrival. The trading banks do not have a waiting period, but they require the applicant to have in hand about one third of the proposed loan. All banks require that the applicant's income be at least four times the amount of the repayments, and in assessing income the wife's earnings are not included. Also, as stated earlier in the chapter, trading banks will only lend 75 per cent of their valuation of an old house, and this is usually considerably less than the market value.

Co-operative housing societies lend up to 95 per cent of the market value for periods up to thirty-two years, and this would be the sort of repayment rate which most migrants could afford. But these societies are always restricted by lack of funds, so that obtaining a long-term loan would involve a long and uncertain waiting period. Also, they only lend on new houses.

The Housing Loans Insurance Corporation insures loans on old as well as new houses up to 95 per cent of the market value, and so encourages lenders to increase the size of loans. But when funds are limited, lenders are more inclined to spread loans over more customers.

The booklet on housing supplied to migrants by the Immigration Department in 1969[3] realistically states that to buy a house in Melbourne with a good loan, a migrant would need to have in hand $3,000. Even if he saved this formidable amount, he would still need a loan of about $7,000. He could get this from a savings or trading bank, but if it were an old house the loan would probably be for fifteen years. The repayment rate would be $58 to $62 per month (at rates of interest current in 1969), and this would require him to be earning at least $60 per week. This would exclude many low wage earners, who must borrow privately on terms which impoverish them for years.

The housing problem focuses sharply the contrast between the skilled high wage earners, mostly from Britain and Northern Europe, and the unskilled low wage earners mostly from Southern Europe.

The typical Northern European comes to Australia on an assisted passage at a cost of only $20; he frequently brings some capital with him; he is a skilled or semi-skilled worker able to earn a high wage; he speaks English or is sufficiently educated to be able to learn it without too much difficulty; and he has grown up in an industrialised society and understands—as far as that is possible—the workings of bureaucracy. In short, he probably arrives in Australia with money in his pocket, will quickly earn a lot more, and knows how to use it to the best advantage. He will probably solve his housing problems without too much difficulty.

[3] *Housing in Australia*, No. 33, May 1969, Information Office, Australian Department of Immigration, Canberra House, London, p. 22

On the other hand, the typical Southern European has had to pay his own passage, and probably had to borrow the money for it; he is unskilled and a low wage earner; he speaks no English and has little education which will help him to learn it; he has grown up in a village and is bewildered by a big industrial city and does not understand our complex institutions. In short, he arrives with little or no money or even in debt, his wages make it hard for him to save and he does not know what services are open to him or how to avail himself of them. Moreover, he may feel obliged to send money back home to support his parents, and he may also be trying to save to bring them, or other members of his family, out to join him. For him housing is a much more difficult problem.

Recommendations

Two things are needed: more housing, preferably in the inner suburbs, at moderate rents for migrants for their first few years and also a better supply of long-term loans on existing houses for purchase.

The provision of housing for rental is particularly difficult. There is no equivalent here of the non-profit-making housing associations in Britain which acquire existing houses and let them out at moderate rents. Such an undertaking here would be costly because of the high current price of houses and the high costs of conversion. In addition, such an association would have to pay dearly for money borrowed at market rates—over 8 per cent. It seems most unlikely that such an operation could provide housing at moderate rents without subsidy.

It would also be difficult to do this by building new housing. Even if land were made available by slum clearance demolitions for such an organisation, it is doubtful if it could build as cheaply as the Victorian Housing Commission which has the advantage of considerable economies of scale. Yet the economic rent for a three-room Housing Commission house can be $14.40 and for a high-rise flat $18.00 per week. (Rents charged for these are very much less because they are averages based on the cost of housing built over several years.)

Large areas of the inner suburbs of Melbourne are scheduled for redevelopment, but the process of rebuilding is so expensive that at the present rate it will take some twenty years. Many of these old houses will therefore stand for ten years or more. So there would seem to be an opportunity for a redevelopment authority to purchase them as they come on the market, and to let them out for the remaining years of their life. In some cases a minimum of repairs and improvements might have to be carried out, or the materials provided for migrants to do the renovation themselves. Public provision of such second-rate housing might be more valuable to migrants than new housing at charges too high for them.

To facilitate purchase of older houses we suggest that the Commonwealth Government should subsidise approved loans. Since the Housing Loans Insurance Corporation has already made a significant contribution towards financing the acquisition of existing houses, it might be a suitable body to approve loans under the subsidy proposed. The guidance that could be offered in this way would also be valuable in helping migrants to avoid entering into contracts to purchase on crippling terms.

It should also be said that, in spite of many imperfections, the market for housing in a city is an inter-connected whole. A high rate of new house building, in excess of demolitions, will reduce scarcity and so tend to modify high rents and prices for all houses. On the other hand, ambitious slum clearance projects that demolish all the houses in large densely populated areas accentuate the scarcity and keep up rents and prices.

Health and Social Services

The booklet on Health and Social Services in Australia[4] issued to migrants by the Immigration Department states that 'Australia has a system of financial help for the sick which brings medical and hospital care within everyone's reach.' The findings of our survey suggest that this paints an unduly optimistic picture. They showed that many recent migrants, especially the Southern Europeans, had no health insurance. In fact over 75 per cent of the Italians and Greeks who had arrived since 1960 were uninsured, and 98 per cent of the Greeks who arrived in the eighteen months before the survey were in the same precarious position. It is not surprising, therefore, to find that illness can be a disaster for these people, and the risk to which they are exposed by this lack of insurance is one more aspect of their vulnerability in their early years in this country. Health problems of migrants are fully described in Chapter 10 and suggestions made for their amelioration.

Social services are no more inadequate for migrants than for the rest of the population except in one important respect; for all migrants except the British, there is a residence qualification for pensions. For the age pension this is ten years, as described earlier; for the invalid

---

[4] *Health and Social Services in Australia*, No. 24, June 1969, Information Office, Australian Department of Immigration, Canberra House, London, p. 9

pension it is five years for those who are fit on arrival, ten years for those who are already incapacitated; for the widows' pension, there is no waiting period if the woman is widowed after arrival in Australia; if she is already widowed on arrival it is five years.

The case for more generous treatment for the aged has already been argued; the residence qualification for women widowed in Australia was dropped in 1968, and it seems reasonable that invalids should be similarly treated. The five-year requirement could cause severe hardship for migrants incapacitated soon after their arrival by sickness or accident, other than those covered by workers' compensation. It is in the early years when they may have little money and few friends to fall back on that they most need the protection of a pension.

All through this chapter it has been evident that for some migrants, especially the Southern Europeans, the years after arrival are a struggle. Perhaps this is best understood through the interviewer's description of a Greek family who arrived in 1964. Their financial position has already been described earlier on page 131. She adds the following general comment.

This couple appear to be fatigued and depressed by their present situation, which they feel is as bad as it can possibly be. They have had problems of illness. Firstly, the wife's long stay in hospital after the birth of the child, which was costly and distressing, and now they are worried about the baby who has had a series of illnesses this winter. Possibly they would be able to see the baby's illness in perspective if they had more understanding of the language and knew exactly what was going on. They both work in order to pay off the house, and as a result have little time to spend together as a family. They resent this, but feel the effort is worth while as eventually things will be better for them when they are out of debt. They appear to be an affectionate, united family whose period of adjustment to a new country is made extremely difficult by their language difficulties, the problem of illness, and by their desire to purchase a house without sufficient financial security.

This is the assessment of a trained and experienced social worker. It reveals some of the defects of our treatment of migrants.

Summary

The survey showed that migrants are spread through every suburb in Melbourne and most have shared the general prosperity. But in the older and sometimes decaying inner city areas, there are big concentrations of Southern Europeans who are less fortunate.

Many live in overcrowded conditions, beset by problems of poverty, poor health and dear housing. Their children go to schools which are old and poorly equipped for both work and play. They often have no money for text books, and little or no special teaching in English. Almost the only good thing about these schools is the devotion of the teachers working in very difficult conditions. The State Schools Relief Committee, a teacher-sponsored group, spent about $32,250 in 1968 providing such basic necessities as clothes and shoes for needy children and had over 7,000 requests for such help in 1969. One headmaster of an inner suburban primary school estimates that 70 per cent of the children are from Greek or Italian migrant families, many of whom are poor.

Housing conditions are one of the greatest problems, and cause many migrants to return home from Australia. The proportion of those doing so increased steadily in the sixties and reached over 5 per cent in 1968-69. The Commonwealth Government plans to maintain a high level of immigration, the target for 1970 being 175,000. If other cities are like Melbourne, one wonders where they are going to live. It is surely evident that further action to improve the housing situation of migrants, especially those of low income groups, is necessary at once.

Migrants have other and perhaps more intractable problems than the economic ones outlined in this chapter: problems of language, of different cultural patterns, of isolation and loneliness. Ignorance of English often leads to a breakdown in communication, so that, as one interviewer commented 'migrants often miss out because they do not know about social services, or how to set about finding out.' More publicity about pensions and benefits in other languages as well as English, the appointment of social workers and welfare officers to work among migrants and the setting up of locally-based welfare services would alleviate some unnecessary poverty.

The picture is not all gloomy. On the contrary most of the great postwar influx of migrants have prospered and settled happily in Australia. They have made a notable contribution to their adopted country. As Dr Charles Price says: 'This massive gain has done great things for the Australian economy, stimulating public and private enterprise, encouraging the development of water, mineral and other resources, and helping overseas capitalists to decide that Australia's future is worth investing in.'[5]

5 C. A. Price, *Migrants in Australian Society*, HRH The Duke of Edinburgh's Third Commonwealth Study Conference, Australia, 1968

They have also added richness and variety to the rather limited pattern of British-Australian life in the visual arts, in the preservation of their own culture through folk music, dancing and handcrafts, in the many excellent national restaurants and food shops and in many other ways. We can justifiably find satisfaction in all that has been given and received. But this does not absolve us from responsibility for the thousands who have to live, for a time at least, in poverty, and from a determination to make a good life available for all.

9 The Unemployed, the Sick and the Other Poor *

In this chapter we consider the problems of poverty among groups other than those specific disability groups previously examined.

The Unemployed and the Sick

Sickness and unemployment benefits in Australia for married couples are now 64 per cent and for a single person 67 per cent of the old age or invalid pension. In the United States they are 106 per cent and in Britain 90 per cent. Thus Australian rates of benefit are low by international standards. It is not surprising that those dependent on sickness and unemployment benefits were found far below the poverty line.

Even a short interruption of earnings can cause hardship to families without reserves. Arrears accumulated over a few weeks may take considerably longer to repay. Nevertheless a short period of unemployment or a short illness is likely to be less devastating than a long one. For analysis we have divided the sick and the unemployed into short-term and long-term groups according to the length of time they were away from work. Only those who were off work for eight weeks or more in the twelve months before the interview were classified in the sickness or accident and the unemployment disability groups.

Unemployment

In the survey week there were very few unemployed. Those described as 'unemployed', 'changing jobs' or 'temporarily laid off' were estimated to number 2,344 or 0·4 per cent of adult working males. When those off work because of an industrial dispute are added the total is 0·7 per cent.[1] The proportion of adult working female heads unemployed was also less than one per cent of those normally working. Of a total of 4,603 income unit heads unemployed, it is estimated that 3,222 had incomes in the survey week which were below the poverty line.

The greatest number of these form a revolving group who are unemployed one week but who will be back at work the next. Most of them are not in need. Table 2·7 shows that the survey estimated the number

* This chapter was written jointly by Ronald F. Henderson and Sheila Shaver.

[1] These figures are lower than published unemployment statistics for several reasons. Because the survey was confined to Melbourne and to occupants of private dwellings, unemployment in rural areas and among a number of homeless men and others was omitted. In addition, the self-employed were included in the survey estimate of the work force, contrary to general practice in the compilation of official unemployment statistics.

of income units suffering long-term unemployment as only 2,349, or twenty-five actual interviews. Of these twenty-five, only four were below the poverty line at the time of the first survey. Some of the others may have been in poverty when unemployed earlier in the year but were in a better position by the week of the survey. In contrast to the circumstances for many years up to 1939, medium-term and long-term unemployment is not now a significant cause of poverty. The numbers of those unemployed for eight weeks or more are small and the proportion in poverty very small. Very few are voluntarily idle.

TABLE 9·1

WORKING INCOME UNIT HEADS WITH REDUCED EARNINGS IN WEEK OF SURVEY

Reason for reduced earnings	Males	Females
Unemployed, changing jobs or temporarily laid off	2,344 ⎫	
Industrial dispute	1,630 ⎬	1,234
Sickness or accident	6,197 ⎭	
Other and unknown	18,014	3,265
Total with reduced earnings	28,185	4,499
Total adult working income unit heads	564,517	84,194

Sickness or Accident

It is estimated that more than 22,000 income unit heads had the disability of sickness or accident. In some cases the period of illness included the week for which income information was collected and in others it did not, as the sickness had occurred earlier in the year. To measure the effect of long-term sickness as a cause of poverty we must therefore limit our analysis to those who were off work at the time they were interviewed. In terms of actual (unweighted) cases there were in the survey only twenty-three such income unit heads, fourteen of whom had incomes below the poverty line and two only marginally above. On the basis of these fourteen cases we estimated that more than a quarter of the 6,802 ill in the survey week were in need because of long-term sickness or accident.

One of several examples of poverty caused by sickness was the case of a Dutch family consisting of parents and four children, two dependent and two independent. The father was self-employed as a painter and the mother worked part-time as a domestic. The eldest boy was an apprentice toolmaker and the girl an office worker. The other two children were still at school. For five months the father had been unable to work because of illness. The working son had also been sick for some of that time. The weekly income of the parents and two dependent children during this period was:

$ 8.25   Sickness benefit
    3.00   Children's allowances
  20.00   Wife's earnings
    1.50   Child endowment

From her earnings of $12, the elder daughter paid $6 per week board. Except for the two periods when he also was unable to work, the working son paid board of $6 out of his weekly earnings of $14. Household rent was $16.80. Adjusted income for the parents and the two younger children was $32.90, just below the poverty line. After payment for housing their adjusted income was only $16.70, far below the corresponding poverty line of $27. Even if the working son and daughter had turned their whole wage over to their parents the family would still have been in poverty.

The number of people in poverty caused by long-term sickness was very small. The first survey estimated that only 22,079, or 2·9 per cent of working income unit heads were sick for eight weeks or longer during the previous twelve months.

These figures do not include two other groups suffering from sickness or accident—those sick for less than eight weeks and those sick and not normally working, such as invalid pensioners. There is hardship among the short-term sick which in some cases may be severe. Some of these were described in Chapter 4. There is also substantial poverty among families in which the head has permanently ceased earning because of sickness or accident. These are not included in the disability groups but are discussed below under the heading 'Invalid Pensioners'.

Recommendations for Sickness and Unemployment Benefit

At the time of the survey and until November 1969 sickness, unemployment and special[2] benefits were paid at the rate of $8.25 per week for adults. Allowances were $6 for a dependent spouse and $1.50 for each dependent child. Thus the total benefit payable to a man with a wife and two children—the standard family—was $17.25. In 1969 benefits were substantially increased. The benefit went up to $10, wife's allowance to

[2] Special benefit, paid at the same rate as unemployment and sickness benefits, is granted on flexible eligibility conditions and serves to fill in gaps left by the more stringent conditions of eligibility for sickness and unemployment benefits.

$7, and children's allowance to $2.50 for the first child and $3.50 for each additional child. A family of four now receives $23 a week in benefits, bringing their total weekly income including child endowment to $24.50. This is still far below the poverty line. For both benefits the minimum waiting period is seven days. Benefits are paid to a married woman only when it is proved that her husband cannot maintain her.

We can contrast the Australian situation with the recommendation of the Royal Commission on Compensation for Personal Injury in New Zealand in December 1967.[3] The Commission suggested immediate compensation for a totally incapacitated worker of 80 per cent of income; accordingly a man earning $40 a week would receive $32 a week. This New Zealand scheme is graduated both for contributions and for benefits. The high wage earner pays more in contributions and receives more in benefits. In Australia, however, social service benefits are not graduated and are paid out of general tax revenue. Thus the New Zealand scheme as a whole would not fit into the present Australian pattern, but a recommendation derived from this study may be applicable to the Australian situation.

The unskilled worker who is unable to work because of accident or sickness should receive a benefit sufficient to give his family no less than 80 per cent of his previous income.

Two arguments are sometimes put forward in defence of the current low rates of sickness and unemployment benefit in Australia:

(i) Rates must be kept down to prevent lazy ne'er-do-wells living in idleness at the expense of the taxpayer.

(ii) The payment of higher rates of benefits would impose an intolerable burden on the taxpayer.

Neither of these arguments will stand up to close examination. Firstly, doctors can and do certify whether a man is sick and unable to work for that reason; and secondly, there is not a large pool of permanently unemployed persons in Australia. The pool is small, less than 2 per cent of the work force, and much of it is composed of people changing jobs. There is no need to penalise them by paying a low rate of unemployment benefit. On the contrary in order to encourage the expansion of fast growing companies there is much to be said for encouraging workers to move to better jobs by reducing the cost to them of being unemployed.

For those such as the aged and invalids, who are dependent on pensions for long periods, we are suggesting that pensions be just sufficient

[3] *Compensation for Personal Injury in New Zealand, Report of the Royal Commission of Inquiry,* Government Printer, Wellington, December 1967

to raise them to the poverty line we have drawn. For those cases of sickness and unemployment, many of which are short-term, perhaps a level of no more than 20 per cent lower than the poverty line might be appropriate.

We estimate that the updated poverty line will be $42.40 by mid-1970. In order to bring a family of man, wife and two dependent children up to a level of income within 20 per cent of the poverty line they will require at least $34. It might be apportioned as follows:

Sickness, unemployment or special benefit	*$17.00*
Wife's allowance	*11.00*
Allowance for first child	*2.50*
Allowance for each additional child	*3.50*

Such a family would receive a further $1.50 in child endowment.

The cost of sickness, unemployment and special benefits in 1968-69 was $16·6 million.[4] Increases contained in the 1969 budget cost another $4·5 million. The further increases proposed above would, at most, cost another $10 million in 1969-70, bringing total expenditure on these benefits to $31·1 million.

This amount seems large in relation to the small numbers of beneficiaries involved, particularly when it is remembered that even expenditures of this magnitude would not bring the sick and unemployed right up to the poverty line. But the magnitude of additional expenditure required is merely another illustration of the depth of poverty among these groups and the urgency of their need.

Of course if the rate of unemployment were to rise sharply to 3 or 4 per cent of the work force, this type of government expenditure would rise accordingly. In such circumstances, a rise in expenditure would be welcome for two reasons. Firstly, in such a recession it is most desirable to maintain the purchasing power of consumers to prevent a further twist of the deflationary spiral in which lower investment leads to lower incomes and lower incomes to lower production and investment. Secondly, in circumstances in which the rate of unemployment has risen to 3 or 4 per cent it is probable that a considerable number will be out of work for several months; thus they will have used up all savings and credit from shopkeepers and will be right down to living on the unemployment benefit. It is, therefore, all the more important that the

[4] *Social Services 1968-69*, Twenty-eighth Report of the Director-General of Social Services, Canberra, 1969, p. 64

rate of unemployment benefit be sufficient to support them near the poverty line.

Sickness and unemployment benefits are means-tested on income but not on property. The unemployment means test is the more severe. Incomes of husband and wife are pooled, and their benefit and allowances reduced by the excess of weekly income over $6. For sickness benefit the wife's income may be disregarded if no allowance is claimed for her. The benefit is subject to a limit of $6 on income. The wife's allowance is reduced by the wife's income in excess of $6. It is partly because of the stringency of these means tests that we recommend such large increases in benefits.

We also recommend some relaxation in the means test applied to the incomes of wives of unemployment beneficiaries.

In a family in which the head suffers frequent episodes of unemployment, his wife's earnings may be the only stable source of income. It is important in such cases that she be not discouraged from continuing to work. Her earnings should be treated in the same way as those of the wife of a sickness beneficiary; so long as no allowance is claimed for her support, her husband's benefit should not be affected. His benefit is urgently needed to help to meet the expenses incurred in seeking work.

Unemployment, sickness and special benefits have been paid at the same rates since the first Commonwealth legislation for them in 1944. However, there is no theoretical reason for a common rate, as the eligibility criteria are conceptually quite distinct. It would be particularly unfortunate if the benefits paid to one category were kept low merely because it seemed desirable that the benefits paid to the others be low. However, there are strong practical arguments for common rates of benefits for sickness and unemployment.

Firstly, the conceptual distinction between being sick and therefore unable to work and being unemployed is sometimes difficult to make in practice. When a man is unable to find a suitable job because of health limitations, is he sick or unemployed? Common rates can help to facilitate transfer between benefits as appropriate in such cases. Secondly, the structure of social service payments is already complex, and there may be some virtue in maintaining as much simplicity as possible in rate structures from the points of view of public understanding and administrative convenience. Clearly this consideration is secondary to that of determining the most effective rate structure for each benefit, but in the absence of evidence clearly favouring different rates of benefit it has some importance.

In Victoria sickness and unemployment beneficiaries who have dependent children may receive further assistance from the State Social Welfare Department. There is a limit on the amount payable so that total weekly income may not exceed an updated basic wage figure, with a small extra allowance made for large families. Unfortunately it appears that few people know that this assistance is available. The survey identified only one case in which a sickness or unemployment beneficiary received this supplement.

The duplication of administration and means-testing involved in payment by both Commonwealth and State governments to the unemployed and the sick is a particularly inefficient use of scarce State resources which has been made necessary by the unrealistically low level of the unemployment and sickness benefits paid by the Commonwealth. The lack of information about State assistance is almost certainly an outcome of the Federal-State financial conflict: to make the availability of State assistance widely known would result in both greater welfare expenditure and the appearance of acceptance of responsibility in an area for which the State has traditionally held the Commonwealth responsible.

It would be more efficient if the administrative mechanism already established by the Commonwealth for the sick and unemployed were used to make payments which were adequate in the great majority of cases. Then State resources could be devoted to a small number of unusual and difficult instances.

Invalid Pensioners [5]

An invalid pension is awarded upon medical certification of permanent 85 per cent incapacity to work. It is subject to means test on income and property. The rates of pension and allowances are the same as for the age pension. Shown in Table 9·2 are the rates prevailing at the time of the survey and in November 1969.

Where both husband and wife are invalid pensioners or where one is an invalid pensioner and one an age pensioner, the combined rate is the same as that for an age pensioner couple: $22 per week in 1966 and $26.50 in late 1969.

We found a number of instances of severe hardship among invalid pensioners. One in four was below the poverty line.

---

[5] We did not initially set up a disability category for invalid pensioners, so that in our totals they are included among the other poor with no disability. We have learnt, however, that they are a sufficiently large category to be treated separately here.

TABLE 9·2

RATES OF INVALID PENSION AND ALLOWANCES IN 1966 AND 1969

	June 1966	November 1969
	$	$
Invalid pension	12.00	15.00
Wife's allowance	6.00	7·00
Allowance for first child	1.50	2.50
Allowance for each subsequent child	1.50	3.50
Supplementary Assistance (standard rate, i.e. single pensioners only)	2.00	2.00

One example was a divorced European woman of forty-three, in very poor health, who lived in part of a very old single storey house in an inner suburb. Her living room had in it a refrigerator and a television set, lent by the agent. Next door was what looked like a very narrow enclosed verandah which was also a passage to the back door. This was the kitchen. The rooms were cold and damp with rotten floors. Her only heating was a kerosene heater which was not effective in heating her whole living area, and the damp and cold aggravated her arthritis. She had no hot water system, only a bath heater. Her name was on the waiting list for a Housing Commission flat. Arthritis and kidney trouble prevented her working. When she was able, she had attended a public hospital outpatients' department, but by the time she was interviewed she was in bed most of the time and the local doctor looked after her. She did her own housekeeping and tried to keep extra supplies of food in the house as she was often too ill to go out. At the time of the survey her invalid pension and Supplementary Assistance came to $14 per week. For her part of the house she paid $10 per week. Her food expenditure was less than $2 per week. During the past year she had used up $140 of her savings to supplement her pension but she obviously could not continue to do this as she had only $100 left. She had stopped working in November 1964 and had used $1,000 of her savings before she began to receive the pension, as she had been unaware that she was eligible for a sickness benefit.

Another example was a cabinet maker, aged thirty-six, with three school-aged children. He had been unable to work for four years as a result of a stroke. The family's weekly income was only $30.50, equivalent to an income of $28.66 for the standard family of man, wife and two children.

As this second example indicates, the plight of the invalid pensioner family may be as bad as that of the widow with young children. The need to care for her husband or young children may prevent the wife from going out to work. Furthermore, the family may have undertaken to buy a house and be committed to payments entered into when the husband was in good health. Supplementary Assistance is not available to house purchasers.

Invalid pensioners are a small group in the community, clearly identified on medical grounds and already receiving pensions. The survey found that at present the inadequacy of the invalid pension condemns their children to a childhood of acute poverty. It should certainly be increased sufficiently to ensure that families dependent upon it are raised above the poverty line. There should be no administrative difficulty in making the necessary increase in pensions, nor will the cost of this reform be great.

TABLE 9·3

EXISTING AND RECOMMENDED RATES OF INVALID PENSION AND ALLOWANCES

	Existing Nov. 1969	Proposed 1970
	$	$
Invalid pension	15.00	17.00
Wife's allowance	7.00	11.00
Guardian's allowance	—	6.00
Allowance for first child	2.50	2·50
Allowance for each subsequent child	3.50	3.50
Total received by family of man, wife and two dependent children (excluding Supplementary Assistance)	28.00	40·00
Child endowment (two children)	1.50	2.50
Supplementary Assistance	2.00	4.00

A conservative estimate of the poverty line updated to June 1970 is $42.40 for a standard family. A standard family wholly dependent on the invalid pension now receives $29.50 per week, including child endowment. *We recommend an increase of about $13.00 a week to bring them up to the poverty line; this might be apportioned as shown in Table 9·3 to correspond with proposals for age pensioners. In addition to increasing rates of the pension and allowances for dependants, we are suggesting that the conditions of eligibility for the guardian's allowance be extended to include married couples with children where both are pensioners or where the husband is a pensioner and the wife receives a wife's allowance.*

In many of these cases it is not possible for the wife to work as she is required at home to care for her husband or her children. Without this allowance many families dependent on invalid pensions have little hope of escaping poverty.

These recommendations are minimal; their effect would be to bring invalid pensioners and their families to a very austere standard. A married invalid pensioner with a wife and two children would receive $40.00 pension income. Child endowment, including the increases proposed in Chapter 7, would bring total weekly income to $42.50, just above the $42.40 which we estimate such a family will require to be above the poverty line in 1970.

We have also recommended that Supplementary Assistance, at present available only to single pensioners, should be extended to married pensioners on the same conditions of eligibility: that they be wholly dependent on their pensions and pay rent or board. We suggest that the rate be $4 each for single pensioners and $4 per married couple.

Young or middle-aged invalid pensioners are unlikely to have completed the purchase of their home, as so many old age pensioners have done. To continue purchasing may be the wisest course for those who have started to buy a house, for in the long run their weekly payments may well be less than they would pay in rent. Thus, it would be highly desirable for both single and married couple invalid pensioners who are buying a house or flat to receive Supplementary Assistance. For families and individuals likely to be dependent on a pension indefinitely the purchase of a home represents an important investment in future security.

In June 1969 there were in Australia 121,744 invalid pensioners, about 80 per cent of whom were receiving pensions at the standard or single rate of $15 per week. About 14,000 of these received allowances for non-pensioner wives. Fifteen thousand age and invalid pensioners had at least one dependent child.[6] Most of these would be invalid pensioners. We estimate that in 1969-70 it would cost about $24 million a year to implement the increases recommended for invalid pensioners and their dependants. Expenditure of this magnitude would bring most of them up to the poverty line. More than half this increase would go to single invalid pensioners. Because of the relatively small number of non-pensioner wives of invalid pensioners, the proposed increase of $4.00 per week would cost less than $3 million per year. Payment of guardians' allowances to married pensioner parents would cost $3·9 million.

[6] *Social Services 1968-69*, pp. 10-11

Repatriation Department Pensioners

Recipients of Repatriation Department pensions for war-caused disablement are substantially better off than other pensioners. War pensioners, including totally and permanently incapacitated (TPI) and war widow pensioners, are not subject to means test on either income or property. Rates vary according to the degree of disability. A TPI pensioner too disabled to work at all received in 1969 $36 a week for himself, $4.05 for his wife and $1.38 per dependent child. Thus if he had two children his weekly pension income would total $42.81, or $44.31 if child endowment is included.

A war widow is also fortunate in comparison with a civilian widow. She receives $15 for herself and a domestic allowance of $7.50 if she has a dependent child or if she is over fifty years of age or if she is unemployable, plus allowances of $5.40 for her first child and $4.25 for each additional child. A war widow with two children would receive, therefore, $33.65 per week including child endowment, an amount which, when adjusted, would put her above the poverty line. A civilian widow with the same number of children would receive at most only $28.50.

Because both the TPI pension and the war widow pension put the recipients clearly above the poverty line and because there is no restriction on non-pension income, we have not included them in our recommendations.

Ex-servicemen who have served in a theatre of war but whose disablement is not war-caused may receive a service pension, which is broadly comparable to civilian age and invalid pensions. It is paid at the same rates as age and invalid pensions and is means-tested in the same way.

We would urge that all the increases we have recommended for age and invalid pensioners should apply equally to service pensioners. We estimate such increases would cost some $3 million to $4 million.

Lone Women

Those lone women most likely to be in poverty, 73,309 women over sixty, have already been discussed in Chapter 5. No detailed analysis has been made of the circumstances of the remaining 84,479 aged between twenty-one and sixty, but certain points can be noted. Of this number, 35,454 were under thirty years of age. These were unlikely to be in poverty unless they were sick, for even a woman's low wage brings a single person above our austere poverty line.

At first sight it seemed as if $11 \cdot 2$ per cent of those between twenty-one and sixty were in poverty. But more than half of these were women with no income at all of their own but not in need, described in Chapter 4. Those with a low income liable to be in poverty include the pensioners and the sick. There were 12,874 recipients of pensions and benefits, mainly invalid and widows' pensions. Widow pensioners without dependent children (Classes B and C)[7] at the time of our survey received a pension of $10.75 a week and in 1969-70 one of $13.25 a week—less than that of a single old age pensioner. This is clearly insufficient by itself to lift them out of poverty.

We recommend that these widows should receive a pension equal to that of a single old age pensioner which should be raised to $17 a week. At the same time it is important that the work training scheme for widow pensioners begun by the Commonwealth Government in 1968 be energetically extended as many of these women need training before they can find employment.

The Other Poor

In this section we shall consider all those who were poor but did not suffer from any disability. As shown in Table $2 \cdot 7$ the incidence of poverty among those with no disability is very low, only 2 per cent. However, since most Australians are in this no-disability group the actual number of them in poverty seems very large. Further consideration of these cases shows that many of them are like some of the cases discussed in Chapter 4; they had low incomes in the week of the survey but were not in need.

There were seventy-three respondents to the survey who did not fall into any of our disability categories and yet had adjusted incomes below $33, and a further twenty-one whose adjusted incomes were just above the poverty line, between $33 and $36. Included in these are a few of the cases with incomes under $3, described in Chapter 4. We studied each of these questionnaires individually and classified them according to the reason for low income. As most of them had been interviewed with the first questionnaire only, the analysis is less thorough than was possible with the aged. Nevertheless sufficient evidence is available for the main circumstances to be identified. They range from a group of invalid pensioners discussed above, clearly in real need, through some

[7] For a description of the Commonwealth Government classification of widow pensioners see footnote 1, Chapter 6, page 96.

cases where the low income is probably temporary, to others 'on holiday' and not in need at all.

The cases in each category of reason for low income are too few to make valid estimates for each separate category, but some very general conclusions can be drawn concerning the proportion which can be regarded as in need. The seventy-three unweighted cases below the poverty line but having no disability represent more than eleven thousand such income units in Melbourne. In very broad terms our study of each individual case leads us to the conclusion that of this eleven thousand about half are not in need. Most of these low incomes are likely to be only temporary. The other half, who 'may be in need', have incomes which are low now and likely to remain so for some time. We may now look at these two groups in more detail (see Table 9·4).

TABLE 9·4

POOR AND MARGINALLY POOR INCOME UNITS WITH NO DISABILITY

Adjusted income	May be in need	Not in need	Total
Below poverty line	5,358	5,921	11,279
Marginally above poverty line	986	99	1,085
Total	6,344	6,020	12,364

Income units below the poverty line but not in need have been so regarded, as mentioned above, because the cause of their low income appears after examination to be only temporary in that the week of the interview was not typical. Some were unemployed but likely to find work soon and therefore are most appropriately described as changing jobs (six cases). Some had been off work because of sickness or accident which did not appear to be serious (thirteen cases, eleven below the poverty line and two just above it). One man had reduced income because of an industrial dispute. In ten cases 'unpaid holiday' was the explanation for low income in the survey week. Some self-employed people had incomes which were highly variable and low in the survey week. One income unit head was not gainfully occupied. Four were living on savings or supported by family members; this group included some migrants not eligible for pensions. Two cases had been mistakenly recorded as having low incomes, because of interviewing or coding errors.

In the group described as 'may be in need' the reasons for low income are less varied and much more grave. The group includes twelve invalid pensioners below the poverty line and another three only slightly above it. Three income unit heads had been sick for at least three months and were living on the very inadequate sickness benefit. Some of the self-employed were not doing well in their businesses and were below the poverty line. Five cases of people who had retired slightly before they became old enough to qualify for age pensions and a few of those living on savings or supported by their families provided clear evidence of the benefits to be derived from a universal superannuation scheme with some flexible arrangements for early retirement.

Finally there was a large group who normally had low incomes. Most of them were just above the poverty line, but five were below—most of them were families with three dependent children.

One was a family of man, wife and three daughters aged eleven, eight and three. The man worked as a labourer. He never stayed long in any job. In the previous three years he had had at least ten jobs and had never earned more than the basic wage. Their income was $36.10, equivalent to an income of $32 for a family of man, wife and two children. They paid $10.50 per week rent for a flat in good condition. Adjusted income after payment for housing was $22.20. Relatives helped out occasionally.

Any family of this size dependent on a basic-wage income will be poor. The most effective policy measure for these cases is the one outlined for large families in Chapter 7, recommending that child endowment be increased greatly. The recurring crises caused by the head's instability of employment could be mitigated by a relaxation of the waiting period for unemployment benefits.

10 Poverty and Health Expenditure*

'To be poor is bad enough. To be poor and sick is just too much.'
—*a survey respondent*

In this chapter we shall turn from discussion of poverty within particular groups to a problem which confronts the whole community: the need for individuals and families to protect themselves against the cost of illness and to pay for treatment when it is required. Low income often means that even after the most careful planning of medical expenditure, the situation of a poor family remains precarious. The survey gathered evidence on three aspects of health care of the poor—entitlement to free care, insurance cover and expenditure on health care.

Pensioner and Repatriation Health Schemes

Free medical care is provided for many of the poor by the Commonwealth Government. About 16 per cent of all income units in the survey and 46 per cent of those below the poverty line were entitled to free or subsidised care through the pensioner medical service and the Repatriation Department.

Respondents expressed no significant dissatisfaction with the care received through pensioner and repatriation schemes. But their replies did point up a major shortcoming of the pensioner medical service—its failure to cover certain health-related expenses. Social Service Department pensioners such as age, invalid and widow pensioners have to pay for dental and optical treatment, appliances, X-rays, physiotherapy and the like, not all of which are available at reduced cost in hospital out-patient departments.

At the time of the survey the most serious of these expenses was the cost of hearing aids. A number of old people interviewed had spent large sums, usually between one and two hundred dollars, on hearing aids. Several had had to undertake substantial and lengthy hire-purchase commitments in order to pay for them; in one case payments of $2 per week stretched over fifteen months. Fortunately this particular gap has since been closed. Hearing aids are now provided to pensioners and their dependants at substantially reduced cost through the Commonwealth Acoustic Laboratories. An initial hiring fee of $10 covers fitting, repairs and servicing and rental for as long as required.

No similar changes have been made to help pensioners with other health-related expenses not covered by the pensioner medical service. Some pensioners interviewed in the survey had had to pay more than

* This chapter was written by Sheila Shaver.

they could afford for spectacles—sometimes as much as $25. Dental expenses sometimes ran as high as $100 for the year. In some cases costly medicines required by pensioner respondents were not available as pharmaceutical benefits under the National Health Scheme.

Present arrangements are seriously inadequate for pensioners who have insufficient extra resources to meet the incidental costs of health care. Repatriation Department pensioners—war, war widow and service pensioners—are substantially better off with regard to health 'extras' such as dental and optical care, physiotherapy, chiropody, X-rays, and surgical appliances.

Provisions similar to Repatriation Department benefits for health-related expenses should be incorporated into the pensioner medical service for needy age, invalid and civilian widow pensioners.

One pensioner in four was found to be insured for medical benefits, chiefly in order to obtain coverage for private specialist consultations. Free specialist care is available to pensioners only in public hospital out-patient departments. One pensioner in three was insured for hospital benefits, which finance more comfortable hospital accommodation than is available in public wards.

Health Insurance[1]

About 19 per cent of all persons and 22 per cent of all income units did not belong to any health insurance scheme or have pensioner entitlement to free care.[2] This high incidence of non-membership was not spread evenly throughout the community but was heavily concentrated among certain groups such as single males, families on low incomes and, most particularly, among migrants from Mediterranean countries.

[1] Stage I survey data on health insurance have been analysed by R. B. Scotton; some of his findings are summarised in this chapter. Detailed accounts of his methods and findings are published in 'Voluntary Insurance and the Incidence of Hospital Costs', *Australian Economic Papers*, Vol. 6, December 1967; 'Voluntary Health Insurance in Australia', *Australian Economic Review*, 2nd Quarter, 1968; with J. S. Deeble, 'Compulsory Health Insurance in Australia', *Australian Economic Review*, 4th Quarter, 1968; 'Membership of Voluntary Health Insurance', *Economic Record*, Vol. 45, No. 109, March 1969; and with J. S. Deeble, 'The Nimmo Report', *Economic Record*, Vol. 45, No. 110, June 1969. These studies by R. B. Scotton and J. S. Deeble were made while they were Senior Research Fellows of the Institute of Applied Economic and Social Research.

[2] Our evidence showed Melbourne to have a higher proportion of people without any health insurance or pensioner entitlement than is true of Australia as a whole. For Australia, excluding Queensland because of its free hospitals, about 15 per cent of people have no insurance or pensioner cover.

Migration: Migrants face considerable barriers in the form of communication and cultural differences. The complexity of the health insurance system and the difficult choices to be made between competing organisations and various possible levels of hospital cover are baffling to many Australians, and still more confusing to new migrants.

One relatively simple reform which would help migrants considerably would be the provision of explanatory information and application and claim forms in the migrants' own languages. Some health insurance funds already do this and we would like to see it made standard practice.

At the time of the survey waiting periods before membership in health insurance schemes became effective also posed special problems for some migrants. Insurance organisations usually waived the two-month qualifying period for migrants who enrolled in a scheme immediately after arrival in Australia. But many were unable to join until they had found employment and were earning. These were perhaps the least likely of all families to be able to pay if an expensive illness occurred during the waiting period required when they had deferred joining an insurance fund.

The provision to migrants of free membership in a health insurance scheme for a substantial period of time after their arrival in Australia should be regarded simply as one cost of a migration programme.

We therefore recommend that this period be made long enough to see most migrants securely established in jobs, with their family finances stabilised after the upheaval of migration. A period of at least six months would give migrants a realistic opportunity to learn the advantages of membership. Their automatic inclusion in the scheme from the date of their arrival would overcome the problem of qualifying periods. The 1969-70 Budget contained measures in this direction. From January 1970 all migrants became eligible for two months' free hospital and medical cover, on the condition that they had joined an insurance scheme by the end of that time. This is a good beginning but the period seems to us far too short. Other reforms planned for the health insurance system, designed to narrow the gap between health costs and insurance refunds (discussed below) would also help to encourage migrants to continue membership in the scheme after they have joined. Many migrants in the survey had discontinued membership when they found that substantial portions of their expenditure on health treatment were not refunded.

Age and Sex: When migrants were omitted from the analysis, single males of any age, but particularly those aged between twenty-five and forty-four, were the group least often insured. The insured proportion of single women aged twenty-five to sixty-four was quite high and the proportion insured among families with at least one dependent child was also higher than the average for the total population. Since age and sex affect the likelihood of requiring medical and hospital treatment, this is the sort of variation to be expected when insurance is voluntary.

Income: Within groups of income units otherwise similar, it was more common for those on low incomes to be uninsured than for those who were better off. Overall, more than a third of those whose actual (unadjusted) weekly incomes were less than $33 had no insurance, compared with less than a fifth of those whose weekly incomes were $59 or more.[3] Thus there is a serious exposure to risk among those in the community least able to afford hospital and medical fees (see Table 10·1).

TABLE 10·1

HOSPITAL AND MEDICAL INSURANCE AND WEEKLY INCOME

Income Units Entitled to Pensioner and Repatriation Benefits Omitted

	Total number of income units	Percentages of income units with weekly money incomes ($) :						
		0–27	27–33	33–39	39–49	49–59	59 or more	Total
No health insurance	204,583	36·2	35·4	36·8	29·1	22·6	17·4	26·0
Insured for hospital and medical benefits	560,059	61·7	61·5	60·0	68·9	75·0	79·3	71·2
Partial or unknown insurance cover	21,711	2·1	3·0	3·2	2·1	2·3	3·3	2·8
Total *	786,353	100·0	100·0	100·0	100·0	100·0	100·0	100·0

*Any inconsistencies between figures and totals is due to rounding.

A given expenditure on health insurance or health treatment costs families with high incomes less than families with low incomes, because it is deductible from income for tax purposes. A concessional deduction of a given size means a greater tax saving to those on high incomes and therefore paying higher marginal rates of tax, than to those on low incomes, who pay lower marginal rates. For example, a man supporting a wife and two children on a weekly income of $40 might have a tax

[3] Income units eligible for free health care under the pensioner medical service and Repatriation Department scheme have been omitted.

saving of about 14 cents for each dollar spent on health or health insurance. A family of the same size on an income of $80 might save about 30 cents per dollar spent, over twice as much.

'I belonged some time ago but I dropped out because I haven't had enough money to keep the payments up.' This comment, made by a poor Greek migrant, is typical of remarks made by many survey respondents when asked why they had no health insurance. This family had a weekly income of only $42.70, equivalent to an income of $36.90 for a standard family. When their rent of $12 weekly was taken into account they were below the poverty line. In their small income there was little margin for either insurance or the costs of illness.

A deserted wife with two young children reported that she had been unable to keep up her payments for health insurance after her husband left her. She had no income until she began receiving a special benefit. The $11.25 a week benefit, when it came, did not leave enough over to pay for health insurance. She intended to join again as soon as she could afford it.

The Commonwealth Committee of Enquiry into Health Insurance, headed by Mr Justice J. A. Nimmo, confirmed many of the serious criticisms which have been levelled against the voluntary insurance system. The most important of these with regard to poverty concerns the cost of insurance. The report said:

. . . it is clear that there are many families on low incomes who cannot afford health insurance at all or for whom payments of the contributions represent severe hardship. Very often these families are large and the incidence of serious illness is high.[4]

The Committee proposed subsidised membership for families below an income level which is very similar to our poverty line. Its terms of reference were limited to the concept of a voluntary insurance system, and the recommendations arising out of its very thorough investigation represented an attempt to remedy the more obvious inadequacies of the present scheme. The limitation of its terms of reference to the present framework of voluntary insurance left the Committee without authorisation to propose basic structural reform of the system.

In 1970 the government announced its intention to implement most of the major recommendations of the Committee, narrowing the gap

[4] *Health Insurance, Report of the Commonwealth Committee of Enquiry*, Commonwealth Government Printing Office, Canberra, 1969, p. 33

between medical costs and insurance rebates and eliminating medical and hospital insurance tables which provided inadequate cover. These efforts to relate insurance rebates more systematically to health care costs can be expected to be of great benefit to the poor, along with the rest of the community. There should be fewer cases of withdrawal from insurance schemes because of disappointment with refunds.

A major reform, introduced in the 1969-70 Budget, was the establishment of a scheme called Subsidised Medical Services, to provide free or subsidised insurance to three groups: low-income families; sickness, unemployment and special beneficiaries; and migrants during their first two months in Australia. Families whose total weekly income is less than $42.50 (20 cents above the Commonwealth minimum wage for Melbourne and 60 cents below the minimum wage for Sydney) are now allowed to join medical and hospital insurance schemes and have their contributions paid by the Commonwealth; they are entitled to full medical benefits and to hospital benefits up to the value of public ward charges in their State. Those with incomes between $42.50 and $45.50 pay one-third of the cost of insurance, and between $45.50 and $48.50 pay two-thirds. Sickness, unemployment and special beneficiaries receive free insurance of the same value as long as they are on benefits, providing they join an insurance scheme. If they are not insured when first entitled to benefit there is a waiting period of two weeks.

Measures to assist these groups were clearly welcome and should do a great deal to remedy the deficiencies of the insurance system found in our survey.

Two difficulties remain with the scheme for low-income families. Firstly, the legislation is written in terms of specific income figures. Thus each time wages increase it must be amended, and a span of time occurs when the minimum wage is above the cut-off point for free insurance. Secondly, the cut-off points for free insurance do not vary to take account of family size. A family of three persons is treated in the same way as a family of nine. The use of such flat cut-off points means that free insurance is not directed necessarily to the poor, and many who are in poverty are excluded. A large family is likely to be below our austere poverty line on a much higher weekly income than $42.50. In June 1970 a family of a man, wife and four children needed an income of at least $50.82, and a family with six children an income of at least $63.64, to be above the poverty line. A family with one child required only $36.24. Under the present legislation a six-child family whose income was $43, well below the $63.64 required to keep them above the poverty line, would not qualify for free insurance, whereas a one-child family whose income was $41, more than they required to be above the poverty line, would qualify. The Nimmo Committee recommended the use of eligibility criteria which included a sliding scale based on the number of dependent children.

We would recommend that in determining eligibility an allowance be made for family size, for without this neither efficiency nor equity is possible in the provision of free health insurance cover to those most in need. A second and to us preferable means of providing health care for everyone at equitable cost has been proposed by R. B. Scotton and J. S. Deeble.[5] They propose replacement of the present voluntary scheme by universal and compulsory health insurance, which would provide entitlement for everyone, without means test, to cover for public ward hospital care and all medical services. Individual contributions would be collected as a small percentage of taxable income and would be paid, together with a matching Commonwealth subsidy and an appropriate levy on workers' compensation and third-party motor insurers, into a separate health insurance fund administered by a statutory Commonwealth health insurance commission. Income tax concessions, more valuable to the rich than to the poor, would be eliminated. The authors of this plan claim that in addition to its social welfare benefits their scheme would make possible substantial administrative savings.

Large medical and hospital bills can affect a closely balanced low-income budget disastrously. Two survey cases demonstrate this point clearly.

One case was that of a carpenter, his wife and their seven dependent children. Their income of $61.50 was equivalent to an income of $32.20 for the standard family of man, wife and two children. Several members of the family were in poor health. A child born during the year suffered permanent injury at birth and a son of fifteen had died recently of kidney disease. Although the family had some hospital and medical insurance cover, their uncovered hospital bills and medical fees after insurance rebates had been collected amounted to $260. Chemist bills for the year were estimated as at least $300. Their dental care had been received at the Dental Hospital without charge.

An aged Italian migrant brought to Australia by his two sons was worried that he had become a burden to them because of his large health expenses. In the last year he had incurred hospital costs of $280

[5] 'Compulsory Health Insurance for Australia', *Australian Economic Review,* 4th Quarter, 1968

and doctors' fees of $220. He had been advised that he needed at least three additional months of intensive hospital care but was unwilling to go to hospital because of the expense. His family was one of many in the survey which replied that they had no health insurance because they they had not understood they were eligible to join.

These two instances illustrate most effectively the human costs of two serious deficiencies of the voluntary insurance system as it was operating at the time of the survey: not all those who would have benefited were members of an insurance organisation, and insurance coverage was often inadequate, leaving a big gap between health costs and insurance rebates.

Health Expenditure and Use of Health Services[6]

Health expenditure data from Stage II were analysed to discover to what extent the use of health services varied with social and economic characteristics.[7] Use of services was measured in terms of expenditure over the previous twelve months on doctors' services, hospital treatment, dental care, drugs and other pharmaceuticals, and other health care. The characteristics examined were family size, migration from Mediterranean countries, health insurance cover and weekly income. Insurance refunds were not deducted for this purpose, as total expenditure was being used as a measure of utilisation of health care resources.

The measurement of utilisation of services in terms of expenditure is complicated by the fact that not only is there variation in the quantity of services used but also in the price charged for these services. At the lowest level of income, expenditure data tend to understate the use of services, because the cost of services is reduced for some poor patients —by doctors' fee concessions, hospital outpatient treatment, means-testing for public ward admission to public hospitals and private charity. This type of price variation affects doctors' charges and the cost of hospital treatment more than it affects the costs of dental care and drugs. Consequently it is important that care be taken in interpreting low expenditure of some kinds as lower use of services. Statistically our findings are not conclusive. Nevertheless they suggest strongly that health expenditure varies for social and economic reasons.

[6] We are grateful for the assistance of R. B. Scotton in the analysis of this section.
[7] Methods and qualifications are set out in Appendix E.

Large Families

Survey findings reflected the obvious fact that the number of persons in the income unit is an important factor affecting expenditure on doctors' services, dental care and drugs and medicines. A second reason for the larger expenditure of large families is the exclusion of independent children from their parents' income unit. Thus large income units are confined to families in an early phase of the life cycle, when more health services are required.

Migrants

Post-1955 migrants from Greece and Italy were shown to have higher health expenditures of every type than non-migrants. The difference was most dramatic in the case of expenditure on hospital care, on which these migrants spent more than twice as heavily as others. It is well known that migrants use public hospitals as a major source of medical care. Reasons for this may be cost, convenience or availability. Our evidence suggests that they use more of all other health services as well. This higher usage implies that migrants from these countries have greater health needs than the community generally, and is especially surprising considering that they must have been certified as fit in order to have been allowed to immigrate.

Effect of Health Insurance on Health Expenditure

Uninsured income units were found to have lower health expenditures of every kind than those who were members of health insurance schemes. This relationship holds true for both migrants and non-migrants. One explanation for this is inherent in the principle of voluntary insurance: people in poor health or who for other reasons expect to incur substantial medical and hospital expenses are much more likely to insure themselves than people who expect to have few or no health expenses.

There was evidence that Mediterranean migrants sort themselves into insured and uninsured groups in this way much more dramatically than do non-migrants. Non-migrants with medical and hospital insurance spent an average of $36 per annum for hospital care; uninsured non-migrants spent an average of $12. Mediterranean migrants with insurance spent $108, and those without insurance $21. The proportion of migrants who are members of insurance organisations is smaller than for the community as a whole (34 per cent of Mediterranean migrants who arrived in Australia in 1955 or later as compared with 77 per cent of non-migrant income units). It is probable therefore that among migrants the proportion who are in poor health or who require health services constitutes a bigger fraction of the total than would apply for the whole community. This sorting is further reinforced by the practice of Melbourne public maternity hospitals (where a high proportion of migrant babies are born) of persuading their pregnant patients to enrol so that the hospital can collect the Commonwealth benefit paid on behalf of insured patients.

Two other factors also contribute to the difference in expenditures between insured and uninsured income units. One is that once the cost of the insurance has been paid, the cost barrier to seeking treatment is significantly lower for the insured than for the uninsured. The other factor is that the lower expenditure by uninsured patients may not entirely reflect lower use of services, as patients without insurance are more likely to benefit from fee reductions and unpaid accounts.

The lower health expenditures of the uninsured reflect partly the causes and partly the effects of an inadequate mechanism for the finance of personal health care. Those least likely to suffer illness do not insure themselves. If they do require treatment they may be unable to pay for it. Their contributions are not available to the rest of the community and the spreading of risk is incomplete. The costs of fee remission and bad debt must be borne by other patients in the form of higher fees. In the case of Greek and Italian migrants, their health problems, their use of services and their low membership of medical and hospital health insurance schemes constitute a social problem of significant dimensions. This situation is likely to be alleviated somewhat by the new scheme of free insurance for migrants during their first two months in Australia. A wider and more satisfactory solution to the health insurance problems of the whole community is contained in the Deeble and Scotton plan.

Income

Table 10·2 shows health expenditures according to actual income. Unstandardised expenditures are simple averages of the expenditures of each income group. Standardised expenditures have been adjusted to correct for variations between income groups, in family size, in the proportions who are migrants and who belong to health insurance schemes. These adjustments correct for the main sources of variation in health expenditure other than income. Differences in standardised expenditures can thus be attributed mainly to differences in income.

TABLE 10·2

AVERAGE ANNUAL EXPENDITURE ON HEALTH CARE

Weekly income	Doctor		Hospital		Dental		Total*	
	Average	Standard-ised** average	Average	Standard-ised** average	Average	Standard-ised** average	Average	Standard-ised** average
Less than $40	21	35	16	28	9	11	65	103
$40 to less than $50	27	18	61	42	13	13	145	112
$50 to less than $70	48	38	41	33	20	20	154	127
$70 to less than $80	68	55	35	27	33	28	208	170
$80 or more	74	61	61	65	55	51	242	218

*Includes expenditure on drugs and 'other' services.
**Standardised to hold constant all factors related to health expenditure other than weekly income.

Total Health Expenditure: There is a wide range of variation in total health expenditure according to income. Average (unstandardised) expenditure among income units whose income was less than $40 a week, or $2,080 a year, was $65 per year. At the other end of the income scale among the few income units whose incomes exceeded $80 a week or $4,160 a year, expenditures on health averaged $242 for the year. Although the span of variation was reduced sharply when the figures were standardised to hold other influences on expenditure constant, the highest income group was still recorded as spending more than twice as much on health care as the lowest income group.

Doctors' Services: Average (unstandardised) expenditure on doctors' services rises sharply with income. As seen in the first column of Table 10·2, these averages rise slowly up to an income level of $50 per week and very steeply thereafter. The standardised figures show the same relationship, with one major exception: with all other influences held constant—migration, family size and insured status—the lowest income group spent almost twice as much as those in the next highest income range, and only three dollars per year less than those whose incomes are between $50 and $70 per week.

In view of the fact that expenditure data understate the use of health services among the poor, the higher expenditure on doctors' services by the lowest income class is even more dramatic than it at first appears. These expenditures obviously indicate a higher level of utilisation of doctors' services among this group than among those with higher incomes. Some confirmation that low income and chronic ill-health are associated has recently been provided in Britain. One group of the poorest families in that country consists of those out of work who are subject to the wage stop: that is, those who when in regular employment earn less than the 'national minimum' provided by Supplementary Benefits. A recent survey by the Supplementary Benefits Commission discovered that only one-third of these said they were in good health, and 'it was clear that in a good many cases ill-health was an important cause of their low earning capacity'.[8]

Hospital Expenditure: Hospital bills showed no consistent variation with income except that they were significantly higher for families whose weekly incomes were around $90 per week. Some relationship between income and hospital expenditure was to be expected because, although illness or injury requiring hospitalisation occurs relatively randomly through the population, the prices charged vary consistently with income. Means tests for public ward status lower the cost of treatment for low-income patients. More expensive private hospital accommodation is available to those who can pay for it. Our findings of higher average expenditure among families with the highest incomes is probably explained by choice to pay for more comfortable hospital accommodation. It may, however, be only an effect of the small number of families in our sample who had such high incomes.

Dental Expenditure: A clear and strong relationship was observed between expenditure on dental care and income. Expenditures on dental care rise slowly over the lower ranges of income and more steeply in the higher ranges. This almost certainly reflects differences in the quantities and kinds of dental care services received at different income levels, as there is little systematic price variation in dental care. Satisfactory dental care cannot be obtained privately at the low levels of expenditure recorded for the lowest income groups. As public provision of free dental care is limited, these figures suggest very strongly that adequate dental care is mostly limited to those in the higher ranges of income.

[8] A. B. Atkinson, *Poverty in Britain and the Reform of Social Security*, Cambridge University Press, 1969, pp. 88-89

Conclusion

These influences on the level of health expenditure do not act singly in isolation from one another. They all operate at once and their effects are cumulative. A survey case illustrates their joint effect on a low-income family.

The husband and wife, both in their late thirties, had migrated from Italy in 1953. When interviewed, he was working as a labourer and the family was wholly dependent upon his earnings of $48 per week. His wife did not work, as all three children were pre-school age. Although both husband and wife had had little formal education, the interviewer reported that they were very capable managers. They had recently undertaken purchase of an old but solid house in a southern suburb, for which they paid $14 in weekly instalments. They would have been getting along quite well had it not been for their medical expenses.

The oldest child was mentally retarded and also in poor health. During the preceding twelve months she had had a large number of minor illnesses and the degree of her retardation also had to be assessed. She had had a good deal of free diagnosis and treatment as an outpatient of a large public hospital. However, outpatient treatment was not altogether satisfactory to the mother. She had to take all three children with her, for there was no one to look after the younger two. Fares for the four of them were more than $2 each time and a visit to the hospital took up an entire day. Whenever special hospital facilities were not required the parents preferred for sake of convenience to visit the local doctor. The family belonged to a health insurance scheme but their biggest expenditures were on drugs and medicines many of which were not available under the pharmaceutical benefits scheme, and which are not covered by insurance. On the day the interviewer called, prescribed drugs had cost $10. For the year they estimated the cost of drugs alone at $100.

This family's circumstances illustrate the effect of factors associated with both high health expenditure and poverty: larger than average family size, migration and having both a low income and frequent need for doctors' services. Their expenses might easily have been higher, as in the year no one in the family except the retarded child had been ill.

11 Domiciliary Services*

Domiciliary services, strictly defined, are those which are supplied to people at home. But the term is often extended to cover other services which make it possible for those who need help to remain at home rather than be transferred to an institution: services such as elderly citizens' clubs and day care centres.

It is difficult to give a clear picture of domiciliary services in Melbourne because they vary so much from one municipality to another. Most, except home nursing, are run by municipal councils, but some rely entirely on church or other voluntary organisations. In some places the attitude towards regulations is flexible and a real effort is made to meet the needs of all; in others the rules about eligibility are closely adhered to and there is unwillingness to extend the service, frequently because of lack of resources. In general, these services seem to be more widely used in middle class districts than in the inner city areas where there is a higher incidence of poverty.

The survey showed that many people need various kinds of domiciliary help. In some cases this help is already available but is not known to those requiring it, in other cases the services needed are not provided. The second questionnaire asked a series of questions about domiciliary needs: What kind of help was needed on a regular basis and in sickness? Could the people needing it pay for it? How were they cared for in the last period of illness? Did they have adequate social contacts? Questions were also asked about the interviewer's judgment of the use being made of present welfare services and the new services required to meet prevailing needs.

Who Needs Domiciliary Care?

The domiciliary services generally available at present are home nursing, provided by the Royal District Nursing Service and certain hospitals; home help and housekeeper services; elderly citizens' clubs and meals on wheels usually centred in the clubs. These services are generally provided by the municipal councils with subsidies from the State Government. All do valuable work, but the survey showed that there are many people in need who are not using them. The following cases illustrate the important role these services can and do play in helping the aged to maintain a reasonable standard of health and comfort in their own homes.

* This chapter was written by Jean McCaughey.

A married couple aged seventy-six and seventy-seven were very contented with their lot although their health was poor. They had council home help service once a week and could have had it more often if necessary. They had a very good relationship with their doctor and this, combined with their awareness of the help available from the council, enabled them to face their health problems without too great anxiety. They were not poor and could afford to pay for the services received.

A widow aged seventy, a quarter-cast aborigine, was completely crippled with arthritis and was bedridden. She lived with and was cared for by her cousin aged fifty-five. The District Nurse visited her four times a week and could come more often if necessary. This made it possible for her to be cared for at home. She was an invalid pensioner and no charge was made for the District Nurse.

Unfortunately many people with equally acute needs are receiving no help at all. One of the most difficult problems is to find out who the needy are and help them to find ways of meeting their needs. It will be discussed later in the chapter.

The largest group needing domiciliary services is the aged. In Stage II of the survey there were 195 aged income units about whose requirements information was collected. (This includes some cases referred to in paragraph 3 of Appendix C.) Several things stand out clearly from these questionnaires: the wretched conditions in which some old people are living; the lack of knowledge and understanding of social and welfare services; the strong desire of many to remain in their own homes and be independent, and the amount of help and support which many receive from their families and friends.

Adequate domiciliary services can alleviate some of the wretchedness. They can make it possible for old people to remain in their homes and be independent; and they can lighten the burden for the families and make it possible for them to continue to support and care for aged parents and relatives. It is quite clear from the survey that, for most old people, this is the most acceptable form of help.

Of the 195 aged income units recorded in the survey 100 would need help in sickness, and a further nineteen aged married couples would need help if both were ill. Twenty-six income units urgently needed permanent help of some kind, often a combination of services. Of these twenty-six,
—ten needed home help, only three were receiving it;
—seven needed home nursing, only three were receiving it;
—nine needed meals on wheels and none were receiving it.

These people were all in immediate need. The figures suggest that an estimated 5,000 people in Melbourne are in need of domiciliary help and are not receiving it. If we were to ask how many would benefit from outside help, or would need it as a preventive measure, the number would be much greater. The following cases illustrate the needs which were not being met.

A widow aged eighty-one, an age pensioner, rented an unfurnished house in an inner suburb. The house was old and dilapidated and damp. It had no sink or running water in the kitchen, no refrigerator, no hot water service and only an open fire for heat, but she wanted to stay on there in spite of its inadequacies. She suffered from diabetes and her health was poor. She could not climb stairs or use public transport. She needed help with housework and shopping and would have benefited from meals on wheels and a visiting nurse or physiotherapist. She had no family, lived entirely alone and needed help if she was to remain at home.

A man aged seventy-two, an age pensioner, was in poor health and lived alone. He had bronchitis, emphysema and heart disease. He was unable to cook proper meals for himself and he lived on a carbohydrate diet. The interviewer said: 'He is probably progressing to a state of mal-nutrition.' He did not know about meals on wheels. In winter he spent most of his day in bed to keep warm, as the radiator was too expensive. He paid $8 per week rent and had no bathroom, refrigerator or hot water service. He was in need of regular household help, especially meals on wheels if he was to continue to live in his own home.

Another case, already described in Chapter 5, illustrates the will to remain independent shown by the aged and the amount of help and support given by their families.

This was an old lady of eighty-seven, an age pensioner, living alone in an inner suburb. In spite of being deaf and almost blind she managed to do all her own shopping and housework. She was very independent but now realised that she needed help and would probably have agreed to have home help service and meals on wheels. She was greatly supported by her stepson who came for his evening meal every day except at week-ends. He paid all her gas, electricity and fuel bills and did all the repairs about her house. This help lifted her out of poverty and she would have been able to retain her independence and remain in her own home if she had had some outside help.

One hundred and thirty-five aged respondents said that their families (or friends and neighbours) would care for them if they were ill. When allowance is made for all those who have no families, or none within reach, this is a remarkably high figure. It seems probable that good domiciliary services are needed if families are to carry this responsibility without undue strain.

While the aged are the largest group in need of domiciliary services, there are others whose needs have to be considered also: one-parent families; the chronically ill; families with a handicapped or seriously ill member or young children, particularly those in which the mother goes out to work; and the considerable number of families who need help temporarily in a crisis, such as the illness of the mother, the arrival of a new baby, etc. The following case studies illustrate some of these needs.

A divorced woman, aged forty-three, Yugoslav, had come to Australia in 1959. She had arthritis and kidney trouble and the interviewer said: 'Should objectively be regarded as permanently in bed, but just manages.' She had no one to look after her. She urgently needed help with shopping and housework and meals on wheels. She had had no help in the last year. She had had to stop work in November 1967 but did not get the invalid pension until late 1968 because she did not know about it. In the meantime she lived on her small savings.

A woman of twenty-five, who had been separated from her husband for over a year, had two children aged five and three. She was a capable woman, and although she had gone through very difficult times, was caring well for her children. In the last year she had qualified as an Infant Welfare Sister—she had been a nurse before her marriage. She needed help with child-minding services, especially during school holidays when existing services closed down.

An Italian woman of forty-eight had come to Australia in 1954. Her husband had died the year before the interview. She had two children, a daughter of eighteen and a boy of fourteen. Although her health was poor she had worked until two months previously to support the family, because she did not know about the widows' pension. Two months earlier she had become too ill to work and had been in bed ever since. She had not applied for a sickness benefit because she did not know about it. The family was living on the daughter's earnings. The mother was alone in the house all day and would have benefited from home nursing.

These are examples of people who need the help which domiciliary services can supply. There is another group who are not physically infirm but who are lonely and isolated and who need help to make social contacts. Their needs must be considered not only on compassionate grounds but also to prevent deterioration to a more serious condition.

A withdrawn isolated woman of fifty-eight lived alone. She was highly strung and had had several breakdowns. She had left her husband early in marriage because of drunkenness. She had worked most of her life and looked after her money well and saved carefully. She had had a breakdown in May 1965 but did not get a sickness benefit until mid-November, because she did not know about it. She was living on her savings. She appeared very tense and nervous and had few social contacts.

Another case is typical of many who were very suspicious and fearful at the beginning of the interview, but who later became friendly and talkative, and frequently welcomed the interviewer at the second visit.

A widow, aged fifty-five, was living alone. She was in a nervous state and had violent trembling of the face throughout the interview. She was extremely lonely and isolated and needed social contacts such as an elderly citizens' club, but found it too difficult to go alone. At first she was extremely reluctant to give the interview, but by the end she was very friendly and talking freely.

The following cases illustrate the loneliness and isolation of migrants, especially the aged, many of whom do not speak English and will probably never learn it.

A Latvian woman, aged sixty-six, had come to Australia in 1952. She was intelligent and well educated and had read widely in English. She was fearful and apprehensive, unwilling to give information in case it would be used against her. She was very isolated and urgently needed social contacts. She had the age pension, out of which she was paying $5 per week rent. She had a little money in the bank.

A Greek widow of sixty-two had come to Australia in 1962. She was living with her son and his family but they were out all day and she was lonely. She spoke no English and would have liked to meet other Greek women. The interviewer said: 'Elderly migrants like her are lonely and isolated.'

These cases illustrate the widespread problem of loneliness in a big city, a problem which is not one which can easily be solved by welfare services. Perhaps the most hopeful sign of a solution is the growth of many voluntary groups in the community which undertake friendly visiting, and often can provide the social contacts so badly needed.

What is Wrong with the Present Services?

It is clear from the survey that many people have needs which are not being met at present, but finding ways of bringing needs and services together is not a simple matter. However, there are some fairly obvious defects of the present services which limit their effectiveness.

Home Help Service: The standard of service and eligibility varies from one municipality to another. This service is subsidised by the State Health Department and officially it is restricted to the aged, except for short-term emergencies. Some municipalities disregard this restriction and try to meet the needs as they arise, but in many places it is hard to obtain help on a long-term basis. Frequently some personal care is also needed which is outside the scope of the existing service. There is also the problem of the 'too dirty' home which sometimes means that families whose need is acute are unable to get help.

Meals on Wheels: Here again eligibility varies. Some municipalities provide only for the aged and so the younger disabled or chronically ill person, or the family in an emergency, are not eligible. Some areas are without services at all. Some services are run by voluntary groups and receive no subsidy. One such group in a Melbourne middle class suburb has to raise $2,000 a year to finance its service. There is no direct subsidy for meals on wheels services and they depend on the elderly citizens' clubs on which they are based. The clubs receive a subsidy from the State Health Department but this is fixed and is often inadequate for both, so that either the meals service has to be restricted, or more finance provided by the municipal government or voluntary gifts. With a fixed subsidy and rising costs many municipalities are finding it an increasingly expensive service to maintain.[1]

Another disadvantage is the Health Department's insistence that wherever possible the meals must be prepared at, and delivered from, the elderly citizens' clubs, even though a more efficient and cheaper service could sometimes be carried out from the local hospital.

[1] In March 1970 the Delivered Meals Subsidy Bill was introduced in Parliament. This provides a direct subsidy of $1 for every ten meals delivered in the previous calendar year. All voluntary and charitable organisations and local governing bodies which provide meals on wheels are eligible. At the time of writing it was not clear how this Commonwealth subsidy was related to the subsidy already available from the State Health Department.

Home Nursing: Home nursing service is also patchy and varies from area to area. Some hospitals provide home nursing for patients in their particular district—for example, St Vincent's Hospital serves Fitzroy. Others provide home care for certain groups of patients, for example, the Peter McCallum Clinic for cancer patients. The Royal District Nursing Service serves the whole metropolitan area but all cases must be referred by a doctor. It could provide care for more patients—and we know there are many who need it—but many doctors do not refer patients who would benefit from it.

General Limitations of Domiciliary Services

Domiciliary services are neither comprehensive nor well co-ordinated. They are not comprehensive in several ways. Geographically, they do not extend to all districts even in the metropolitan area, much less to rural areas. There is uncertainty about eligibility which is often limited to those with medical certification. At present the services are administered through the State Department of Health and so tend to be regarded as health services. Ideally they should be community services available to all who need them, whether their needs are medical, social or financial. Para-medical services such as physiotherapy and chiropody are frequently not available except from private practitioners. All services are available only in the daytime, not at week-ends, and frequently not during holiday periods.

In many cases social diagnosis is as necessary as medical diagnosis if the real problems are to be identified and needs met. This requires the help of a social worker which frequently is not available. Where it is available, social workers as well as doctors should have the power of referral to all services.

Lack of co-ordination of services is also a serious defect. Each is run from a different centre and there is no framework of communication between them. Communication may sometimes occur on a personal basis, but as far as the organisation is concerned it is quite fortuitous. The exceptions to this are the municipalities which employ a social worker or welfare officer who does co-ordinate services at the local level. There is considerable evidence in the survey of the lack of co-ordination and even where a family has one kind of domiciliary help there is no guarantee that other services which are needed will be called in. These cases illustrate this point.

A husband and wife both sixty-five, lived in an outer suburb. The husband was bedridden and the wife suffered from an acute nervous disorder. The District Nurse called each day to attend to the husband, but they urgently needed home help as the wife was quite unable to cope. The doctor said the wife's condition was aggravated by home conditions, but no one had suggested home help to them.

A widow aged seventy lived alone in an old house. In winter she had bronchitis almost continually. When she was able she went to the elderly citizens' club for her midday meal, yet when she had a long period of sickness she did not receive meals on wheels which would have helped her greatly.

The seriousness of this generally unsatisfactory state of domiciliary services is increased by other factors. There is a shortage of all kinds of accommodation for the aged, including those who need some care. Old people often have to wait for years before they can be accommodated, and in spite of the efforts of the Housing Commission and voluntary agencies the situation is steadily getting worse. In this waiting period their condition can deteriorate rapidly if help is not available.

Facilities are equally inadequate for the frail aged and the chronically sick who need hospital care. Waiting lists for hospitals and nursing homes are lengthening. This growing pressure on hospital and medical services, and their soaring costs, are compelling those concerned with welfare to look for alternatives to institutional care for as many people as possible.

An effective network of domiciliary services could relieve the hospitals by enabling people to be cared for much longer in their homes. Hospitals could strengthen domiciliary services by providing day care centres, specialised clinics and para-medical services such as physiotherapy and occupational therapy. Already some hospitals make laundry and kitchen facilities available at an economic price.

It is sometimes advocated that domiciliary services should be attached to hospitals, but there are powerful arguments also for community based services. In Newcastle NSW, a comprehensive home care service has been developed, based on the Royal Newcastle Hospital. In South Australia, pilot projects are being worked out for rural and metropolitan areas, one of which is centred in an elderly citizens' club. Whether the services are hospital or community based, close co-operation between hospital and municipal welfare services is essential.

Two important developments give grounds for hope that a much better network of services will be evolved. These are the developments of locally based welfare services, and the Commonwealth offer in May

1969 of substantial aid to the States for the provision of comprehensive services of home care for the aged.

The Development of Locally Based Welfare Services

In the past six years there has been a rapidly growing concern for community welfare and a realisation that this cannot be left entirely to Federal and State government departments. This concern has shown itself in the increasing readiness of municipal councils to take responsibility for providing welfare services such as home help and elderly citizens' clubs and in the growth of voluntary groups willing to devote time and energy to meeting the needs of their own community.

In Victoria twenty-one municipalities or shires now employ a social worker or welfare officer, and a further twenty are considering such an appointment. South Melbourne, an inner suburban municipality of 30,000 inhabitants, provides a good example of what can be done. The municipal council has had a social worker on the staff for over twenty years and now has an established social work department. This has enabled the municipality to cope with the considerable social problems associated with large scale Housing Commission development, a big influx of migrants (especially Greeks) and a high proportion of old people—15 per cent of the population is of pensionable age. The Annual Report of South Melbourne's Social Work Department for the year ending 30 September 1968 states: 'While many agencies, both voluntary and statutory, provide a variety of forms of assistance, the help is mostly fragmented. The Council's social workers, being close to the person in trouble are able to co-ordinate the available resources to meet the needs of the individual.' Many municipal councils now recognise the importance of this kind of work.

Parallel with these developments has been the growing awareness of the responsibility of the ordinary citizen in social welfare, leading to the formation of many voluntary groups to supplement the established voluntary organisations like Rotary and Red Cross. These groups are doing an excellent job running advisory and information bureaux and community aid centres. The following are examples of this kind of activity, and many more could be given.

Knox, a semi-rural municipality of 49,000 people on the edge of Melbourne, has over 200 volunteers mobilised in groups to undertake a wide variety of services such as child-minding, visiting the aged and the housebound, providing transport and gardening. Much of the effectiveness of this centre depends upon a capable welfare officer employed by the municipal council.

In Box Hill, a middle class suburb of 60,000 inhabitants, a group of people from the churches met together in 1966 to consider the needs of their community. They decided to organise an advisory and referral centre where anyone with a problem could seek help and advice. In the first year they had 985 enquiries, 191 of which were concerned with personal and family problems. To have got such a centre going and to have enlisted and trained eighty-three active voluntary workers is a considerable achievement. This group has clearly demonstrated the need for such a centre, and they now need a full-time trained worker to supplement and direct the work of volunteers. The municipal council has provided facilities for them at the Town Hall and it is hoped they will support the centre further by employing a municipal social worker.

The widespread interest in community based welfare services is reflected in the fact that early in 1969 the Victorian Council of Social Service was in consultation with twenty-five municipal councils and fifty-four civic groups and welfare organisations about the establishment of these programmes. The Council now has a trained and experienced social worker on its staff to maintain contact with these groups and assist in their development.

The Commonwealth Offer of Finance for Domiciliary Services

With all this ferment in the local community, the Commonwealth offer of substantial aid to the States on a dollar for dollar basis for the establishment of a programme of home care for the aged is timely.

The States Grants (Home Care) Act, 1969, offers financial assistance for (i) the provision of home care services and (ii) the provision of welfare services associated with senior citizens' centres, including half the salary of a welfare officer. The offer recognises the importance of community-based welfare services. Announcing it in Parliament,[2] the Minister for Health said:

> The Government recognises the importance of community participation in the proposed home care programme, and therefore wants to see the State Governments play their rightful part, the municipalities play theirs and, perhaps most importantly of all, the voluntary agencies and groups bring their enthusiasm and experience into the programme.

[2] *Commonwealth Parliamentary Debates*, House of Representatives, 26 February, 1969, p. 161

This offer promises a break-through in the provision of better domiciliary services centred in the local community. It is a new thing for the
Commonwealth government to provide assistance to the States and
municipalities for such services. In an article in the March 1969
Council Newsletter of the Victorian Council of Social Service, the Minister said, 'I would point out that the Commonwealth Government has no
direct constitutional power for what we are proposing to do. This is a
case where the Commonwealth Government has chosen to initiate action
by means of grants to and through the State Governments.'

This initiative should be welcomed, but there are many difficulties to
be overcome, not least the problem of Commonwealth-State financial
relationships. At the time of writing all the States except Victoria had
accepted on varying terms the Commonwealth offer. It would be unfortunate if this opportunity to provide better domiciliary services were lost
because of failure on the part of the Victorian and Commonwealth
governments to agree on the financial arrangements.

Financial considerations apart, the legislation has some serious defects.
The services are to be provided 'wholly or mainly for aged persons' and
the subsidised welfare officers are to be attached to senior citizens'
centres. Many people in the community besides the aged are in need of
help, domiciliary and otherwise. But will a deserted wife left with the
care of young children seek help at an elderly citizens' club; or the family
with personal problems; or migrants unable to understand social and
welfare services? Many of the cases presented in this chapter show situations of acute need close to break-down point. It is to be hoped that help
will be made available at a much earlier stage to prevent break-down and
that it will be made available to all in need.

Such a centre providing widespread help would be best located at the
Town Hall or municipal offices. This would probably also ensure a better
use of trained social workers or welfare officers, who would be responsible for the direction and co-ordination of the whole municipal welfare
programme, including senior citizens' centres.

It is to be hoped that the Victorian government will make a sub-
mission on the form of its participation in the Commonwealth home care
programme, and that its proposals will enable these services to become
more comprehensive and effective. More evaluation of present programmes is needed, and more research into the structure and function
of locally based welfare services and their relationship to municipal
and regional structures. Perhaps this evaluation could be done most
effectively by setting up an advisory committee on domiciliary services

to consult with the relevant government departments, local governing bodies and voluntary organisations and to report to the government. Such a committee has been established in South Australia and is preparing pilot projects for their participation in the Commonwealth programme, as described above.

A detailed analysis of the present situation, and proposals for the development of domiciliary services have been prepared by a special committee of the Victorian Council of Social Service and were submitted to the Commonwealth Minister for Health late in 1969.

How can a Comprehensive and Co-ordinated Service be Provided?

In the present fragmented stage of domiciliary services a properly co-ordinated scheme will not be easy to achieve. The provision of the services now involves several different departments of Commonwealth and State governments, municipal councils and many voluntary groups and organisations. In the article in the March 1969 *Council Newsletter* of the Victorian Council of Social Service mentioned above the Minister said:

We have in this country a very complex interlacing of health and welfare services provided through three main channels—the Commonwealth government, the State governments and their local authorities and through voluntary community groups. There are very sound reasons why the pattern has evolved in this way and I want to emphasise that the Commonwealth has no ambitions to disturb this pattern.

It may be rather optimistic to describe the present picture as a pattern. It looks more like a muddle and the Minister's unwillingness to interfere with its complexities is understandable. But it seems doubtful whether a comprehensive and co-ordinated service can be achieved with the present structure. The appointment of municipal social workers and welfare officers should certainly help, but it cannot be regarded as a panacea for all present ills. Proper lines of communication have to be worked out centrally as well as locally so that hospitals and domiciliary services, doctors, social workers, welfare officers and voluntary groups can all work together for the greatest possible benefit of the whole community.

The organisation of this co-ordinated network of services will not be easy, nor will the financing of such a scheme be a simple matter. A truly comprehensive network of domiciliary services can not be achieved cheaply. Certainly it will be less expensive than caring for people in institutions, but it will be costly and it is reassuring to find that this is being recognised by the Commonwealth government. No domiciliary services at present are comprehensive. They operate only from Monday to Friday, and some close down at holiday times. They are only available from 9 a.m. to 5 p.m.—a serious limitation if they are to provide an alternative to institutional care.

Another problem about financing these services is that many of the municipalities most needing help are least able to pay for it. It will be necessary to work out a scale of subsidies or grants which will enable the poorer municipalities to claim more funds to provide the services needed. There are statistical criteria available on which such a distribution of funds could be based; a grants commission could be established to study and apply them.

The success of the programme also depends on the availability of a considerable number of social workers and welfare officers. In his article in the Victorian Council of Social Service *Newsletter* referred to above the Minister went on to say, 'These centres would need to employ welfare officers to work for the development, co-ordination and continuing provision of the most appropriate services. . . . The success of the centres would naturally depend very much on the human qualities of the people appointed to them. They would, I think, need to be qualified social workers or people with equivalent qualifications or experience.'

Such trained workers are in short supply and if this programme were to be initiated many more would be needed, but how or where they are to be trained is far from clear. It is timely that the Australian Council of Social Service, the Association of Teachers in Schools of Social Work, and the Australian Association of Social Workers have set up a joint committee to prepare a report on Social Welfare Education in Australia.

At the present time the only training for social workers in Victoria is a course for the Diploma of Social Studies in the University of Melbourne, which takes three or four years. Numbers are so strictly limited by the quota system that they can only accept a proportion of graduates who wish to enrol for the Diploma. At the undergraduate stage, the level of entry for the combined course in Arts and Social Studies is very high indeed. Perhaps in this new kind of welfare service there is room for a greater diversity of workers. Fully trained social workers will continue to be key personnel in any social welfare system, but there will

be many administrative jobs for which a shorter training in social administration and community organisation might be adequate. In 1970 the Victorian Social Welfare Training Institute initiated a one-year course for
welfare workers. The enlisting and training of workers needs to be investigated and pursued energetically if the scheme is not to be held up for
want of trained staff.

Training for volunteers is also needed. Since 1967 the Victorian Council of Social Service and the Mental Health Authority have jointly
offered a course for volunteers working in Citizens Advice Bureaux and
the Personal Emergency Service. This provides a weekly three-hour
training session for fourteen weeks. The Cairnmillar Institute[3] also
offers short training courses for volunteers in citizens' advisory services,
and several centres have used them, sometimes supplemented by the
Mental Health Course. These courses offer an introduction to the skills
of interviewing and enable those concerned to have enough understanding of the problems brought to them to be able to refer them to
the appropriate centre. Such training has the additional advantage of
providing some screening of voluntary workers, so that those who are
not suitable for personal interviewing can be directed into some other
form of service.

The increase of voluntary workers has created an increased demand
for training. In response, the Institute of Training for Community Service came into being in 1969. Its first objective will be to train volunteers
and in June 1970 it will take over the training course previously run by
the Mental Health Authority and the Victorian Council of Social Service. Its future development is still tentative, and depends to some extent
on the financial support it can command.

Availability of Domiciliary Services

We must now return to the problem mentioned at the beginning of this
chapter—that of finding out who the needy are and helping them to find
ways of meeting their needs. If most people lived in villages or small
towns this would be relatively easy, but in Australia most seem destined
to live in larger and larger cities, in which it is all too easy for those in
trouble to be left to struggle along on their own. A great number of
social and welfare agencies offer a wide variety of services; at the same

[3] The Cairnmillar Institute is a community mental health organisation concerned
with preventive as well as therapeutic work. It offers counselling and psycho-
logical services, courses in human relations and community affairs. It is community based and is entirely self-supporting financially.

time there is a great deal of human need, and it is often a matter of chance if the two meet. How can domiciliary and other help be made so easily available that the greatest number of people in need will be reached?

Locally based welfare centres along the lines already described should help. Many who would find it difficult to travel into the city and approach a large Commonwealth or State organisation might be willing to go to a local centre. Friends or neighbours concerned about some needy family would have a place and a person to whom they could be referred. Volunteers willing to give their time could be directed to those who need their help. In fact, these centres could become a focus of community responsibility for people in need.

More should be done about advertising social welfare services. Perhaps the most striking fact which emerges from the questionnaires in Stage II of the survey was the widespread ignorance about these services. This is particularly true of migrants but it applies to the Australian-born as well. There is also considerable ignorance, especially among widows and the sick, about Commonwealth social service pensions and benefits. We had many cases in the survey where people did not receive the statutory benefits to which they were entitled because they did not know about them. Several of these have already been quoted, and only one more will be added.

A widow, aged fifty-three, came to Australia from Malta in 1960. Her husband died in 1964 and the family were in extreme poverty. They even had trouble finding the money for the funeral. She did not apply for the widows' pension because she did not know about it. They attended their local church regularly, but no one had suggested that she should apply for a pension. Her two daughters, aged seventeen and fifteen, had to leave school to support the family. Quite by chance they found out about the pension several months later.

It is quite unacceptable that invalids and widows should live on their savings because they do not know about the statutory benefits to which they are entitled. More publicity is needed. We therefore welcomed the large advertisements which appeared in the press after the 1969 Budget, setting out new pension rates and entitlements and telling people how to apply. This should be done regularly.

Application forms for benefits need to be simplified and written in plain English. An experienced social worker confessed that she found the widows' pension application form too difficult to tackle, so it is not surprising that it is bewildering to most widows. Other application forms and information sheets are similarly complicated and incomprehensible. Another discouraging practice for migrants is that they are printed only in English.

Perhaps the change which is most needed to make domiciliary services readily available is a change in the attitudes of those who provide them and of those for whom they are provided. On one side there is a reluctance to publicise them widely and make them open to all, in case the demand should increase and swamp the resources available to meet it. In fact, there is a good deal of evidence that in some areas the services are not being fully used at present. Many of the cases of urgent need quoted existed in areas where the services were available, but clearly not available enough. It is also a fact that, although the numbers of old people in the Melbourne city area is increasing, fewer meals on wheels are being served. If the Commonwealth offer to help to provide greatly expanded services is accepted, it is to be hoped that a greatly increasing demand would be met.

On the side of those who need the services, especially the aged, there is evidence in the survey of some reluctance to use them. When asked if they would need help with meals, shopping or housework, respondents frequently answered: 'I would rather manage on my own.' One old lady of seventy-seven, who did all the housekeeping for herself and two unmarried sons, when asked: 'Would you need help in sickness?' replied: 'I hope not, I never have and I hope I never will.' Others said they would not like a strange person coming into the house. This attitude may be much more true of old people than of those who are now middle-aged and are more accustomed to their privacy being invaded in various ways. Even in the case of the aged it can often be overcome by patience and tact. In the survey, interviewers often found that old people who initially were very reluctant to be interviewed, in the end were willing to talk freely and even welcomed them back if a second visit were necessary.

The reluctance to use the services frequently springs from a strong desire of many to be quite independent, and also from a feeling that these services are a sort of hand-out to the poor. The limitation of eligibility encourages this attitude. There is some feeling that you must prove you are a deserving case. One old lady in the survey, an age pensioner living alone, had applied for free blankets, in a much publicised local relief scheme. When the social worker questioned her about her income to make sure she was eligible, her pride was so offended that she flatly refused to have them, saying: 'there are probably many who are worse off than I am.'

How can this reluctance to accept help be overcome? The services need to be widely advertised and attractively presented. People have to know not only that they exist, but that they would be good for *them*, which is surely the aim of all advertising.

They could be made available to all in need, regardless of age or income. Domiciliary services might be as valuable to those who can afford to pay for them as to those who cannot. Then there need be no more social stigma about accepting them than about having one's rubbish collected. Far from being hand-outs to the poor who could prove they were eligible, domiciliary services could offer possibilities of free choice to those unable to care for themselves. This sort of service is provided in a centre for old people in Oegstgeest, Holland, visited by one of the directors of this survey. The warden there said: 'The aged want to use this centre like a bank; to choose what they want from the services available, not to be treated as cases.'

Some of the case studies described earlier—and there were many more in the survey—showed old people clinging to homes which were lacking in the bare essentials of comfort. If they wish to move into elderly citizens' flats or homes, these should be available. If they want to live in squalor and look after themselves, they should be allowed to do so. But domiciliary services could give them the choice of being cared for in their own homes with the minimal comfort of at least one hot meal a day, a clean house and a visiting nurse if necessary.

Many social workers think that our welfare services should be more 'consumer-oriented' and provide more opportunities for consumer participation. It is too often true that planners and providers make decisions about the nature and scope of services without reference to the wishes of the consumer. He is treated as a dependant who has no say in the matter. Welfare services might be more closely related to needs and more effective if there were better lines of communication. As the Seebohm Report[4] says: 'For those it is intended to serve, "effectiveness" implies a service which is accessible and acceptable and which meets the need promptly, that is, a service which is as far as possible community based. "Effectiveness" in terms of the service offered implies one which has adequate skills to cope with needs; sufficient manpower to maintain the

---

[4] *Report of the Committee on Local Authority and Allied Personal Social Services*, July 1968, Her Majesty's Stationery Office, London, p. 181

service under all conditions; comprehensive training facilities to provide a progressive and expanding service, and a wide variety of physical resources to support the field workers. "Effectiveness" in terms of democratically controlled local government service implies a service with assured communication between the "consumer" of the service and those responsible for policy and for provision of the necessary resources.'

It will take time to overcome the attitudes inherited from the past, but there is much promise of change in the present concern of many people for the well-being of their own community. There is a growing sense of responsibility for those in need and especially for those who seem unable to fend for themselves.

We must aim to develop the kind of services described in the summary of findings in the Seebohm Report:

A community based and family oriented service, which will be available to all. This will, we believe, reach far beyond the discovery and rescue of social casualties, it will enable the greatest possible number of individuals to act reciprocally, giving and receiving service for the well-being of the whole community.

12 Summary of Findings and Recommendations

The Survey of Living Conditions in Melbourne measured income in relation to the needs of families. It took as a benchmark in 1966 an income of $33 for a man, wife and two children—approximately the total of the basic wage and child endowment. Those who were worse off were described as being below the poverty line. More than 7 per cent of income units were estimated to be below the poverty line, and included in these numbers were more than 42,000 children. In the main survey, information was collected for one particular week's income and for some of this 7 per cent, weekly income figures did not reflect accurately the resources available to meet the family's needs. Some modification had to be made for instances in which income in the week surveyed was abnormally low because of situations which were likely to be temporary and for persons whose low incomes were supplemented by drawing upon assets of substantial value. Still others, although clearly in poverty, were enabled to live at a more satisfactory standard by the generosity of friends and relatives. If we regard these three groups as not in need, we reach a minimum estimate of 4 per cent of income units in need.

Principal Findings

Most of the poor were found to suffer from one or more of the following disabilities: old age, lack of a male breadwinner, a large number of dependent children, recent migration to Australia or prolonged illness. The incidence of poverty was much higher among people in these categories than among those without any of these disabilities.

The Aged

More than 15 per cent of aged income units were below our poverty line when measured in terms of annual income in the second stage of the survey. Because many in this group owned their homes and had relatively small housing costs, the proportion in poverty when housing costs were taken into account was smaller, just below 9 per cent. Some of the aged were also found to have assets of substantial value, and when both housing costs and assets were considered some 6 per cent remained below the very stringently defined poverty line. This estimate regards as not poor those whose low incomes were compensated for by low housing costs; it takes no account of the standard of their accommodation. Some of the aged achieved low housing expenditure by living in substandard housing.

Briefly, those who were in need were mostly single old people who had few resources other than the pension, some pensioners who had to pay more in rent than they could afford, and a few aged migrants not eligible for pensions and entirely dependent on their families for support. Much of the poverty among the aged was not obvious. More than half of the poor were able to live more comfortably than their incomes would imply because they received regular assistance from their families, friends and charitable organisations. There remained more than 2 per cent of aged income units living in chronic economic need.

Fatherless Families

Thirty per cent of women bringing up children alone were found to be in poverty and another 14 per cent were only marginally above the poverty line. The incidence of poverty was higher in this group than in any other group in the survey. Because fatherless families comprised less than 2 per cent of all income units it would cost relatively little to bring them above the poverty line.

Large Families

Among families with at least four dependent children about 8·5 per cent were found to be below the poverty line. Another 14 per cent were very little above. These families were poor or nearly poor not because their incomes were lower but because their needs were greater. Their already difficult situation was frequently aggravated by high housing costs. When housing costs were considered, the number in poverty was even greater: 10 per cent were below the poverty line.

Migrants

The degree of poverty among migrants was found to depend on country of origin and length of residence in Australia. Hardship was concentrated most heavily among Southern Europeans, especially Greeks and Italians who had arrived in Australia after 1954, and least heavily among Dutch and Germans. When rent or house-purchase payments were taken into account, some 23 per cent of Greek householders who had settled in Australia between 1960 and 1966 were poor or marginally poor. There was also significant poverty among recently arrived Italians. Thirty per cent were below the poverty line or only marginally above. The proportions in poverty were almost as high among Greek and Italian householders arriving between 1954 and 1960. British migrants also experienced hardship associated with housing costs. More than 17 per cent of householders who had arrived after 1960 were poor or marginally so. The most important problem faced by many migrants was the high cost both of rented accommodation in their early years in Australia and of buying a home later on.

Unemployment, Sickness and Accident

There was little evidence of poverty caused by long-term unemployment, although some hardship of only short duration was found.

Prolonged illness and serious accident were clearly shown as causes of poverty. In one quarter of all instances in which the head of the income unit had been off work for a substantial period of time because of ill health, the income unit was in need. One invalid pensioner in four was also poor. Those who were receiving an invalid pension or sickness benefit had required medical certification of their inability to work, yet levels of pension and benefit were inadequate to meet the needs of many who had to depend on them.

Health Insurance

The survey showed that health insurance poses particular problems for groups which suffer economic hardship, such as migrants from Southern Europe and low-income families. These people were much less commonly contributors to health insurance schemes than were members of the community as a whole. Poverty was especially frequent among them, and their unpreparedness in the event of expensive illness sometimes brought tragic results. Large families, too, often had large health expenses.

Domiciliary Services

The present circumstances and past experiences of survey respondents showed a need for welfare services which extend beyond income support through pensions. Comprehensive domiciliary services such as housekeeping, the provision of meals on wheels and home nursing would enable many of the aged and handicapped to continue living independently in their own homes. Without help many could not manage alone. Such services could provide a cheaper and more satisfactory alternative to special housing or institutional care. Besides aged and invalid persons there are others in the community who need help in the home, usually at times of crisis. The range and adequacy of services at present available was found to vary greatly from municipality to municipality, and where services existed a serious lack of communication was revealed between providers of care and their potential consumers.

Recommendations

Pensions and Benefits

The disabilities which were associated with poverty—particularly old age, lack of a male head of the income unit, sickness and unemployment —corresponded closely to the criteria upon which Australian social service payments are based. Survey findings have therefore led directly to recommendations concerning the rates of age, invalid and widow pensions and sickness, unemployment and special benefits. From our evidence about poverty among large families we have drawn conclusions about rates of child endowment. Suggestions have also been made regarding housing, health insurance, and domiciliary services. Most of our recommendations concerning social services fit generally within the existing framework and preserve the traditional relationships between categories of pensions and benefits.

At the time of writing four years have passed since the survey was undertaken in the June quarter of 1966. The poverty line then drawn at $33 for a standard family of a man, wife and two children was 54·55 per cent of average weekly earnings per employed male unit in Victoria, which was $60.50. Since we maintain that the living standard of people dependent on pensions should not be allowed to drop in relation to that of the average worker, we have up-dated the poverty line to keep pace with the rise in average earnings. In the June quarter of 1969 these were $73.70. On this basis the poverty line became $40.20 in the June quarter of 1969.

If average earnings continue to rise as we expect by a further 5·4 per cent to $77.68 by the June quarter of 1970, the poverty line will then be about $42.40. This is the figure which will be relevant for the 1970 budget, so we have proposed increases in basic pension rates on this basis.

In 1969 age, invalid and Class A widows' pensions were brought to $15 for a single pensioner and $26.50 for a married couple both eligible for a pension. At those levels the single pensioner with no other income was below the poverty line and the married couple above. We believe that at that time the single rate should have been $16. By mid-1970 it will have to be raised to $17 if single pensioners without additional resources are to be near the poverty line. If pensions are to maintain their existing relationship to average earnings the married rate should rise correspondingly to $28.

Survey data showed the needs of widows who have no dependent children to be at least as great as the needs of single age pensioners, and this finding has led us to favour a move away from the existing practice of paying pensions to such widows at lower rates than those applying to single age pensioners.

Similarly the needs of a married couple are the same, irrespective of whether one is a pensioner and one not, or both are pensioners. In cases where the husband is an age or invalid pensioner but his wife is not entitled to a pension, the wife's allowance is much too small. We have recommended that in such cases the total payment to a pensioner and his non-pensioner wife should be equal to the total paid to a couple both of whom are pensioners.

A widow or a single age or invalid pensioner who has at least one dependent child receives at present a guardians' allowance (or mothers' allowance) of $6 if there is a child under six years of age and $4 if all the children are six or over. As children grow older their needs are more likely to increase than to decline, and consequently we believe the guardians' allowance should be brought up to $6 for mothers of older children as well as of young ones. We have also proposed that it be paid to married-couple invalid-pensioner parents. In view of our recommendation for substantial increases in child endowment (summarised below), we have not argued for increases in the pension allowances for children of age, invalid and widow pensioners.

Single pensioners who have little or no other income and who pay rent or board receive Supplementary Assistance, currently paid at the rate of $2 a week. Survey evidence proved this amount to be no longer adequate as a significant contribution to the rents paid by many pensioners. We have recommended $4 as a more realistic figure. Supplementary Assistance should also be extended to married couples in the same circumstances, at the rate of $4 per couple. We also favour financial assistance from the Commonwealth government to enable the practice of some local councils of deferring rates owed by needy pensioners owning their homes to be extended.

Sickness, unemployment and special benefits have always been paid at very low rates in Australia. Many such beneficiaries in the survey, especially those who were sick, were found to be in acute need and consequently we have thought it important that these benefits be substantially increased. They should be brought high enough to provide an income floor no lower than 80 per cent of the poverty line. To accomplish this the basic benefit should be $17 a week and the allowance for a dependent spouse $11. Furthermore, benefits should cover the whole period without earnings. The restrictive means tests applied to these benefits ensure that these large increases will go only to those in need.

Child Endowment

To supplement the earnings of heads of large families substantial increases in child endowment are needed, especially for third, fourth and subsequent children. Therefore we have recommended that child endowment be raised to $3.50 for third and $4.50 per week for fourth and subsequent children. Such an increase would bring the incomes of most poor large families up to the poverty line. Most of this increase could be financed by abolishing concessional deductions for children in the calculation of taxable income. If this were done it would be appropriate to increase child endowment rates for first and second children as well. The following schedule of weekly child endowment rates for children under 16 years would result.

First child	$1.00
Second child	1.50
Third child	3.50
Fourth and subsequent children	4.50

Costs of Main Recommendations

Had our main recommendations—those already summarised in this chapter—been put into effect for the year 1968-69 we estimate that they would have cost about $100 million, as shown in Table 12·1. The estimates, although necessarily approximate, show that the increased expenditure needed is not unduly great.

If child endowment were increased without removal of concessional deductions for children the increased expenditure recommended would be $108 million instead of $19 million, an increase of 58 per cent in actual expenditure on child endowment. In this case the total cost of our proposals would be $189 million.

Our proposals would have raised total Commonwealth expenditure on cash social benefits in 1968-69 from 5·3 per cent of gross national product to 5·7 per cent (6·0 per cent if concessional deductions for children were not removed)—a moderate level in comparison with the average 5·9 per cent per annum spent in the four years 1960-61 to 1963-64.

The modest cost of our proposals is explained partly by the fact that they are designed to raise only to an austere poverty line the relatively small number of people below that line; and partly by the fact that the proposals are designed to concentrate extra expenditure as far as possible on subgroups of people identified as likely to be in poverty.

TABLE 12·1

ESTIMATED COST OF MAIN RECOMMENDATIONS IF IMPLEMENTED IN 1968-69

Recommendations for:	Actual expenditure in 1968-69	Estimated additional expenditures recommended	
	$ million	$ million	%
Age pensions*	476	42	9
Invalid pensions	82	18	22
Widows' pensions	69	13	19
Unemployment, sickness and special benefits	17	8	47
Child endowment**	193	19	10
Total	837	100	12

*Expenditures on age and invalid pensions have been broken down according to the number of pensioners in each category.
**Assuming withdrawal of concessional deductions for children in assessment of taxable income. With no change in these deductions the estimated cost of our recommended increases is $108 million, bringing the total estimated cost of all our main proposals to $189 million.

Costs of Subsidiary Recommendations

There are a number of other proposals which have been made in previous chapters which are not included in Table 12·1. Some of them, such as the increased endowment to tertiary student children, are not specifically directed to assisting those discovered to be below the poverty line. Other examples are recommendations concerning domiciliary care, assistance to elderly migrants and Subsidised Medical Services. It has not been possible to make a detailed estimate of the cost of all of these.

Housing

The Victorian Housing Commission has done much to provide low-cost housing for purchase and rental. But still more low-cost housing is needed, for there remain many who must pay more for housing than they can afford. What is needed is both more low-rent housing and greater availability of low-interest loans on old houses. We have also suggested that it might be possible for houses in areas to be redeveloped in the distant future to be bought by housing authorities as they become available and let at low rents until redevelopment actually takes place.

Health Insurance and Domiciliary Care

A system of universal and compulsory health insurance financed as a small percentage of income tax would provide protection from the expense of sickness to everyone, with an equitable distribution of cost. We have regarded this as the most desirable change; however we have also made secondary recommendations which fit within the present framework of voluntary insurance. Both migrants who have been less than two months in Australia and low-income families have recently become entitled to free membership in health insurance schemes. These measures are too narrow. Migrants need to be insured at no cost for at least six months. The cut-off point in income for determining the eligibility of low-income families for free insurance should be both higher than the $42.50 (approximately the Commonwealth minimum wage for Melbourne) at which it is now fixed, and made flexible to take account of the number of persons in the family.

If domiciliary services are to be effective they must be comprehensive and available in all districts at all times. Co-ordination of services must be well planned, so that those who need them receive immediately the kind of help which is most appropriate. These services must also be well publicised; deficiencies in communication constitute a fundamental problem at the present time, not only in the realm of domiciliary services but throughout the whole range of social services.

Appendix A

The Questionnaire used for Stage I

CONFIDENTIAL

UNIVERSITY OF MELBOURNE

INSTITUTE OF APPLIED ECONOMIC RESEARCH

SURVEY OF LIVING

CONDITIONS IN MELBOURNE

	Date
Interviewed	
Checked	
Edited	
Coded	
Punched	

-2-

1   Could you tell me what kind   1   detached house   4   flat
     of accommodation you have?   2   semi-detached house   5   room/rooms
                                      3   terrace house   6   other (specify)

2   We are interested in the size
     of families and households.
     Could you tell me who normally
     lives here with you?

     Household   1   ....

                       2   ....

                       3   ....

                       4   ....

                       5   ....

3   How many rooms do you have?

	living & dining	kitchen	bedrooms
Number	....	....	....

4   *ASK ONLY IF MORE THAN 1 HOUSEHOLD LISTED IN Q2*

Are any of the rooms you have
just mentioned solely used by
anyone else? *(i.e. another*
household)

	living & dining	kitchen	bedrooms
Number	....	....	....

5   *ASK ONLY IF MORE THAN 1 HOUSEHOLD LISTED IN Q2*

Are any of the rooms you have
just mentioned *(i.e. in Q3)* shared
with anyone else?
(i.e. another household)

	living & dining	kitchen	bedrooms
Number shared	....	....	....
Shared with	....	....	....

Do you *(i.e. your household)* share
any of the following with anyone
else? *(i.e. another household).*

	bath or shower	lavatory	laundry facilities
Shared with	....	....	....

-3-

6	A	Do you own this house or are you renting it?	Own	Renting	-0 Unknown
					1 Owner - no mortgage
	B	*IF OWN* Do you own it outright or are you making any payments on it?	Outright	Buying	2 Owner - with mortgage 3 Buyer - H.C. 4 Buyer - not H.C. 5 Tenant U.H.C.w/o subs.
	C	*IF OUTRIGHT* Does anyone have a mortgage on the property?	Yes	No	6 Tenant U.H.C. with subs. 7 Tenant U. not H.C. 8 Tenant F 9 Tenant Rent Free
	D	*IF BUYING OR RENTING* Are you buying (or renting) from the Housing Commission?	Yes	No	
	E	*IF BUYING* How much do you pay each week in instalments?	....		
	F	*IF RENTING* How much rent do you pay each week?	....		
		Is this furnished or unfurnished?	Furnished	Unfurnished	
	G	*IF RENTING FROM HOUSING COMMISSION* Is your rent subsidised?	Yes	No	
		IF YES How much per week is this subsidy?	....		

7   How many places have you lived in
during the last two years?   ....

Dwelling Number			Household Number	C.D. Number				Interviewer	Number of Visits	Number of Contacts	Length of Interview	Number of IU's in Household	No. of Persons in Household	Type of Accommodation	Number of Rooms - Own	No. of Rooms - Shared	No. of Outside Sharers	Shared Kitchen	Shared Facilities	Amount of Rent		Occupancy of Household	Number of Dwellings
1	2	3	4	5	6	7	8	9	10	11	12	13	14	15	16	17	18	19	20	21	22	23	24	25	26	27	28

↑

Household Data Only - Punch on this Number of Cards

-4-

8　Would you mind giving me some details about yourself and the other people who live here?

RECORD ANSWERS IN A TO E FOR ALL PERSONS　　　　　*ASK F TO H OF ALL PERSONS WHO*
　　　　　　　　　　　　　　　　　　　　　　　　　　　　WORK FULL OR PART TIME

		A	B	C	D	E	F	G	H
IU Number	Person Number	RELATIONSHIP TO HOUSEHOLDER	AGE	MARITAL STATUS	COUNTRY OF BIRTH	EMPLOYMENT	WORK STATUS	OCCUPATION	TIME OFF DURING PAST YEAR
		Wife W Son S Daughter D Mother M Father F Brother BR Sister SI Boarder m/f B Other specify O Respondent X		Single S Married M Widowed W Divorced D Separated P	If born outside Australia - state year of arrival	Works Full Time F Works Part Time P At Home H Tertiary Student T School Pupil S Infant - pre school I	Employs Others E Works on Own O Account Works for Wage W or Salary Helps without H Payment	Describe in detail	Yes　　No IF YES How many weeks? Why? Unemployed U Changing Jobs C Industrial Dispute D Temporarily Laid Off T Accident A Sick S Family Responsibility F Other specify O
	1	Householder m/f							
	2								
	3								
	4								
	5								
	6								
	7								
	8								
	9								
	10								
	11								
	12								
	13								
	14								

9 Could you tell me something about your family income? -5-

RECORD ANSWER FOR ALL PERSONS	ASK B OF EACH PERSON RECORDING INCOME				
		ASK C TO E OF ALL PERSONS WHO WORK FULL OR PART TIME			

IU Number	Person Number	A	B	C	D	E	F
		Could you tell me which of the people we have just listed have no income of any kind of their own?	Could you tell me, of each person or married couple, whether their total income last week was more or less than $80? (after tax)	Did last week's earnings include payments over and above standard pay because of overtime or a second job?	IF YES IN C In how many weeks over the past year have you received extra earnings because of overtime and/or second job?	IF NO IN C Did you receive less than your standard pay last week?	TO ALL What do you usually earn for a standard working week? i.e. without overtime and/or second job after tax
		No Yes	More Less Record answer for all persons with income	Yes No IF YES How much? (i) Overtime (ii) Second Job		Yes No IF YES Why? Unemployed U Changing Jobs C Industrial Dispute D Temporarily Laid Off T Accident A Sick S Family Responsibility P Other specify O	
	1						
	2						
	3						
	4						
	5						
	6						
	7						
	8						
	9						
	10						
	11						
	12						
	13						
	14						

I.U. No.	Household Composition	IU Number	Relation of IU to Householder	IU Head	Respondent	No. of Dep. Children in IU	Indep. Single Child in H'hold.	Age of IU Head	Age of Wife of I.U. Head	Age and Sex of Dependent Children						Marital Status of IU Head	Origin of IU Head	Year of Arrival of IU Head	Employment of IU Head	Employment of Wife	Work Status of IU Head	Occupation of IU Head	Time Off Last Year - IU Head	Reasons for Time Off	Income Level of IU	Extra Work of IU Head	Earnings from Overtime and/or Second Job	Extra Work Last Year	Reduced Earnings of IU Head	Standard Earnings of IU Head
										M less than 6 years	F less than 6 years	M 6-14 years	F 6-14 years	M 15 years & over	F 15 years & over															
	29	30	31	32	33	34	35	36	37	38	39	40	41	42	43	44	45	46	47	48	49	50	51	52	53	54	55	56	57	58	59	60	61	62	63	64	65	66	67
1	1																														
2	2																														
3	3																														
4	4																														
5	5																														
6	6																														
7	7																														
8	8																														

-6-

ASK 10 ONLY IF ANSWER TO 9B IS 'LESS'

10   Could you give me some more details about your family's income?

		A							B				C
		How much income, after tax, did you have last week from ......?							Do you have any annual income from other sources like ......?				ASK WOMEN WITH ELIGIBLE CHILDREN
IU Number	Person Number	(i) earnings	(ii) social service pension or benefit specify	(iii) super-annuation annuity or private pension	(iv) gross amount from pro-fessional boarders full or b/b record each amount	(v) scholar-ship or student-ship	(vi) other specify	(vii) total	(i) interest. dividends and income from property	(ii) non-weekly earnings	(iii) other probe tax refund specify	(iv) total	How much child endowment do you receive per week?
										DO NOT DEDUCT TAX			
	1												
	2												
	3												
	4												
	5												
	6												
	7												
	8												
	9												
	10												
	11												
	12												
	13												
	14												

	Last Week's Income - I.U. Head				Card Number	Identification			H'ld No.	Last Week's Income of I.U. Head			Last Week's Income - Wife of I.U. Head						Last Week's Income of School Pupil
	Earnings	Pensions	Super-annuation	Boarders		Dwelling Number				Scholar-ship	Other		Earnings	Pension	Super-annuation	Scholar-ship	Other		
I.U No.	68 69 70 71 72 73 74 75 76 77 78 79				80	1 2 3 4		5		6 7 8	9 10 11		12 13 14 15 16 17	18 19 20	21 22 23	24 25 26			27 28 29
1					1														
2					1														
3					1														
4					1														
5					1														
6					1														
7					1														
8					1														

-7-

ASK 11 IF HOUSEHOLD CONTAINS PERSONS OVER 16 YEARS OF WHOM Q10 WAS NOT ASKED

11   A   Apart from *(see 10A(ii)),* whom
             you have already mentioned, is
             there anyone living here who   Yes   No
             receives a social service or
             repatriation pension?

             IF YES

      B   Who receives this pension?   Person Number ......

                                                                         ....

      C   What kind of pension is it?   ....

                                                         ....

I.U. No.	IU Number	Last Week's Child Endowment					Last Week's Amount Paid by Professional Boarders		Type of Board	Last Year's Income - I.U. Head										Last Year's Income - Wife of I.U. Head										Pensioner Head of IU	Pensioner Wife of IU Head
										Interest Dividends		Earnings			Other			Interest Dividends		Earnings			Other				
	30	31	32	33	34	35	36	37	38	39	40	41	42	43	44	45	46	47	48	49	50	51	52	53	54	55	56	57	58	59	60	61	62	63
1	1																																	
2	2																																	
3	3																																	
4	4																																	
5	5																																	
6	6																																	
7	7																																	
8	8																																	

-8-

	ASK 12 *ABOUT ALL PERSONS RELATED TO HOUSEHOLDER WHO MIGHT PAY BOARD*	ASK 13 *ABOUT ALL PERSONS*	ASK *ABOUT ALL PERSONS EXCEPT WIVES, CHILDREN AND RETIRED PERSONS*	ASK 15, 16 *AND* 17 *OF ALL HOUSEHOLDS*
	12	13	14	15
	Did you receive anything last week for board or lodging from relatives living with you? Yes No *IF YES* From whom? How much? *Show amount opposite payer*	Are any of the people in your household covered by hospital or medical benefits? Yes No *IF YES* What Organisation? H.B.A. B Other F What Cover? Hospital Only H Medical Only M Hosp. & Med. HM *IF NO*, or H or M Only Why Not? C Too Costly X Against in Principle I Ignorance P Pensioner A Apathy D Dissatisfied O Other *specify*	Can you tell me if you are making provision for your retirement? Yes No *IF YES* What Provision? S Superannuation I Insurance O Other *specify* *IF S or I* How much per week?	How much do you spend each week on food? ....
IU Number / Person Number				16
1				Do you have enough income to meet your family's needs each week?
2				
3				
4				
5				
6				
7				
8				
9				
10				
11				
12				
13				
14				

I.U. No.	Last Week's Receipt of Board from Family Boarders	Last Week's Payment of Board by Family Boarders	Membership of H.B.A. etc.	Reason for Non-Membership	Retirement Provision IU Head	Payment for Super. & Insurance	Interviewer's Assessment	Receiver of Board	Number of Households	Identification Number	Card Number	
	64	65 66 67	68 69	70	71 72	73	74 75	76	77	78 79	80	
1												2
2												2
3												2
4												2
5												2
6												2
7												2
8												2

17

Which people in the community do you think have most difficulty in making ends meet?

18

Interviewer's assessment of housing
1   2   3   4   5

We are likely to be making a second visit to many families within the next few weeks. If we call on you we hope you will help us again. Thank you very much.

The previous eight pages contain a facsimile of the questionnaire that was used in the Stage I interview. This questionnaire was used in the collection of information about all persons who were living together in one household. Pages two and three contain questions that relate to the household as a whole. The individuals comprising the household were listed on page four—a line being allowed for each of them—and data relating to each person were recorded there and on the following pages on the appropriate line.

The coding of the data was also done on the questionnaire. At the bottom of several of the pages the relevant parts of the coding frame are set out, indicating the detail that was recorded on the two eighty-column punch cards.

Appendix B

Standard Costs used in the Adjustment of Income

TABLE B·1

STANDARD COSTS USED IN THE ADJUSTMENT OF INCOME

Part A: Food, clothing and other costs that vary with family status, age, sex and work status of individuals.

I STANDARD COST OF INCOME UNIT HEADS

(i) Where income unit head lives alone

Age	Under 40		40–65		65 and over	
Employment status	Works	At home	Works	At home	Works	At home
Males	20.80	14.80	20.30	14.30	20.00	12.95
Females	20.40	12.75	20.15	12.50	19.85	10.85

(ii) Where income unit head lives with other people

Age	Under 40		40–65		65 and over	
Employment status	Works	At home	Works	At home	Works	At home
Males	19.70	13.70	19.20	13.20	18.90	11.85
Females	20.40	12.75	20.15	12.50	19.85	10.85

II STANDARD COST OF WIVES

Age	Under 40		40–65		65 and over	
Employment status	Works	At home	Works	At home	Works	At home
Wife	20.70	10.00	17.45	9.75	17.15	8.10

III STANDARD COST OF CHILDREN

Age	Under 6	6–15	15 and over
Males	5.08	8.48	13.00
Females	5.08	8.23	11.05

Part B: Housing and other costs that vary with the size of the household.

STANDARD COST OF HOUSING AND POWER, FURNITURE, EQUIPMENT, ETC.

Number of persons in household	1	2	3	4	5	6	7	8
Housing	11.20	10.85	11.95	12.95	12.95	16.00	16.00	16.00
Power, furniture, equipment, etc.	6.05	9.30	10.80	11.10	12.95	14.65	16.40	18.05

To calculate the standard costs of an income unit the appropriate costs for the head, his wife and each child are taken from Part A of the table and added to the appropriate housing and other costs from Part B. The housing and other costs for an income unit are calculated as a fraction of the costs of the appropriate sized household, the fraction depending on the ratio of the number of persons in the income unit to the total number of persons in the household.

Appendix C

The Poverty Classification of the Aged

The poverty classification of aged income units in Melbourne is a best estimate, involving adjustments to the sample results for several reasons.

1. The weighted results of the Stage I survey yielded an estimate of 142,019 aged income units in Melbourne. For 9·0 per cent of these units there was inadequate information about income. For 52·1 per cent, income data suggested they were sufficiently above the poverty line to require no further investigation. The remaining 38·9 per cent were possibly in poverty and one-half of this population was randomly sampled for further investigation. The 80 per cent response rate to this Stage II survey yielded 186 usable replies to the second questionnaire. We are aware of the substantial margins of error attaching to comments based on this second sample and realize that the margin of error increases for increasingly fine subdivisions of the sample. All statements in Chapter 5 should accordingly be read with appropriately severe reservations.

2. In grossing up data from the Stage II sample, allowance had to be made for income units about whom there were inadequate or no data on income. From other information collected at Stage I, we estimated that of the 9 per cent in this category, 6·2 per cent were probably in the group presumed to be not in poverty and the other 2·8 per cent in the group thought to be possibly in poverty. The Stage II data were accordingly grossed up to represent 41·7 per cent of the original population of aged income units: that is, the 38·9 per cent for whom income data were available and the 2·8 per cent for whom the data were inadequate.

3. The remaining 58·3 per cent of income units were presumed to be above marginal poverty. A small (2·5 per cent) random sample of those in this category with incomes of up to $80 a week was also approached with the second questionnaire. The results confirmed our expectation that none of this group would prove, on closer examination, to be in poverty. In particular, information collected at the first stage about income over a short period was unlikely to be unrepresentative of the position of the aged, as it might be for the earning members of the population.

In only one case in this small sample was the respondent worse off than at Stage I, due to a change of circumstances. At Stage I both husband and wife had been earning good incomes and were well able to afford the high rent they were paying for their house. Between the two enquiries, the wife had become ill, had ceased work and was unlikely to resume. The husband's earnings were, at the time of Stage II of the survey, high enough to keep them out of poverty. But when they became dependent on the pension (they had virtually no assets), they would move down into poverty unless they were able to secure cheaper accommodation.

4. In the poverty classification, income units above marginal poverty have adjusted incomes of $39 or more, and $33 after housing costs. Those in marginal poverty have adjusted incomes of between $33 and $39, and/or adjusted incomes after housing costs of between $27 and $33. Those in poverty have adjusted incomes of less than $33, and/or adjusted incomes after housing costs of less than $27.

Those in poverty but not in need have adjusted incomes of less than $33, but their adjusted incomes after housing costs are brought above $27 by the cheapness of their accommodation, by the annuity value of their assets, or by the help they receive from families, friends and charitable organisations.

5. The composition of the second sample, in respect of several aspects relevant to the poverty classification, was checked against the first sample from which it was drawn. For some of these aspects, differences in the composition of the second sample were either negligible or irrelevant. For three aspects, the differences affected the poverty classification as shown in Table C·1.

TABLE C·1

POVERTY CLASSIFICATION OF AGED INCOME UNITS REPRESENTED BY THE SECOND SAMPLE

	Stage II sample as originally constituted	Stage II sample reconstituted to conform to Stage I sample in respect of :		
		Sex and marital status	Housing status	Pensioners and non-pensioners
	%	%	%	%
Above marginal poverty	15·9	16·5	16·1	15·9
In marginal poverty	10·6	10·3	11·3	10·5
In poverty but not in need —by accommodation	6·5	6·2	6·6	6·4
—by assets	2·9	2·9	2·8	2·9
—by family help	3·5	3·4	2·7	3·7
In poverty and in need	2·3	2·4	2·2	2·3
Total percentage of all aged income units	41·7	41·7	41·7	41·7

Inspection of these results showed, however, that the differences are not large and to some extent offset each other. It was decided that it would be best to use the Stage II sample as originally constituted.

6. The poverty classification used in analysis of Stage I data had only four groups—above marginal poverty, in marginal poverty, in poverty but not in need by cheapness of accommodation, and in poverty and in need. Additional information from Stage II questionnaires permitted a further two groups to be established—in poverty but not in need by the annuity value of assets, and by family help.

A study of changes in the poverty classification between Stages I and II shows that, of total aged income units, the poverty classes of 74·4 per cent remained unchanged. For 3·4 per cent, changed circumstances led to changes in their classification, with 1·5 per cent moving up to a higher group, 1·0 per cent moving down, and 0·9 per cent moving into the two new groups. For the remaining 22·2 per cent, new information revealed at the second stage moved 16·4 per cent into a higher group, 0·3 per cent into a lower group, and 5·5 per cent into the two new groups.

Allowing for some of these movements offsetting each other, the net changes in the classification affected 20·0 per cent of aged income units, of whom 6·4 per cent moved into the two new groups.

TABLE C·2

CHANGES IN THE POVERTY CLASSIFICATION BETWEEN ESTIMATES AT STAGES I AND II

Poverty classification	Poverty classification Stage I	Net changes of poverty classification			Poverty classification Stage II
		To a higher group	To a lower group	To a new group	
Above marginal poverty	86,114	+19,188			105,302
In marginal poverty	22,122	—3,740	—1,623	—1,633	15,126
In poverty but not in need —by cheapness of accommodation	16,113	—7,279	+1,428	—1,096	9,166
—by annuity value of assets				+4,158	4,158
—by family help				+4,994	4,994
In poverty and in need	17,670	—8,169	+195	—6,423	3,273
Total	142,019				142,019

7. For allocation of respondents to the first three categories in the poverty classification of aged income units, we used information about income from all sources, including rent, interest or dividends received on property, and about payments of rent, instalments or on mortgages. For the fourth category, in poverty but not in need by the annuity value of assets, we used as a measure of assets essentially the rules laid down by the Commonwealth Department of Social Services. We ignored altogether the value of a house owned and occupied by a respondent, its land and contents, a car, clothing and other personal effects, together with $800 of property for a married couple and $400 for a single person. Income from unsaleable assets, such as flats which were an integral part of the house owned and occupied by the respondent, was retained as income. Income from all other assets was deducted and, instead, we added back 10 per cent of the value of those assets. If the adjusted income after housing cost was then above the $27 poverty line, the respondent was classed as not in need by annuity value of assets.

Few Australians—and none of our respondents—actually buy annuities. Some aged people—especially married couples, and females not much above 60—would not be able to buy annuities on a 10 per cent basis. These rules impute, therefore, to asset holders larger incomes than they actually receive.

People have many valid reasons for not using their assets to buy annuities; they may want to keep capital in order to leave something to their children, or to have by them to meet emergencies that may arise; they often do not know about or understand annuities or, if they do, they may fear to lose either by dying younger than average or from the rise in prices likely to occur during the currency of fixed-value annuities. Thus some of these people may be suffering the hardships and deprivations of those with incomes below the poverty line since their disposable income—what they feel they can spend without reducing their assets— is lower than the poverty line. None of these arguments, however, can be expected to sway a government department concerned to assess the means of an applicant for pension.

The departmental rules are quite properly concerned to put a holder of assets on a footing comparable with the recipient of superannuation benefits who leaves no capital equivalent behind him when he dies, and with the recipient of part-time earnings who has no capital reserve— and whose earnings anyhow will diminish as his health deteriorates. The Department does not argue that aged people should buy annuities, but merely treats them as if they had.

The current departmental treatment of assets is, it should be noted, a great advance on its practice right up to 1960. Until then, the pension was reduced by $2 for every $20 by which the value of assets exceeded $400 (or $800 for a married couple). Since 1960, ten per cent of the value of assets in excess of $400 per head is included in means as assessed. It is in respect only of means in excess of $10 a week ($17 for a married couple) that the pension is reduced.

For the category, in poverty but not in need by family help, we made individual judgments based on the description, in answers to the second questionnaire, of the nature and amount of help received. Where the help was given by the family with whom the aged respondent was residing, we allowed also for the impact on the poverty classification of the family as a whole, including the aged persons in receipt of help.

Appendix D

Effects of Proposed Increases in Child Endowment

These calculations all relate to families earning $45 a week before payment of tax. The only deductions for tax purposes which are considered are those for wife and children. All other deductions depend on certain types of expenditure; we are concerned to measure the adequacy of income for all types of expenditure. The poverty line has been updated to June 1969 in line with the rise in average earnings since the survey was carried out in June 1966.

TABLE D·1

EFFECT OF PROPOSED INCREASES IN CHILD ENDOWMENT

Column	1	2	3	4
	$	$	$	$
Weekly earnings	45	45	45	45
Annual earnings	2,340	2,340	2,340	2,340
Deductions for tax purposes:				
Wife	312	312	312	312
Child 1	208	208	208	208
Child 2	156	156	156	156
Child 3	156	156	156	156
Child 4	156	156	156	156
Child 5	—	—	156	156
Child 6	—	—	156	156
Taxable income	1,352	1,352	1,040	1,040
Tax	103	103	60	60
Annual net income after tax	2,237	2,237	2,280	2,280
Child endowment:				
Child 1	26	26	26	26
Child 2	52	52	52	52
Child 3	78	182	78	182
Child 4	91	234	91	234
Child 5	—	—	104	234
Child 6	—	—	117	234
Total annual income net	2,484	2,731	2,748	3,242
Total weekly income net	47.77	52.52	52.85	62.35
Income equivalent to poverty line *	52.22	52.22	60.31	60.31

*This is the income required to equate such a family's income to the poverty line updated to June 1969. It is derived from the standard cost calculations.

In our calculations of adjusted income a child over six years of age costs more than a younger one. A family of four is assumed to have two younger and two older children, a family of six to have four younger and two older children. If the children were assumed to be older, a higher income would be required.

Table D·1 shows the effect of raising child endowment for the third child to $3.50 and for the fourth and subsequent children to $4.50 each. As no balancing changes in taxation are proposed this would be expensive, costing about $108 million in 1968-69.

In Table D·1:
Column 1 shows the present position of a four-child family.
Column 2 shows the effect of increasing child endowment to $3.50 for the third child and $4.50 for the fourth child.
Column 3 shows the present position of a six-child family.
Column 4 shows the effect of increasing child endowment to $3.50 for the third child and to $4.50 for the fourth and each subsequent child.
Each of these families would be raised above the poverty line by these increases in child endowment.

In Table D·2 the effects are shown of a combined operation—abolition of deductions for children for tax purposes and increases in child endowment for all children to form the following scale:

First child	$1.00
Second child	1.50
Third child	3.50
Fourth and each subsequent child	4.50

Since it is estimated that the net saving to the Treasury from the abolition of tax deductions would have been $160 million in 1968-69, the net cost of these combined proposals would be quite small—only $19 million.

In Table D·2:
Column 1 shows the present position of a four-child family.
Column 2 shows the effect of the combined operation on this family.
Column 3 shows the present position of a six-child family.
Column 4 shows the effect of the combined operation on a six-child family.

TABLE D·2

EFFECT OF PROPOSED INCREASES IN CHILD ENDOWMENT WITH TAXATION CONCESSIONS
FOR CHILDREN ELIMINATED

Column	1	2	3	4
	$	$	$	$
Weekly earnings	45	45	45	45
Annual earnings	2,340	2,340	2,340	2,340
Deductions for tax purposes :				
Wife	312	312	312	312
Child 1	208	—	208	—
Child 2	156	—	156	—
Child 3	156	—	156	—
Child 4	156	—	156	—
Child 5	—	—	156	—
Child 6	—	—	156	—
Taxable income	1,352	2,028	1,040	2,028
Tax	103	224	60	224
Annual net income after tax	2,237	2,116	2,280	2,117
Child endowment :				
Child 1	26	52	26	52
Child 2	52	78	52	78
Child 3	78	182	78	182
Child 4	91	234	91	234
Child 5	—	—	104	234
Child 6	—	—	117	234
Total annual net income	2,484	2,662	2,748	3,130
Total weekly net income	44.77	51.19	52.85	60.19
Income equivalent to poverty line *	52.22	52.22	60.31	60.31

*This is the income required to equate such a family's income to the poverty line updated to June 1969.
It is derived from the standard cost calculations.

TABLE D·3

EFFECT OF PROPOSED INCREASES IN CHILD ENDOWMENT WITH CHILD ENDOWMENT ADDED
TO TAXABLE INCOME

Column	1	2
	$	$
Weekly earnings	45	45
Annual earnings	2,340	2,340
Taxable child endowment:		
Child 1	52	52
Child 2	78	78
Child 3	182	182
Child 4	234	234
Child 5	—	234
Child 6	—	234
Earnings plus child endowment	2,886	3,432
Deductions for tax purposes:		
Wife	312	312
Child 1	208	208
Child 2	156	156
Child 3	156	156
Child 4	156	156
Child 5	—	156
Child 6	—	156
Taxable income	1,898	2,054
Tax	198	230
Total annual net income	3,688	3,124
Total weekly net income	57.70	60.08
Income equivalent to poverty line *	52.22	60.31

*This is the income required to equate such a family's income to the poverty line updated to June 1969.
It is derived from the standard cost calculations.

Table D·3 shows the effect of raising child endowment rates as in Table D·2, leaving concessional deductions as at present but making child endowment payments taxable as part of the income of the father. These proposals would also bring the four-child and six-child families almost up to or above the poverty line. But these would be quite expensive, costing the Treasury some $129 million.
Column 1 shows the effect on a four-child family.
Column 2 shows the effect on a six-child family.

Appendix E

Analysis of Health Expenditure

The technique used in the analysis of health expenditure was multiple linear regression after a model developed by G. Wirick and R. Barlow, explained in 'Social and Economic Determinants of Demand for Health Services', *The Economics of Health and Medical Care*, University of Michigan, Ann Arbor, 1964.

The procedure by which income was adjusted to correct for varying ages, family sizes and work status could not be used in the analysis of health data as the regression method itself contains an implicit correction similar in its effects.

The Stage II sample had been constructed so as to concentrate interviewing on the poor and the near-poor, and no sample had been drawn from among some groups obviously not poor. Because it was not possible to restore the original composition of the population by any system of weighting, the regressions were performed on the unweighted data. Thus the sample is poorer, less well insured, and has a larger average family size and a higher proportion of migrants than the Stage I population from which it was drawn.

Because health expenditure and income data were collected for income units rather than for individuals, demographic characteristics such as age and sex which would have helped to predict the need for health care had to be omitted. A degree of homogeneity was achieved by excluding from the analysis all income units in which the head received a pension carrying an entitlement to free medical care and all income units in which the head was of pensionable age. There remained observations for 269 income units.

Index

Accident
  association with poverty 38-40, 58, 59, 147-50
  benefits *see* Sickness benefits
Acts of Parliament (Commonwealth)
  Delivered Meals Subsidy Act, 1970 178n
  States Grants (Deserted Wives) Act, 1968 60, 97n, 98
  States Grants (Home Care) Act, 1969 182-3
Aged
  assets and retirement provision 8, 10, 62-4, 69, 75-83 *passim*, 191, 211-4
  family help for 62-5, 68-9, 75-6, 83-6, 192, 211-2, 214
  housing 62-3, 68-9, 74-9, 191, 210-3
  pensions 3, 9, 10, 65, 70-3, 88, 191-5, preface
  poverty classification and determinants 3, 37-42, 62-70, 191, 192, 210-4
Allowances
  see Children's, Guardians', Maternity, Mothers', Wife's Allowances
Association of Teachers in Schools of Social Work 185
Atkinson, A. B. 171n
Australian Association of Social Workers 185
Australian Council of Social Service 185

Barlow, R. 219
Basic Wage
  as income component 29
  definition 1
  families on 159

Benefits (Commonwealth Cash Social)
  allowances *see* Children's, Guardians', Maternity, Mothers', Wife's Allowances
  annual expenditure on 2, 3, 10, 13
  as components of income 24
  comparison of expenditure with other countries 4, 13, 59
  cost of recommended increases in 2, 196-7
  definition 3
  eligibility for 3, 8, 9
  financing of 8
  ignorance concerning 8, 57, 187-8
  means-testing for 8-13
  waiting period for 58-60
  weekly rates of 8, 9
  see also Allowances; Child endowment; Deserted wives', Health, Hospital and Medical, Pharmaceutical, Repatriation, Sickness and Accident, Special, and Unemployment benefits; Pensions
Benefits (State)
  deserted wives' 96-7
  sickness and unemployment 152
Blind pensions 9
Bolte, Sir Henry 97
Box Hill, City of 182
British migrants
  numbers in poverty 126-7, 130-1, 192
  numbers in survey 119
  occupations and earnings of 123-6
  pattern of settlement of 120-3
  see also Migrants
Brotherhood of St Laurence 93, 112n
Budget Standard Service of New York 26
Bureau of Census and Statistics (Commonwealth) 15